First World War
and Army of Occupation
War Diary
France, Belgium and Germany

1 INDIAN CAVALRY DIVISION
Headquarters, Branches and Services
Adjutant and Quarter-Master General
16 October 1914 - 31 December 1916

WO95/1168/1

The Naval & Military Press Ltd
www.nmarchive.com
Published in association with The National Archives

Published by

The Naval & Military Press Ltd

Unit 10 Ridgewood Industrial Park,

Uckfield, East Sussex,

TN22 5QE England

Tel: +44 (0) 1825 749494

www.naval-military-press.com

www.nmarchive.com

This diary has been reprinted in facsimile from the original. Any imperfections are inevitably reproduced and the quality may fall short of modern type and cartographic standards.

© Crown Copyright
Images reproduced by permission of The National Archives, London, England, 2015.

Contents

Document type	Place/Title	Date From	Date To
Heading	WO95/1168/1		
Heading	B E F 1 Indian Cav. Div. A Q 1914-Oct To 1916 Dec		
Heading	B E F 1 Indian A Q June 1915 Starts With 2 Days Of Late May 1915 But May June 80c 60 End Of Month		
Heading	War Diary of Q M G. 1st Indian Cavalry Division From 16-10-14 To 17-12-14 Volume I		
War Diary	Bombay	16/10/1914	16/10/1914
War Diary	Morsvilles.	10/11/1914	14/11/1914
War Diary	Aire	26/11/1914	26/11/1914
War Diary	Lozinghem	27/11/1914	27/11/1914
War Diary	Berguette.	07/12/1914	07/12/1914
War Diary	Berguette & Lillers	08/12/1914	10/12/1914
War Diary	Lozinghem	13/12/1914	13/12/1914
Miscellaneous	Appendix I The General Officer Commanding, Indian Cavalry Division, I.E.F. "A"	30/10/1914	30/10/1914
Miscellaneous	Hired Transport "Ballarat."	28/10/1914	28/10/1914
Miscellaneous	Appendix II Report On Billets In Marseilles.		
Heading	War Diary of 1st Ind, Cav. Divn. Admn. Staff (C A A & Q M G) From 18-12-14 To 31-12-14 Volume I		
War Diary	Lozinghem	18/12/1914	23/12/1914
War Diary	Bourecq	23/12/1914	24/12/1914
War Diary	Bourecq Midnight	24/12/1914	24/12/1914
War Diary	Norrent	25/12/1914	31/12/1914
Miscellaneous	Appendix A Order By Major General H.D. Fanshawe C B Bourecq	24/12/1914	24/12/1914
Heading	War Diary of A & Q. 1st Indian Cavalry Division January 1915		
Heading	War Diary of DAA & Q.M.G. 1st Indian Cavalry Division From January 1st To 31st 1915 Volume III		
War Diary	Norrent Fontes	31/12/1914	31/01/1915
Miscellaneous	Appendix "A"		
Miscellaneous	Appendix B	03/01/1915	03/01/1915
Miscellaneous	Appendix-C.	10/01/1915	10/01/1915
Miscellaneous	Appendix D.	10/01/1915	10/01/1915
Miscellaneous	Appendix E	17/01/1915	17/01/1915
Miscellaneous	Appendix F.	17/01/1915	17/01/1915
Miscellaneous	Appendix G	24/01/1915	24/01/1915
Miscellaneous	Appendix "H"	24/01/1915	24/01/1915
Miscellaneous	Appendix I		
Miscellaneous	Appendix J.		
Heading	War Diary of A & Q 1st Indian Cavalry Division February-1915		
Heading	War Diary with Appendices. of D.A.A. And Q.M.G. 1st Indian Cavalry Division. 1st February 1915 To 28th February 1915		
War Diary	Norrent Fontes.	01/02/1915	28/02/1915
Miscellaneous	Appendix "A"		
Miscellaneous	Appendix "B"		
Miscellaneous	Appendix "C"		
Miscellaneous	Appendix "D"		

Type	Description	From	To
Miscellaneous	Appendix "E"		
Miscellaneous	Appendix "F"		
Miscellaneous	Appendix "G"		
Miscellaneous	Appendix "H"		
Heading	War Diary of A & Q 1st Indian Cavalry Division March-1915		
Heading	War Diary with Appendices of D.A.A. and Q.M.G. 1st Indian Cavalry Division. From 1st March 1915 To 31st March 1915		
War Diary	Norrent Fontes.	01/03/1915	10/03/1915
War Diary	Marles.	11/03/1915	14/03/1915
War Diary	Bourecq	15/03/1915	17/03/1915
War Diary	Enquin.	18/03/1915	31/03/1915
Miscellaneous	Appendix. "A"	01/03/1915	01/03/1915
Miscellaneous	Appendix. "B"	01/03/1915	01/03/1915
Operation(al) Order(s)	Operation Order No 1 By Major General H.D. Fanshawe, C.B., Commanding 1st Indian Cavalry Division. App "C"	10/03/1915	10/03/1915
Miscellaneous	Appendix "D"		
Miscellaneous	Appendix E	14/03/1915	14/03/1915
Miscellaneous	Appendix F	14/03/1915	14/03/1915
Miscellaneous	Appendix G	21/03/1915	21/03/1915
Miscellaneous	Appendix H	21/03/1915	21/03/1915
Miscellaneous	Appendix I	28/03/1915	28/03/1915
Miscellaneous	Appendix J	28/03/1915	28/03/1915
Heading	War Diary of A & Q. 1st Indian Cavalry Division April-1915		
Heading	War Diary with Appendices of D.A.A & Q.M.G. 1st Indian Cavalry Division From 1st April 1915 To 30th April 1915		
War Diary	Enquin	01/04/1915	24/04/1915
War Diary	St Marie Cappel	25/04/1915	28/04/1915
War Diary	Watou	29/04/1915	01/05/1915
Miscellaneous	Appendix "A"	04/04/1915	04/04/1915
Miscellaneous	Appendix "B"	04/04/1915	04/04/1915
Miscellaneous	Appendix "C"	11/04/1915	11/04/1915
Miscellaneous	Appendix "D"	11/04/1915	11/04/1915
Miscellaneous	Appendix "E"	18/04/1915	18/04/1915
Miscellaneous	Appendix "F"	18/04/1915	18/04/1915
Miscellaneous	Appendix "G"		
Operation(al) Order(s)	1st Indian Cavalry Division Order No. 3		
Miscellaneous	Headquarters 1st Indian Cavalry Division. 24th April 1915	24/04/1915	24/04/1915
Miscellaneous	Appendix "H"	25/04/1915	25/04/1915
Miscellaneous	Appendix "I"	25/01/1915	25/04/1915
Heading	War Diary with Appendices of Administrative Branch, 1st Indian Cavalry Division From 1st May 1915 To 31st May 1915		
War Diary	Watou.	01/05/1915	01/05/1915
War Diary	St. Marie Cappel	02/05/1915	03/05/1915
War Diary	Roquetoire.	03/05/1915	16/05/1915
War Diary	Roquetoire Allouagne.	17/05/1915	19/05/1915
War Diary	Roquetoire	20/05/1915	26/05/1915
War Diary	Roquetoire Staple	27/05/1915	27/05/1915
War Diary	Staple Rubrouck.	28/05/1915	28/05/1915
War Diary	Rubrouck.	29/05/1915	31/05/1915

Miscellaneous	Appendix "A"	02/05/1915	02/05/1915
Miscellaneous	Appendix "B"	02/05/1915	02/05/1915
Miscellaneous	Appendix "C"	09/05/1915	09/05/1915
Miscellaneous	Appendix "D"	09/05/1915	09/05/1915
Miscellaneous	Appendix "E"	16/05/1915	16/05/1915
Miscellaneous	Appendix "F"	16/05/1915	16/05/1915
Miscellaneous	Appendix "G"	23/05/1915	23/05/1915
Miscellaneous	Appendix "H"	23/05/1915	23/05/1915
Miscellaneous	Appendix "I"	30/05/1915	30/05/1915
Miscellaneous	Appendix "J"	30/05/1915	30/05/1915
Heading	War Diary of A & Q. 1st Indian Cavalry Division June-1915		
Heading	War Diary of Administrative Branch, 1st Indian Cavalry Division From 1st June 1915 To 30th June 1915		
War Diary	Reninghelst Roubrouck	28/05/1915	13/06/1915
War Diary	Rubrouck	14/06/1915	14/06/1915
War Diary	Rubrouck Roquetoire	15/06/1915	15/06/1915
War Diary	Roquetoire	16/06/1915	19/06/1915
War Diary	Rocquetoire	20/06/1915	30/06/1915
Miscellaneous	App I Report On 1st Indian Cavalry Division Supply Column, Inspected On 12/13th May 1915	23/05/1915	23/05/1915
Miscellaneous	App II Headquarters, 1st Indian Cavalry Division. 2nd June 1915	02/06/1915	02/06/1915
Operation(al) Order(s)	Extract From Divisional Orders No. 149 Dated 6th June 1915	06/06/1915	06/06/1915
Miscellaneous	Appendix IV	06/06/1915	06/06/1915
Miscellaneous	Appendix V.	06/06/1915	06/06/1915
Miscellaneous	App VI		
Miscellaneous	Appendix VII	13/06/1915	13/06/1915
Miscellaneous	Appendix VIII	13/06/1915	13/06/1915
Miscellaneous	Appendix IX	20/06/1915	20/06/1915
Miscellaneous	Appendix X	20/06/1915	20/06/1915
Miscellaneous	Appendix XI	27/06/1915	27/06/1915
Miscellaneous	Appendix XII	27/06/1915	27/06/1915
Heading	War Diary of A & Q. 1st Indian Cavalry Division July-1915		
Heading	War Diary with Appendices of Administrative Branch, 1st Indian Cavalry Division From 1st July 1915 To 31st July 1915		
War Diary	Roquetoire	01/07/1915	31/07/1915
Miscellaneous	Appendix I.	04/07/1915	04/07/1915
Miscellaneous	Appendix II.	04/07/1915	04/07/1915
Miscellaneous	Appendix III	11/07/1915	11/07/1915
Miscellaneous	Appendix IV.	11/07/1915	11/07/1915
Miscellaneous	Appendix V	18/07/1915	18/07/1915
Miscellaneous	Appendix VI	18/07/1915	18/07/1915
Miscellaneous	Appendix VII	25/07/1915	25/07/1915
Heading	War Diary with Appendices of Administrative Branch 1st Indian Cavalry Division From 1st August 1915 To 31st August 1915		
War Diary	Domart	01/08/1915	29/08/1915
Miscellaneous	Appendix I	01/08/1915	01/08/1915
Miscellaneous	Appendix II	01/08/1915	01/08/1915
Miscellaneous	App III	09/08/1915	09/08/1915
Miscellaneous	App IV	07/08/1915	07/08/1915
Miscellaneous	Appendix V	08/08/1915	08/08/1915

Miscellaneous	Appendix VI	08/08/1915	08/08/1915
Miscellaneous	Appendix VII	15/08/1915	15/08/1915
Miscellaneous	Appendix VIII	15/08/1915	15/08/1915
Miscellaneous	Appendix IX	22/08/1915	22/08/1915
Miscellaneous	Appendix X	22/08/1915	22/08/1915
Miscellaneous	Appendix XI	29/08/1915	29/08/1915
Miscellaneous	Appendix XII	29/08/1915	29/08/1915
Heading	War Diary of A & Q. 1st Indian Cavalry Division September-1915		
Heading	War Diary with Appendices Administrative Branch, 1st Indian Cavalry Division From 1st September 1915 To 30th September 1915		
War Diary	Domart	03/09/1915	19/09/1915
War Diary	Domart Le Millard	22/09/1915	22/09/1915
War Diary	Lemillard	25/09/1915	28/09/1915
Miscellaneous	Appendix "A"		
Miscellaneous	App. B	05/09/1915	05/09/1915
Miscellaneous	App "C"	05/09/1915	05/09/1915
Miscellaneous	App "D"	18/09/1915	18/09/1915
Miscellaneous	App. "E"	12/09/1915	12/09/1915
Miscellaneous	App "F"	12/09/1915	12/09/1915
Miscellaneous	App. "G"	19/09/1915	19/09/1915
Miscellaneous	App "H"	19/09/1915	19/09/1915
Heading	App I.	19/09/1915	19/09/1915
Miscellaneous	App J	23/09/1915	23/09/1915
Miscellaneous	App "K"	26/09/1915	26/09/1915
Miscellaneous	App. "L"	26/09/1915	26/09/1915
Heading	War Diary of A & Q 1st Indian Cavalry Division October-1915		
Heading	War Diary with Appendices of D.A.A. and Q.M.G. 1st Indian Cavalry Division From 1st October 1915 To 31st October 1915		
War Diary	Lemeillard	02/10/1915	10/10/1915
War Diary	Domart	13/10/1915	14/10/1915
War Diary	Le Quesnoy	22/10/1915	31/10/1915
Miscellaneous	App. "A"	02/10/1915	02/10/1915
Miscellaneous	Appendix "B"	03/10/1915	03/10/1915
Miscellaneous	Appendix "C"	03/10/1915	03/10/1915
Miscellaneous	Appendix "E"	10/10/1915	10/10/1915
Miscellaneous	App."F"	14/10/1915	14/10/1915
Miscellaneous	Appendix "G"	14/10/1915	14/10/1915
Miscellaneous	Appendix "H"	17/10/1915	17/10/1915
Miscellaneous	App. "I"	28/10/1915	28/10/1915
Miscellaneous	Appendix "J"	24/10/1915	24/10/1915
Miscellaneous	Appendix "K"	24/10/1915	24/10/1915
Miscellaneous	Appendix "L"	03/10/1915	03/10/1915
Miscellaneous	Appendix "M"	31/10/1915	31/10/1915
Heading	War Diary of A & Q 1st Indian Cavalry Division November-1915		
Heading	War Diary of Administrative Branch, 1st Indian Cavalry Division From 1st November 1915 To 30th November 1915		
War Diary	Le Quesnoy	01/11/1915	28/11/1915
Miscellaneous	Appendix I	07/11/1915	07/11/1915
Miscellaneous	Appendix II	07/11/1915	07/11/1915
Miscellaneous	Appendix III	14/11/1915	14/11/1915

Miscellaneous	Appendix IV	14/11/1915	14/11/1915
Miscellaneous	App. V	19/11/1915	19/11/1915
Miscellaneous	Appendix VI	21/11/1915	21/11/1915
Miscellaneous	Appendix VII	21/11/1915	21/11/1915
Miscellaneous	Appendix VIII	28/11/1915	28/11/1915
Miscellaneous	Appendix IX	28/11/1915	28/11/1915
Heading	War Diary of A & Q 1st Indian Cavalry Division December-1915		
Heading	War Diary of D.A.A. & Q.M.G. 1st Indian Cavalry Division. From 1st December 1915 To 31st December 1915		
War Diary	Le Quesnoy	05/12/1915	15/12/1915
War Diary	Dargnies	16/12/1915	26/12/1915
Miscellaneous	Appendix I	05/12/1915	05/12/1915
Miscellaneous	Appendix II	05/12/1915	05/12/1915
Miscellaneous	Appendix III	12/12/1915	12/12/1915
Miscellaneous	Appendix IV	12/12/1915	12/12/1915
Miscellaneous	App V	14/12/1915	14/12/1915
Miscellaneous	App VI	17/12/1915	17/12/1915
Miscellaneous	Appendix VII	19/12/1915	19/12/1915
Miscellaneous	Appendix VIII	19/12/1915	19/12/1915
Miscellaneous	Appendix IX	26/12/1915	26/12/1915
Miscellaneous	Appendix X	26/12/1915	26/12/1915
Heading	War Diary of D.A.Q.M.G. 1st Indian Cavalry Division From 1st January 1916 To 31st January 1916		
War Diary	Dargnies	09/01/1916	30/01/1916
Miscellaneous	Appendix I	08/01/1916	08/01/1916
Miscellaneous	Appendix II	09/01/1916	09/01/1916
Miscellaneous	Appendix III	15/01/1916	15/01/1916
Miscellaneous	Appendix IV	16/01/1916	16/01/1916
Miscellaneous	Appendix V	22/01/1916	22/01/1916
Miscellaneous	Appendix VI	23/01/1916	23/01/1916
Miscellaneous	Appendix VII	29/01/1916	29/01/1916
Miscellaneous	Appendix VIII	30/01/1916	30/01/1916
Heading	War Diary of D.A.A. & Q.M.G. 1st Indian Cavalry Division From 1st February 1916 To 29th February 1916		
Heading	War Diary Administrative Branch 1st Indian Cavalry Division February 1st To 29th 1916		
War Diary	Dargnies	31/01/1916	29/02/1916
Miscellaneous	Appendix I	06/02/1916	06/02/1916
Miscellaneous	Appendix II	06/02/1916	06/02/1916
Miscellaneous	Appendix III	13/02/1916	13/02/1916
Miscellaneous	Appendix IV	13/02/1916	13/02/1916
Miscellaneous	Appendix V	20/02/1916	20/02/1916
Miscellaneous	Appendix VI	20/02/1916	20/02/1916
Miscellaneous	Appendix VII	27/02/1916	27/02/1916
Miscellaneous	Appendix VIII	27/02/1916	27/02/1916
Heading	War Diary Administrative Branch-1st Indian Cavalry Division March 1st To 31st 1916		
War Diary	Dargnies	02/03/1916	20/03/1916
War Diary	Wail	26/03/1916	31/03/1916
Miscellaneous	Appendix I	05/03/1916	05/03/1916
Miscellaneous	Appendix II	05/03/1916	05/03/1916
Miscellaneous	Appendix III	12/03/1916	12/03/1916
Miscellaneous	Appendix IV	12/03/1916	12/03/1916

Miscellaneous	Appendix V	19/03/1916	19/03/1916
Miscellaneous	Appendix VI	19/03/1916	19/03/1916
Miscellaneous	Appendix VII	21/03/1916	21/03/1916
Miscellaneous	Appendix VIII	27/03/1916	27/03/1916
Miscellaneous	Appendix IX	26/03/1916	26/03/1916
Miscellaneous	Appendix X	26/03/1916	26/03/1916
Heading	War Diary Administrative Branch-1st Indian Cavalry Division April 1st To 30th 1916		
War Diary	Wail	02/04/1916	16/04/1916
War Diary	Yvrench	22/04/1916	30/04/1916
Miscellaneous	Appendix. I	02/04/1916	02/04/1916
Miscellaneous	Appendix. II	02/04/1916	02/04/1916
Miscellaneous	Appendix. III	09/04/1916	09/04/1916
Miscellaneous	Appendix. IV	09/04/1916	09/04/1916
Miscellaneous	Appendix. V	16/04/1916	16/04/1916
Miscellaneous	Appendix. VI	16/04/1916	16/04/1916
Miscellaneous	Appendix VII	23/04/1916	23/04/1916
Miscellaneous	Appendix. VIII	23/04/1916	23/04/1916
Miscellaneous	Appendix IX	23/04/1916	23/04/1916
Miscellaneous	Appendix X	30/04/1916	30/04/1916
Miscellaneous	Appendix XI	30/04/1916	30/04/1916
Heading	War Diary Administrative Branch-1st Indian Cavalry Division May 1st To 31st 1916		
War Diary	Wail	07/05/1916	07/05/1916
War Diary	Le Cauroy	10/05/1916	28/05/1916
Miscellaneous	Appx. I	07/05/1916	07/05/1916
Miscellaneous	Appx. II	07/05/1916	07/05/1916
Miscellaneous	Billeting Area-1st Indian Cavalry Division. Appx III	11/05/1916	11/05/1916
Miscellaneous	Appx. IV	14/05/1916	14/05/1916
Miscellaneous	Appx. V	14/05/1916	14/05/1916
Miscellaneous	Appx. VI	21/05/1916	21/05/1916
Miscellaneous	Appx. VII	21/05/1916	21/05/1916
Miscellaneous	Appx. VIII	28/05/1916	28/05/1916
Miscellaneous	Appx. IX	28/05/1916	28/05/1916
Heading	War Diary of D.A.A. & Q.M.G. 1st Indian Cavalry Division From 1st June 1916 To 30th June 1916		
War Diary	Le Cauroy.	01/06/1916	29/06/1916
War Diary	Doullens	30/06/1916	30/06/1916
Miscellaneous	Appx I	10/06/1916	10/06/1916
Miscellaneous	Appx II	15/06/1916	15/06/1916
Miscellaneous	Appx III	26/06/1916	26/06/1916
Miscellaneous	Appx IV	28/06/1916	28/06/1916
Miscellaneous	Appendix "A" Billeting Accommodation		
Miscellaneous	Billeting Area-1st Indian Cavalry Division.	30/06/1916	30/06/1916
Heading	War Diary Administrative Branch-1st Indian Cavalry Division. July 1st To 31st 1916		
War Diary	Doullens	02/07/1916	02/07/1916
War Diary	Auxi-Le-Chateau	12/07/1916	18/07/1916
War Diary	Villers Chatel	19/07/1916	31/07/1916
Miscellaneous	Billeting Area 1st Indian Cavalry Division. Appx I	03/07/1916	03/07/1916
Miscellaneous	Administrative Instructions Issued in accordance with "G". Appx II	18/07/1916	18/07/1916
Miscellaneous	Billeting Area-1st Indian Cavalry Division. Appx III	19/07/1916	19/07/1916
Heading	War Diary Administrative Branch-1st Indian Cavalry Division. August 1st To 31st 1916		
War Diary	Villers Chatel.	01/08/1916	29/08/1916

Miscellaneous	Administrative Instructions. The following changes will take place in billeting areas on the morning of the 10th instant. Appx I	09/08/1916	09/08/1916
Miscellaneous	Billeting Area-1st Indian Cavalry Division. Appx II	10/08/1916	10/08/1916
Heading	War Diary Administrative Branch-1st Indian Cavalry Division. September 1st-30th. 1916		
War Diary	Villers Chatel	01/09/1916	01/09/1916
War Diary	Frohen Le Grand	03/09/1916	03/09/1916
War Diary	St Riquier	04/09/1916	09/09/1916
War Diary	Doullens	11/09/1916	11/09/1916
War Diary	Allonville	13/09/1916	13/09/1916
War Diary	Morlancourt.	15/09/1916	25/09/1916
War Diary	Bussy Les Daours	27/09/1916	27/09/1916
War Diary	Picquigny	28/09/1916	28/09/1916
War Diary	Ailly Le Haut Clocher	29/09/1916	29/09/1916
War Diary	Ligescourt	30/09/1916	30/09/1916
Miscellaneous	Administrative Instructions. Reference O.O. 22. Appx I	01/09/1916	01/09/1916
Miscellaneous	Billeting Area-1st Indian Cavalry Division. Appx II	04/09/1916	04/09/1916
Miscellaneous	Billeting Area-1st Indian Cavalry Division. Appx III	03/10/1916	03/10/1916
Heading	War Diary Administrative Branch-1st Indian Cavalry Division. 1st October To 31st October. 1916		
War Diary	Ligescourt.	01/10/1916	28/10/1916
Heading	War Diary Administrative Branch, 1 Cavalry Division. November 1st To 30th, 1916		
War Diary	St Valery	02/11/1916	30/11/1916
Miscellaneous	Billeting Area-1st Indian Cavalry Division. Appx I	24/11/1916	24/11/1916
Heading	War Diary Administrative Branch-(1 Div) Division 1st To 31st December, 1916		
War Diary	St Valery	01/12/1916	31/12/1916
Miscellaneous	Divisional Orders by Major-General A.A. Kennedy.C.M.G. Commanding 4th Cavalry Division. App 1	05/01/1917	05/01/1917
Miscellaneous	Divisional Orders by Brigadier-General N.A.Haig. Commanding 4th Cavalry Division.	27/12/1916	27/12/1916
Miscellaneous	Divisional Orders by Brigadier-General N.A.Haig. Commanding 4th Cavalry Division.	08/12/1916	08/12/1916

WO 95/11811

BEF

1 Indian Cav. Div.

A & Q

1914 Oct — 1916 Dec

BEF / Indian
A+Q

June 1915

starts with

2 days

of late

May 1915

but May file goes to end of month

121/4046

War Diary of
D.M.G. 1st Indian
Cavalry Division
from 16.10.14
to 17.12.17.

Volume I
pp 1 to 6

Army Form C. 2118.

WAR DIARY
Q. M. G's. Staff (or) Indian Cavalry Division
INTELLIGENCE SUMMARY.
(Erase heading not required.)

Instructions regarding War Diaries and Intelligence Summaries are contained in F. S. Regs., Part II, and the Staff Manual respectively. Title pages will be prepared in manuscript.

Hour, Date, Place.	Summary of Events and Information.	Remarks and references to Appendices.
Bombay 16.10.14	Indian Cavalry Division landed, 2 brigades from Bombay, 1 from Liverpool: stand at Marseilles between Nov 7 & 10th.	W.S.
Marseilles 10.11.14	A report submitted to the Q.M.G. in India on the arrangements for embarkation with fifteen of ships is given in Appendix I.	
	The Division is placed fresh in camp huts in billets. The camps were muddy roads; it was a severe strain on the horses to be taken out of life ships & through sand storms. The watering troughs were insufficient, & efforts to be made to establish, whenever tubs were found the heating them in camp. More tubs were available, & could have been used, if tubs had been placed on them previously.	Appx II Report on Marseilles
	The Division was equipped with warm caps, etc. with warm clothing at Marseilles, the remaining	W.S.

Army Form C. 2118.

WAR DIARY
or
INTELLIGENCE SUMMARY.

(Erase heading not required.)

Instructions regarding War Diaries and Intelligence Summaries are contained in F. S. Regs., Part II, and the Staff Manual respectively. Title pages will be prepared in manuscript.

Hour, Date, Place.	Summary of Events and Information.	Remarks and references to Appendices.
Nov. 10-14. 1914.	Regt. finished training reserved at ORLEANS. Machine Gun & transport were handed into MARSEILLES, & now on their return to ORLEANS. All base regiments were also transferred to bayonets. Division entrained to ORLEANS, then placed in Camp. Horse Transport — to the Baggage Wagons, lorries brought from ENGLAND; but owing to an outbreak of Pink eye, only one Brigade (UMBALLA) & a small portion of Div. Troops could be equipped. Officers of the Divisional Staff, & Staff Captains & Supply Officer of Brigades were entrained at the Place of Concentration, & Billeting area. The HQ as follows. Div. H.Q. LOZINGHEM Div. Troops AVRHEL Sialkot Brigade BURBURE & neigh bourhoods	(MS)

Army Form C. 2118.

WAR DIARY
INTELLIGENCE SUMMARY.
(Erase heading not required.)

Hour, Date, Place.	Summary of Events and Information.	Remarks and references to Appendices.
AIRE. 26.10.14	Lucknow Brigade Ammunition Park arrived in the Lucknow area.	
LOZINGHEM. 27.10.14	The Supply Column ALLOUAGNE (Amn. Park) and Field Ambulances LILLERS. Over the days before the first Troops arrived by train. & The Lucknow Brigade arrived on 27th & 28th. at HAZEBROUCK. the regulating station, & was detrained at LILLERS & ERQUETE. On troops on detrainment taking 2 days' supplies in the train with them (1 iron ordinary ration — 30 hours, they carry with 1½ days' rations); for three transports there was [?]. This was done by the Supply Column but complications arose because the Advanced Base lorries had been lent up from the Advanced Base lorries in bulk by Division weekly transport. The remainder of the Division were held up by	[SD] [SD] [illegible notes]

Army Form C. 2118.

WAR DIARY
or
INTELLIGENCE SUMMARY.
(Erase heading not required.)

Instructions regarding War Diaries and Intelligence Summaries are contained in F. S. Regs., Part II, and the Staff Manual respectively. Title pages will be prepared in manuscript.

Hour, Date, Place.	Summary of Events and Information.	Remarks and references to Appendices.
BERGUETTE 7.12.14.	continued further cases of puntures among the Horses. Transport. It has only been possible to bring them into billets with their transport by using the Supply Columns, many of them refused to receive them till they were mobilised. Lt. Col. Vaughan, A.D.S.T. was accordingly dis-patched to ROUEN to take over inquiries for and transport short time had - coming under Col. Vaughan, were kept and brought back unit to, to it came.	WD
BERGUETTE + LILLERS 8 - 10.12.14.	Remainder of Division determined proceeded to billets. The whole supply organization & system being entirely different to the Indian, it has been necessary to reorganize entirely; this has entailed many changes which have been too great & too numerous to give in detail. Certain information have also been necessary	WD

Army Form C. 2118.

WAR DIARY
or
INTELLIGENCE SUMMARY.
(Erase heading not required.)

Hour, Date, Place.	Summary of Events and Information.	Remarks and references to Appendices.
10.21 N6 H.E.M. 13.12.14.	Telegram from G.H.Q. illustrating the personnel of S.A.A. section. Am. Col. & Signal Troop in extra to the establishment of regiments & numbers on theatre to be filled up.	WB

Wm Brown More
Brig Genl g.
1st Ind. Cav. Division.

17.12.14

No. 21   Appendix I

S.S. "Ballarat,"

Port Said, the 30th October 1914.

From

The General Officer Commanding,
    Indian Cavalry Division, I.E.F. "A".

To

The Quartermaster-General in India,
                    Simla,

Sir,

After very careful investigation and consideration I forward herewith some suggestions as to arrangements at the Port of Embarkation and on board ships carrying horses.

(1) When such large convoys (in this case 46 ships) have to be dealt with, it is essential that the Embarkation Staff should be increased and especially the S. and T. portion. As temporary increases and reductions would not conduce to efficiency it is therefore desirable that the whole-time Staff should be permanently augmented.

(2) The object to be aimed at is to reduce the period during which horses have to remain on board ship, especially in harbour, to a minimum. In my opinion this can only be done by ensuring that practically all the ships of the convoy are ready for the embarkation of troops and horses before the latter arrive at the port. In this way the full berthing accommodation can be utilised simultaneously for the embarkation of troops and horses. The only limit to this arrangement would be the capacity of the railways. All surplus baggage should be sent on ahead of the troops with an advance party and could be loaded before the troops arrive. If the capacity of the railways admit of it the arrangements would probably be found to expedite the sailing of the convoy even though no embarkation of troops and horses would take place until practically all the ships were ready. This would also reduce the period of detention in relief camps to a minimum. Even a few days delay in the sailing of a convoy would be preferable to the very serious risk of losses in horseflesh involved by premature

"Lockeley Hall" and "Franz Ferdinand" are very unsuitable and are slow. If the general speed of the convoy could be quickened up even to 12 knots the conditions on board ship would be improved and the worst parts of the voyage would be accomplished more rapidly and with less risk.

3. I attach a list of fittings, etc., which are authorised by regulations but which were not supplied. Naturally, in time of emergency it is not always possible to provide everything but I consider that most of the items named are essential and should not have been overlooked. Their provision would have saved much loss in horseflesh.

I am,

Sir,

Your obedient servant,

Major-General,
Commanding Indian Cavalry Division, I.E.F. "A".

or two plates on each side of the ship could be opened up and made to work on hinges and be capable of being securely fastened in case of bad weather. This would provide a good draught through the ship which is so essential to the welfare of the horses.

(8) If the stall arrangement be continued the floor board battens should be bolted. The screws used are too short and the battens come off causing risk of damage to the horses. The floor baulks should be raised three or four inches to facilitate cleaning out the stalls. At present urine and dung lodge against them and are difficult to remove. A passage way of at least 18 inches should be left between the rear of the stalls and the side of the ship for the same reason.

(9) More and larger windsails are required and large square sails should be provided for each hatchway to catch every breath of wind and carry it below.

(10) Suction fans should be provided wherever possible.

(11) Steam ventilators should be fitted in all ships carrying horses to blow out the foul and draw in fresh air.

(12) Instead of salt water tanks on the horse decks it would be preferable to run pipes, provided with taps at intervals, along the top of the stalls or pens.

(13) Under the present arrangement of loading S. & T. stores there is great difficulty in finding them on the ships. The ship's people are responsible but the tallying in is not satisfactory. I recommend that an officer or quartermaster-serjeant of the unit should be present at the loading of S. & T. stores on his ship to note the location of the various articles and facilitate subsequent handling.

(14) Fresh potatoes and onions are not suitable rations for long voyages in hot climates. They very soon go bad. On most of the ships of the convoy they had to be thrown overboard.

(15) No salt for horses was provided in the "Ballarat."

2. I am aware of the difficulties experienced in taking up sufficient ships but now that the initial stress is over I strongly recommend that slow ships and those unsuitable for carrying horses be eliminated. Several of the ships of this convoy, notably the

embarkation.

(3) One of the chief causes of delay at the docks was the time spent in moving ships from one berth to another for the various operations involved in fitting, coaling, watering, loading S. & T. stores and Ordnance stores. I am fully aware that only a certain number of ships can be fitted at one time with the present establishment and labour but, given the necessary increase in this respect, it seems to me that the dock accommodation admits of this part of the work being expedited provided, of course, that the ships are available.

(4) Again, something might perhaps be done to quicken matters by the sub-division of the Base Supply Depot and Ordnance Depot between the various docks so as to ensure simultaneous loading and obviate the movement of ships about the docks.

(5) For a voyage across the Indian Ocean and through the Red Sea the location of horses in ill ventilated pockets and corners of the ship should be absolutely prohibited. It was in such places that the greatest trouble arose. The congestion was so great and the ventilation so deficient that we were in great danger of losing a large percentage of horses. Consequently officers and men were engaged day and night tending the horses and removing them alternately to places where it was possible for them to breathe. Temperatures rose rapidly to great heights and it was only by constant and unremitting attention that the percentage of deaths was kept within reasonable limit.

(6) In continuation of my telegram of the 24th October 1914, despatched from Aden, I attach a plan of this ship showing that it is possible to provide for the same number of horses on the pen system which gives the horses more freedom and breathing space and is, in my opinion, far preferable to the stall system if some suitable form of foothold such as cinders, coarse matting, and sand is provided. This would reduce the expense and time, required for fitting, considerably.

(7) On ships which are badly ventilated between decks, one

HIRED TRANSPORT "BALLARAT."

Various stores, fittings, etc., allowed under (I) Regulations for H.M. Transport Service, 1908, and (II) Marine Regulations, India, Vol. II, 1914, and found deficient.

Regulation and paragraph	Article deficient.	Remarks and recommendations.
Regs. for H.M. Transport Service, 1908.		
Para.54	Dung Ports	Considered absolutely necessary.
Para.56	Steam Boats	
Para.98	Ventilation	Scuttles and air-scoops fitted, ventilation improved by opening coal shoots and recess on port side. Windsails should all be long, short ones of no value.
Appx.I	Ventilation	No arrangement for up-draught or exhausting foul air. Steam jetters (vide page 181) or similar device most necessary. 25 electric fans were fitted by men of U Battery, R.H.A., on horse decks, after sailing, with marked success.
Appx.XII	Hose on 'tween decks	No arrangements. Flexible hose had to be brought down from Saloon Deck. A clumsy and unsatisfactory method.
Appx.XII	Gratings over Hatchways	Should be fitted instead of boards and booby-hatches.
Appx.XIX	Combined brushes and squeegees.	No squeegees supplied. Considered absolutely necessary for 'tween decks.
Appx.XIX	Baskets, ballast ½ ton, fitted with slings complete.	None supplied.
Appx.XIX	Wire nippers	None supplied. Considered desirable
	Wooden tubs	do. do. do.
	Thermometers	do. do. do.
	Portable horse boxes	do. do. do.
Appx. XX	Carrots, oatmeal, rocksalt, linseed.	None supplied. Considered most necessary
Appx XX	Corn-crusher	None supplied. Consider necessary
	Chaff-cutters	do. do. do.
	Scuppers	Only 7 on each side of 'tween decks of which some were cut after embarkation. Should be as laid down.
Appx.XXIII	Orderly-Room and Helmet Room	None supplied. Considered desirable
	Isolation Hospital for horses	None supplied. Consider necessary.
Appx.XXIII	Hose with nozzle for scuppers	None supplied. Consider necessary.

Regulation and paragraph.	Article deficient.	Remarks and recommendations.
Appx.XXIII, Part 3, para.6	–––	No horse to stand against bulkhead. This precaution entirely neglected. Should be rigidly insisted on.
-do.-para.5	Platforms	Crossbars should be clamped on, not merely nailed.
Marine Regs., India, Vol.II.		
Sec.III, para.231	Animals near boilers	This precaution neglected with result that atmosphere for most of voyage was very nearly unbearable and 7 horses died before reaching Suez.
	Loose boxes	None supplied.
	Rear gangway	Not nearly large enough, consequently no room for men to work.
	Stalls on middle line	This para. was not complied with.
	Ventilation	Artificial ventilation most necessary. No arrangements made for up-draught.
	Electric Lighting	<u>Double</u> contact lamps fitted in middle of gangways 'tween decks. Ships lamps are all <u>single</u> contact and lamps were constantly broken by horses heads and men carrying trusses of hay, etc., along gangway. Should have been fitted to one side.

H.T. "Ballarat",
At Sea, 28th October 1914.

Sd. J.G.Dennistoun, Major, R.H.A.,
Commanding Troops on Board.

Appendix II.

REPORT ON BILLETS IN MARSEILLES.

Appended is a list of the billets formed in Marseilles for the Indian Cavalry Division. Private houses were avoided; and barns, stables and factories made use of. The inhabitants were most willing to lend their property, and the services of the Maire were not made use of.

2. Mr. H. Pigeord, House Agent and Contractor, was absolutely invaluable, in finding places, and in getting the necessary alterations and clearances carried out. I trust that his services will not be forgotten.

3. The cost of the billeting is not known to me. Mr. Pigeord was asked to submit an account to the Billeting Officers. It will probably be found that the cost is much less than that spent in preparing a camp for the same number of men.

4. Barrels were placed in each large billet for the treating of the water, but it is desirable that arrangements should be made for this treatment to be carried out before the troops arrive. In one case, that of the Distillery Bonneveine, the Medical Officer reported that he was unable to obtain the necessary ingredients from the Supply Depot.

5. Troops using billets were obliged to indent daily at the Charles Roux for transport to draw their rations. This meant a 5 to 10 mile journey and the same on return for the N.C.O. drawing the transport. It would probably have been more economical of transport, and would have certainly have been more convenient for the troops, if the transport could have been supplied daily at the issue point, viz. the nearest camp.

6. The list of billets is as follows:-
   A. La Valentine.
     1. Moulin Escudeau. Half Squadron.
     2. " Marcel Freres. Half Squadron.
     3. Scattered billets through the village. 1 Squadron.

B. La.Penne.

    1. Chateau Riqneau: Headquarters & 1 Section R.H.A.
    2. Hotel de Ville: 1 Section R.H.A.
    3. La Grande Auberge: 2 Sections R.H.A.
    4. House of M.Fabre: 1 Section R.H.A.
    5. Small billets in the village: 1 Section R.H.A.

C. La.Barasse and part of S.Marcel, used by R.F.A., not reported on by me.

D. Part of S.Marcel east of the camp,

    1. Glass factory of M.Gueylan: used for 260 men & horses of XX Deccan Horse; not used by the remainder of the Division, which arrived later.
    2. Soapworks opposite the Commissaire of Police: room for half squadron; prepared but not used.
    3. Various barns & stables: prepared but not used.

E. Pont de Vivaux, Gr. Chômine de Toulon

    1. Glass factory of M.Gueylan.
    2. Locale Gries. *Guis*
        These two places were side by side. A Regt was put into them, 19th Lancers. Most of the houses in Locale Gries, most of the men in the Factory.
    3. Usine of Moral Freres, a disued Foundry. 1 Regt, 3oth Lancers.

F. Bonne-Veine, near Parc Borély.
    1. Distillery. 200 men & Horses. 1 Squadron & Hdqr-s K.D.G.
    2. Soapworks. 1 Squadron K.D.G.
    3. Tramway Coy Stables. About 50 Horses Headquarter Staff
    4. Pink Cottage. A Racing Stable & covered riding school. 40 horses of Headquarter Staff.

7. Any number of other billets could have been found in addition, but this would have involved scattering troops; and they would have had to be content with the ordinary conveniences of the inhabitants in the way of water and sanitation.

War Diary of
1st Ind: Cav: Divn: Admin: Staff
(b's A & QMG)
from 16-12-14
to 31-12-14.

121/4046

Volume I
Pp 1.6 to 2

Confidential.

Indian Cavalry Corps
Army HQ Staff

Army Form C. 2118.

WAR DIARY
or
INTELLIGENCE SUMMARY.

(Erase heading not required.)

December 1914

Army Form C. 2118.

Instructions regarding War Diaries and Intelligence Summaries are contained in F.S. Regs., Part II, and the Staff Manual respectively. Title pages will be prepared in manuscript.

Hour, Date, Place.	Summary of Events and Information.	Remarks and references to Appendices
LOZINGHEM Dec 18th	Corps was formed, in A.R.O. but no actual separation of Staffs occurred.	
" 22.	Maj. Gen. Fanshawe assumed command of 2nd Cav. Div. Staff under usual orders. G.S.O.I G.S.O.2. Major E.C. Conran-Gordon G.S.O.3 A.A.& Q.M.G. Major W.K. Bonner D.A.A.& Q.M.G. Capt. H. Lewis.	
" 23	Left LOZINGHEM to take up new billets.	
BOURECQ 23	Took up billets. SIALKOTE Bde - RELY - AUCHY - WESTREHEM - FEBVIN - PIPPEMONT - LIGNY-LES-AIRES. AMBALA Bde. LA COUTURE, FLECHIN, BONCOURT, ESTRÉES BLANCHES, LIETTRES. LUCKNOW Bde. - ST HILAIRE, NORRENT FONTES, HAM. DIV. TROOPS - BOURECQ, ESPERUES, LIERRE. Supply railhead - BERGUETTE " " - ST VENANT DIV. H.Q - BOURECQ.	
" 24	Rec'd orders to move brass billets to make room for MEERUT DIV..	

WAR DIARY
or
INTELLIGENCE SUMMARY.
(Erase heading not required.)

Army Form C. 2118.

Hour, Date, Place.	Summary of Events and Information.	Remarks and references to Appendices
Bourecq Midnight 24	Orders were received for LUCKNOW Bde to move into new billets in area LIBOURG - PREDEFIN - FIEFS - HEUCHIN. 9 Div troops to area - ST HILAIRE, NORRENT-FONTES.	Appendix A.
NORRENT 25	Moved to new billets.	
do 26	Reinforcement arrived - 17 Lrs. 38 O.R., 38 horses 8" Hussars 23 " 23 " 1 K.D.G. 10 " 10 " 	
27	Major R.O.B. Taylor took over duties of G.S.O I Capt A. Evan R.E. took over command of Signal Sq. but not posted.	
28	Lt. Brooke Hunt joined Signal Sq.	
29		
30	Lt Col Simpson Baikie R.H.A left to take up appoint at LINDENHOEK 2nd Army	
31	Capt. Kirkwood, 19th Cav. & Capt Gulley, 32nd Lancers reported arrival as Gde. T.O's. Capt Molesworth, Comdg 2nd Sikh Troop accidentally shot.	New Cot S KL b/t 2nd Cav St

Appendix A.

Copy No 13

Q 596   24t

Orders by Major General H.D. FANSHAWE C.B.
BOURECQ 24-12-14.

Refer ST OMER and ARRAS maps 1/80000

(1) The Lucknow Cavy Bde will move to morrow 35th into new billets in the area LISBOURG PREDEFIN FIEFS HEUCHIN

(2) The main road AIRE - LILLERS between FONTES and BOURECQ will be kept clear of all other troops and transports between 10.0 and 11.0 a.m. the Bde will clear the junction of that road and the road to AUCHY AU BOIS by 11.0 a.m.

(3) The Regiment in HAM will move by the road from HAM to BORECQ and will join the Bde at the above mentioned junction of roads it will not leave HAM before 9.45 a.m.

(4) The Divl Troops will move into billets on the AIRE-LILLERS road as follows :-

(5) Billeting parties from each unit will meet the A A & Q M G at Divl Hdqrs at 10.30 a.m.

(6) The Divl Amn Col will leave LIERES at 10.30 a.m. and march by the road which leaves LIERES due North. It will receive instructions when the Head of the Column reaches the North end of ST HILAIRE.

(7) The Sialkote and Ambala Field Ambulances will be ready to march at 11.0 a.m. and will stand fast till orders reach them.

(8) The Lucknow Field Ambulance will remain at LINGHEM.

(9) Divl Hdqrs and the Field Troop will be ready to march at 1.0 p.m. the Amn Park at 2.0 p.m. These units will also stand fast till orders reach them.

(10) The Supply Col for Sialkote, Ambala & Lucknow Bdes will march by road ST HILAIRE AUCHY AU BOIS and will be west of the main road AIRE-LILLERS by 10.0 a.m.

(11) The Supply Col of the Lucknow Bde will halt on the ST HILAIRE - AUCHY AU BOIS - HEUCHIN road South of FEBVIN till it is known where it is to distribute

(12) The Supply Col of the Divl Troops will leave railhead at 2.30 p.m.

Copy

Copy No. 1 to Lucknow Bde by D/R   Cpl. LUPTON
Copy No. 2 to Divl Amn Col by D/R ⎫
Copy No. 3 to Sialkot Field Amb: by D/R ⎬ Cpl. WALDRON
Copy No. 4 to Ambala — " — by D/R ⎪
Copy No. 5 to O/C Divl Amn Park by D/R ⎭

Copy No. 6 to Divl Troops Supply Officers ⎫ by D/R
Copy No. 7 to D.E.C. for Field Troops   ⎬ Cpl.
Copy No. 8 to O/C Divl Supply Col   ⎭ Simmonds

Copy No. 9 to O/C S.T.
Copy No. 10 to A.D.M.S.
Copy No. 11 to Camp Comdt
Copy No. 12 to C.R.A.
Copy No. 13 Office Copy
Copy No. 14 — " —

W.C. Bourne Major
D.A.A. & Q.M.G.
1st Ind. Cav. Div.

WAR DIARY

OF

A & Q.

1st INDIAN CAVALRY DIVISION

JANUARY 1915.

A 2213

CONFIDENTIAL

WAR DIARY OF DAA&QMG 1st INDIAN CAVALRY DIVISION

from JANUARY 1st to 31st 1915

VOLUME III

No 3 Section
A. G's Office at Base
I.E. Force
Passed to W. S. Sectⁿ
on

Army Form C. 2118.

WAR DIARY
or
INTELLIGENCE SUMMARY.
(Erase heading not required.)

Instructions regarding War Diaries and Intelligence Summaries are contained in F. S. Regs., Part II, and the Staff Manual respectively. Title pages will be prepared in manuscript.

Hour, Date, Place.	Summary of Events and Information.	Remarks and references to Appendices
31-12-14 IN	Capt. Kirkwood 1/C & Capt. Molloy 32 Lrs reported arrival on Bn. T.O's. Capt. Molloy with Con 2" Field (rear accidentally shot.	
1-1-15 NORREST IN FONTER	8 dispatch riders with mot. cycles & 4 litographs (Lines) arrived Q.S. began arrival for Signal Sqn.	
2-1-15 ,, IN	Capt. Molloy buried at 2.30 p.m. 5 chop bean opened.	
3-1-15 ,, IN	Depriving is establishment for hipsting units were Signal of automatic sigs to Reinforcement team rather slow. 16 officers chargers remounts arrived, did not go notice reported. Indian mule cart unsatisfactory, horses badly debilitated. Lt Col Home relieved Lt Col Vaughan in AD S.T. Public body rather inefficient Command 2nd lr. aps; hopes head of a sack pulled up. him both bad + looks bad.. Horse rake recommend Debors not with out replaced.	APPENDIX A.
	Weekly wastage • sick for week ending 3rd ·/	APPENDIX B.

Army Form C. 2118.

WAR DIARY
or
INTELLIGENCE SUMMARY.

(Erase heading not required.)

Instructions regarding War Diaries and Intelligence Summaries are contained in F. S. Regs., Part II, and the Staff Manual respectively. Title pages will be prepared in manuscript.

Hour, Date, Place.	Summary of Events and Information.	Remarks and references to Appendices
4-1-15 W	NORRENT	
5-1-15 W	FONTES NIL	
6-1-15 W		
7-1-15 W	3.52 p.m. 2nd Echelon to return 1st & 110 & 43 O.R. 9" Horse D.1. 2.0 & 270 I.R. 20 2nd mi am in air at 12.45 a.m. Sirhind Bde. entrained at 16 m.p.h. duty to Trenches near BETHUNE.	
8-1-15 W	O.C. Div Troops established. Div. troops, for purposes of Adm. organized — Div Amm Column } under C.R.A. Field Troops under Amm Park } O.C F.T Field Ambulance } under A.D.M.S Supp & al Signal Sq. } under A.D.S.T Mob Workshop Unit } Div Troops Supp }	

Army Form C. 2118.

WAR DIARY
or
INTELLIGENCE SUMMARY.
(Erase heading not required.)

Instructions regarding War Diaries and Intelligence Summaries are contained in F. S. Regs., Part II, and the Staff Manual respectively. Title pages will be prepared in manuscript.

Hour, Date, Place.	Summary of Events and Information.	Remarks and references to Appendices
8-1-15 NORREMFONTES	Div. H.Q under Camp Commandant.	
9-1-15 "	Casualties of 2nd SIALKOTE Bde in trenches near GORRE Farm evening 7th - evening 9th. 17th Lancers. wounded 2nd Lt STANYFORTH, 1 O.R. C. Cor. Ind. O.R Killed 2, O.R. wounded 3 19. L.rs. wounded Maj F.F. LANCE, Jem BAWA SINGH other ranks wounded 5.	
10-1-15 "	Casualties of LUCKNOW Bde in trenches in relief of SIALKOTE Bde evening 9th - evening 11th. K.D.G's wounded O.R. 5 29 L.rs wounded O.R. 13, 36 Horse Killed O.R. 2 wounded O.R. 13, Killed Jem. SHAM SINGH. O.R. 5, wounded O.R. 4.	
11-1-15 "	Weekly un live n sick for week ending 10th. Weekly statement showing deficiencies in fighting units	App. C. App. D.

Army Form C. 2118.

WAR DIARY
or
INTELLIGENCE SUMMARY.
(Erase heading not required.)

Instructions regarding War Diaries and Intelligence Summaries are contained in F. S. Regs., Part II, and the Staff Manual respectively. Title pages will be prepared in manuscript.

Hour, Date, Place.	Summary of Events and Information.	Remarks and references to Appendices
12-1-15 NORRENT FONTES	Numbers of Sialkot Bde temporarily unfit owing to exposure in trenches evening 11th to 9th:— 17th Lancers — 19 men } Practically all will be 6th Cavy — 69 " } fit in 4 days. 19th Lancers — 130 "	
13-1-15 " "	Casualty return Lucknow Bde. shows total casualties in trenches for whole period evening 9th to evening 11th as follows:— K.D.Gs. wounded O.R. — 5 29th Lancers killed O.R.— 2, wounded O.R. 15, missing O.R.1. 36th Horse wounded Lt. R.D.S. Owen Jones, missing Jemadar Sham Singh. Killed O.R. 5, wounded O.R. 6, missing O.R. 6.	
13-1-15 " "	Numbers Sialkot Bde. temporarily unfit owing to exposure in trenches.— 17th Lancers — 19 men unable to walk 24 " excused duty 6th Cavy — 1 Ind. Off. & 28 men unable to walk 19th Lancers 120 " " "	
14-1-15 " "	Men temporarily unfit in Sialkot Bde. from exposure in trenches 17th Lancers — 16 19th Lancers — 93. 6th Cavy. 6.	

Army Form C. 2118.

WAR DIARY
or
INTELLIGENCE SUMMARY.

(Erase heading not required.)

Instructions regarding War Diaries and Intelligence Summaries are contained in F.S. Regs., Part II, and the Staff Manual respectively. Title pages will be prepared in manuscript.

Hour, Date, Place.	Summary of Events and Information.	Remarks and references to Appendices
15-1-15 NORRENT FONTES	Sialkote Bde return of men with sore feet from exposure in trenches	
"	17th Lancers — Hospital 21 — Line Sick 12	
"	6th Cavy — " — 29 — " — 3	
"	19th Lancers — " — 25 — " — 13.	
16-1-15 "	Addl. Casualties Lucknow Bde - Operations evening 9th-11th	
"	36th Horse - Wounded O.R. 2	
"	" Missing O.R. 10	
16-1-15 "	Sialkote Bde return of men with sore feet from trench exposure	
"	17th Lancers — Hospital 20 — Line Sick 10	
"	6th Cavy — " — 26 — " — 14	
"	19th Lancers — " — 25 — " — 41	
17-1-15 "	Daily return Sore Feet - Sialkote Bde. —	
"	17th Lancers — Same as on 16th	
"	6th Cavy — Hospital 24 — Line Sick 2	
"	19th Lancers — " — 25 — " — 25	

Army Form C. 2118.

WAR DIARY
or
INTELLIGENCE SUMMARY.
(Erase heading not required.)

Instructions regarding War Diaries and Intelligence Summaries are contained in F. S. Regs., Part II, and the Staff Manual respectively. Title pages will be prepared in manuscript.

Hour, Date, Place.	Summary of Events and Information.	Remarks and references to Appendices
18-1-15. NOGRENT FONTES	Amended Casualty Return 36th Horse - evenings 9th to 11th. Wounded - Lt. R.D.S. OWEN JONES. Missing - Jemadar SHAM SINGH. Killed - O.R. 5, Wounded O.R. 12, Missing O.R. 1. Weekly wastage in sick for week ending 17-1-1915. Weekly statement showing deficiencies in fighting units 14-1-15.	App. E. " F.

19-1-15	Daily Report sore feet or safe trench exposure of units of Sialkot Bde.
	  14th Lancers. Hospital - 18. Line Sick 8
	  6th Cavy. — 24 5
	  19th Lancers — 25 17.	

20-1-15	nil	
21-1-15	nil	
22-1-15	nil	
23-1-15	Reinforcements arrived.	
24-1-15	nil	
25-1-15	Wastage in sick for week ending 24-1-15 Statement re deficiencies in fighting units	App. G " H.

Army Form C. 2118.

WAR DIARY
or
INTELLIGENCE SUMMARY.
(Erase heading not required.)

Instructions regarding War Diaries and Intelligence Summaries are contained in F. S. Regs., Part II, and the Staff Manual respectively. Title pages will be prepared in manuscript.

Hour, Date, Place.	Summary of Events and Information.	Remarks and references to Appendices
26-1-15. NOFFRENTANTES	nil	
27-1-15 "	"	
28-1-15 "	Reinforcements arrived.	
29-1-15 "	nil	
30-1-15 "	nil	
31-1-15 "	nil.	

H Lewis Captr.
D.A.a.Q.M.G. M'Ind C.F.
2/2/15.

APPENDIX 'A'. Deficiencies in estabs: fighting units on 3-1-15.

Unit	Offrs. Br.	Offrs. Ind.	Other Ranks Br.	Other Ranks Ind.	Offrs. Ch.	Horses Riding	Horses Draught	Mules	Remarks
17th Lancers	4	–	–	–	–	14	1	1	
6th Cavy.	1	1	–	34	–	36	1	1	
19th Lancers	1	1	–	29	–	25	–	–	
A. Bty. R.H.A.	1	–	4	1	3	–	–	–	
8th Hussars	1	–	–	–	–	–	6	–	
9th Horse	1	3	–	54	–	4	–	–	
30th Lancers	3	3	–	57	–	28	–	–	
'U' Bty. R.H.A.	–	–	1	–	–	–	–	–	
1st K.D.G's	–	–	3	–	–	4	–	–	
29th Lancers	–	–	–	42	–	14	–	–	
36th Horse	1	2	–	30	–	35	–	–	
Total. –	13	10	8	253	3	160	8	2	

H Lewis Capt.
D.A.A.+Q.M.G.–S.C.8.

APPENDIX B

Weekly Wastage in Sickness
For week ending Jany. 3rd 1915.

Unit	Officers		Other Ranks		Remarks
	Br.	Ind.	Br.	Ind.	
17th Lancers			4		
6th Cavalry				1	
19th Lancers				1	
8th Hussars			4		
30th Lancers	2			11	
U Bty. R.H.A			1	1	
K.D.G's			3		
29th Lancers				2	
36th Horse				2	
C.R.A's Staff			1		
No.2 Fd Troop				5	
Divl. Ammn. Col.				4	
Divl. Supply Col.	1		4		
Divl. Ammn. Park			4		
TOTAL	3	–	21	30	

Hewis Capt.
D.A.A.& Q.M.G, 1st Ind. Cav. D.

APPENDIX - C.

Weekly wastage in sickness – week ending 10/1/15.

Unit	Officers		Other Ranks		Remarks
	Br.	Ind.	Br.	Ind.	
Q Bty. R.H.A.			1	1	
17th Lancers.			20		
6th Cavalry				2	
19th Lancers.	1				
8th Hussars.			4		
9th Horse.				21	
30th Lancers.	3			33	
K.D.G's	1		2		
29th Lancers.				2	
36th Horse.				2	
Dil. Ammn. Col.				8	
Divl. Supply Col.			13		
Divl. Ammn. Park.			3		
TOTAL.	5	.	43	69	

Meuris Capt.
D.A.A. & Q.M.G. 1st I.C.D.

APPENDIX D

Deficiencies in establishments of fighting units on 10-1-15.

Unit.	Offrs. Br.	Offrs. Ind.	Other Ranks Br.	Other Ranks Ind.	Offrs. Ch.	Horses Riding	Horses Draught	Mules	Remarks
'Q' Bty. R.H.A.	-	-	-	-	1	-	1	-	
14th Lancers	5	-	19	-	-	14	2	1	
6th Cavalry	-	1	-	25	-	-	2	+	
19th Lancers	2	2	-	21	-	-	-	-	
'A' Bty. R.H.A.	-	-	4	1	3	2	1	-	
8th Hussars									
9th Horse	-	2	-	32	-	-	-	-	
30th Lancers	1	5	-	41	-	-	-	-	
'U' Bty. R.H.A.									
1st K.D. Gs.	-	-	5	-	-	4	-	-	
29th Lancers	-	-	-	15	-	6	-	-	
36th Horse	-	1	-	8	-	-	-	-	
Total.	8	11	28	143	4	26	6	1	

Hewis Captn
D.A.A. & Q.M.G 1st Ind. Cav. D.

APPENDIX 'E'

Weekly Wastage in Sickness – 14-1-15.

Unit	Officers		Other Ranks		Hos	Remarks
	Br.	Ind.	Br.	Ind.		
14th Lancers			19			
6th Cavalry		2		28		
19th Lancers				13		
9th Horse				16		
30th Lancers				4		
H. Bty. R.H.A.				1		
29th Lancers		1		14		
36th Horse	1	1		32		
Divl. Ammn Column			5			
Signal Squadron			1			
Total	1	4	25	111		

Newis Captn.
D.A.A.Q.M.G.

APPENDIX 'F'

Deficiencies in establishment of fighting units on 14-1-15.

Unit	Offrs Br.	Offrs Ind.	Other Ranks Br.	Other Ranks Ind.	Offrs Ch.	Horses Riding	Horses Draught	Mules	Remarks
17th Lancers	4	-	19	-	-	14	2	1	
6th Cavalry	-	3	-	46	2	-	2	-	
19th Lancers	-	2	-	31	-	-	-	-	
B Bty. R.H.A	-	-	1	-	-	-	-	-	
A Bty. R.H.A	-	-	-	1	3	2	1	-	
8th Hussars	-	-	2	-	-	-	-	-	
9th Horse	-	2	-	32	-	-	-	-	
30th Lancers	1	3	-	25	-	-	3	-	
K.D.Gs	1	-	41	-	-	-	-	-	
29th Lancers	-	1	-	41	-	-	-	-	
36th Horse	3	3	-	52	1	-	-	-	
Total	9	14	93	228	6	16	8	1	

H Lewis Capt
D.A.A. & Q.M.G.

APPENDIX G
Weekly wastage in Sickness - 24-1-15.

Unit	Officers		Other Ranks		Folls.	Remarks
	Br.	Ind.	Br.	Ind.		
Q. Bty. R.H.A				1		
17th Lancers			28			
6th Cavalry	1	–		12		
19th Lancers				3		
A. Bty R.H.A			2			
9th Horse				7		
30th Lancers				3		
K.L. Gs.	1	–	11	–		
29th Lancers				2	1	
36th Horse				5		
Lucknow Bde S&T					1	
Signal Squadron			1			
No. 2 Fd Troop			1			
Divl. Ammn. Column	1	–	–	–	1	
Divl. Supply Column			5		2	
	3	–	48	33	5	

Nevin Capt.
D.A.A & Q.M.G

APPENDIX 'H'

Deficiencies in establishments of fighting units on 26-1-15.

Unit	Officers Br.	Officers Ind.	Other Ranks Br.	Other Ranks Ind.	Offrs Ch.	Horses Riding	Horses Draught	Mules	Remarks
Q. Bty. R.H.A.	–	–	–	1	–	–	–	–	
14th Lancers	4	–	44	–	–	1	2	–	
6th Cavy.	1	3	–	44	2	1	–	–	
19th Lancers	–	1	–	4	–	–	–	–	
A. Bty. R.H.A.	–	–	–	–	–	4	–	–	
8th Hussars	–	–	–	–	–	–	3	–	
9th Horse	1	2	–	31	–	–	1	–	
30th Lancers	1	1	–	9	–	–	3	–	
U. Bty. R.H.A	–	–	–	–	5	–	33	–	
K.D. Gs.	2	–	71	–	–	9	–	–	
29th Lancers	–	1	–	36	–	–	–	–	
36th Horse	2	2	–	45	–	–	–	–	
Total	11	10	115	173	7	15	42	–	

Mewis
Captn
L.a.a.Q.M.G.

APPENDIX I

Weekly wastage in Sickness – 31-1-1915.

Unit.	Officers.		Other Ranks.		Folls.	Remarks.
	Br.	Ind.	Br.	Ind.		
14th Lancers.	1	–	3	–	–	
6th Cavalry	–	–	–	5	–	
19th Lancers	–	3	–	11	–	
8th Hussars.	–	–	1	–	–	
30th Lancers.	–	–	–	4	–	
Ambala Bde Sig. Troop	–	–	1	–	–	
'U' Bty. R.H.A.	–	–	3	–	–	
29th Lancers.	–	–	–	5	–	
36th Horse	–	1	–	45	1	
Divl. Signal Squadron	–	–	1	–	–	
No. 2 Field Troop.	–	–	–	4	–	
Divl. Supply Column	–	–	7	–	–	
Senior Engnr. Offr.					1	
Total.	1	4	16	74	2	

Mewis
Captn.
D.A.A.&Q.M.G.

APPENDIX J.

Deficiencies in establishments - fighting units - 31-1-15.

Unit.	Officers.		Other Ranks		Offrs. Ch.	Horses Riding	Horses Draught	Mules	Remarks.
	Br.	Ind.	Br.	Ind.					
17th Lancers	5	-	47	-	-	5	-	-	
6th Cavalry	1	2	-	33	-	-	-	-	
19th Lancers	-	4	-	14	-	-	-	-	
8th Hussars	-	-	2	-	-	-	-	2	
9th Horse	-	1	-	-	-	-	1	-	
30th Lancers	1	1	-	-	-	-	3	2	
K. D. Gs.	2	-	69	-	-	9	-	-	
29th Lancers	1	1	-	10	-	-	-	-	
36th Horse	1	2	-	83	-	-	-	-	
Total.	11	11	118	140	-	14	4	4	

Hewis Captn
D. A. A. & Q. M. G.

WAR DIARY
OF
A & Q

1ST INDIAN CAVALRY DIVISION

FEBRUARY - 1915

Serial No 2.

121/4719

WAR DIARY
With Appendices.
OF
D.A.A. and Q.M.G: 1st Indian Cavalry Division.

From 1st February 1915 to 28th February 1915

Army Form C. 2118.

WAR DIARY

INTELLIGENCE SUMMARY.

(Erase heading not required.)

Instructions regarding War Diaries and Intelligence Summaries are contained in F. S. Regs., Part II, and the Staff Manual respectively. Title pages will be prepared in manuscript.

Hour, Date, Place.	Summary of Events and Information.	Remarks and references to Appendices
1-2-15. NORRENT FONTES.	Lt-Col Covington, S.& T. Corps joined the S.T. in relief of Lt-Col Moore, A.D.S.T. Appointment A.D.S.T. abolished. Lt-Col Covington assumed title & duties of O.C. 1st Indian Cavy. Div. S.& T. Corps. Lt-Col Moore proceeded to Ind. Cavy Corps to take up duties of A.D.S.T. Ind. Cavy. Corps. A.T. Carts & mules in L.A.A. destn. with Ammn Col. unsatisfactory. Carts in bad condition, also mules. Column short of 3rd & more or less immobile. Replacements demanded.	
2-2-15.	Major H.A. Young, S.& T. Corps, assumed duties of Senior Supply officer. Revised orders received regarding indenting for remounts to replace deficiencies — Previous system of indenting thro' D.R. Commt. not entirely satisfactory as certain amount of delay incurred. Orders now received are that	

Army Form C. 2118.

WAR DIARY

INTELLIGENCE SUMMARY.

(Erase heading not required.)

Instructions regarding War Diaries and Intelligence Summaries are contained in F.S. Regs., Part II, and the Staff Manual respectively. Title pages will be prepared in manuscript.

Hour, Date, Place.	Summary of Events and Information.	Remarks and references to Appendices
2-2-15. NOTRENT FONTES. W	that all deficiencies in animals to be shown in weekly state of "Present + Fit". This return forwarded by a.g.m.R. to A.G. Rouen. Latter arrange to co-ordinate supply of Brit. + Indian Personnel + Animals.	
3-2-15 4-2-15 5-2-15 6-2-15 } W	nil	
4-2-15. W	Weekly wastage in sick. Deficiencies in fighting units. Notices that supply of reinforcements is slow. ~~[crossed out]~~	APP "A" " — B"
8-2-15. W	Field Sqdn moved into billets at St. HILAIRE, vacated by 2nd Armd Column Sqdn incomplete, consisting of 2 officers, 51 men + 86 horses. Latter personnel not yet arrived. Reinforcements arrived.	

Army Form C. 2118.

WAR DIARY
or
INTELLIGENCE SUMMARY.

(Erase heading not required.)

Instructions regarding War Diaries and Intelligence Summaries are contained in F. S. Regs., Part II, and the Staff Manual respectively. Title pages will be prepared in manuscript.

Hour, Date, Place.	Summary of Events and Information.	Remarks and references to Appendices
9-2-15 NORRENT FONTES	Inf. Exercise. Transport was not entirely satisfactory. Several minor points, easily remediable, were noticed.	
10-2-15. "	10 officers changes indented for. Representation put up to Ind. Cavy. Corps re delay experienced in obtaining reinforcements.	
11-2-15 " 12-2-15 " 13-2-15 "	nil.	
14-2-15 "	Weekly wastage from sickness. Deficiencies in establishments of fighting units. G.H.Q. report that reinforcements for Ind. units or way up. Men being sent from Home to fill shortages in Brit. units.	APP "C" " "D"
15-2-15 "	nil.	
16-2-15 "	Reinforcements arrived for Indian units.	
17-2-15 " 18-2-15 " 20-2-15 " 21-2-15 "	nil.	
22-2-15 "	Weekly wastage from sickness. Deficiencies in establishments of fighting units	APP "E" " "F"

Army Form C. 2118.

WAR DIARY

INTELLIGENCE SUMMARY.

(Erase heading not required.)

Hour, Date, Place.	Summary of Events and Information.	Remarks and references to Appendices
23-2-15 NORRENT FONTES	nil	
24-2-15	"	
25-2-15	"	
26-2-15	Reinforcements & Remounts arrived.	
27-2-15	nil.	
28-2-15	Weekly Wastage from sickness. Deficiencies in establishment of fighting units	APP "G" " "H"

Henri
Capt?
D.A.A. & Q.M.G, 1st Ind Cav. S.
1/3/15.

APPENDIX 'A'

Weekly Wastage from Sickness – 4-2-1915.

Unit	Officers Br.	Officers Ind.	Other Ranks Br.	Other Ranks Ind.	Folls.	Remarks
17th Lancers.	–	–	10	–		
6th Cavalry.	–	–	–	3		
19th Lancers.	–	–	–	7		
8th Hussars.	1	–	3	–		
9th Horse.	–	1	–	6	–	
29th Lancers.	–	–	–	9	–	
36th Horse.	–	1	–	3	–	
Lucknow Bde Signal Troop	–	–	–	1		
No. 2 Field Troop.	–	–	1	5		
Divl. Ammn Column.	–	–	–	–	1	
Divl. Supply Column	–	–	8	–	–	
Total. –	1	2	22	34	1	

Heuri Capt.
D.A.A & Q.M.G.

APPENDIX "B"

Deficiencies in establishments – Fighting units – 4-2-15.

Unit	Officers Br.	Officers Ind.	Other Ranks Br.	Other Ranks I.A.	O/pr Ch.	Horses Riding	Heavy Draught	Light Draught	Pack Horse	Mules	Remarks
17th Lancers	5	–	56	–	–	5	–	–	–	–	
6th Cavalry	1	2	–	30	–	–	–	–	–	–	
19th Lancers	–	4	–	23	–	–	–	–	–	–	
8th Hussars	–	–	6	–	4	4	2	–	–	–	
9th Horse	–	2	–	4	–	–	–	1	–	2	
30th Lancers	1	1	–	–	–	–	2	–	–	2	
K.D.G.	2	–	70	–	–	15	–	–	–	1	
29th Lancers	1	1	–	18	–	–	–	–	–	–	
36th Horse	–	3	–	81	–	–	–	–	–	–	
Total	10	13	132	156	4	24	4	1	–	5	

H Lewis Capt.
D.A.A. & Q.M.G.

APPENDIX "C"

Weekly Wastage from Sickness — 14-2-1915.

Unit	Officers		Other Ranks		Follrs	Remarks
	Br.	Ind.	Br.	Ind.		
Hd. Qrs. Sialkot Bde.	–	–	1	–	–	
17th Lancers.	–	–	4	–	–	
Hd. Qrs. Ambala Bde.	–	–	1	–	–	
9th Horse.	–	–	–	3	–	
30th Lancers.	–	–	–	1	–	
K.D.Gs.	–	–	2	–	–	
29th Lancers.	–	–	–	1	–	
36th Horse.	–	–	–	2	1	
Lucknow Bde. Signal Troop.	–	–	–	1	–	
'A' Bty. R.H.A.	–	–	2	–	–	
'Q' — " — " —	–	–	1	–	–	
'U' — " — " —	–	–	2	–	–	
Field Squadron.	–	–	2	–	–	
No. 2 Field Troop.	–	–	–	1	3	
Divl. Ammn. Column.	–	–	–	–	1	
" " Park	–	–	1	–	–	
" Supply Column	–	–	7	–	–	
Total	–	–	23	9	5	

H. Lewis Capt.
D.A.A. & Q.M.G.

APPENDIX "D"

Deficiencies in establishments – Fighting units – 14-2-1915.

Unit	Officers		Other Ranks		Offrs. Ch.	Horses Riding	Heavy Draught	Light Draught	Pack Horses	Mules	Remarks
	Br.	Ind.	Br.	Ind.							
17th Lancers.	4	–	15	–	5	4	2	–	–	–	
6th Cavalry.	2	2	–	30	3	–	–	–	–	–	
19th Lancers.	–	4	–	23	–	–	–	–	–	–	
8th Hussars.	–	–	3	–	5	10	–	–	5	–	
9th Horse.	–	2	–	9	3	–	1	–	–	–	
30th Lancers.	1	–	–	–	–	–	2	–	–	2	
K.D.Gs.	–	–	30	–	–	1	–	–	–	–	
29th Lancers.	1	1	–	16	4	–	–	–	–	–	
36th Horse.	–	3	–	80	2	–	1	–	–	–	
"A" Bty. R.H.A.	–	–	4	–	–	–	–	7	–	–	
"Q" " " "	–	–	4	4	3	–	–	6	–	–	
"U" " " "	–	–	12	–	–	–	–	6	–	–	
Total	8	12	68	162	22	15	6	19	5	2	

Lewis Capt.
D.A.A. & Q.M.G.

APPENDIX "E"

Weekly Wastage from Sickness – 21-2-1915.

Unit	Officers		Other Ranks		Foll.	Remarks
	Br.	Ind.	Br.	Ind.		
14th Lancers	1	–	6	–	–	
6th Cavalry	–	–	–	1	–	
19th Lancers	–	–	–	1	–	
Sialkot Bde. Transport H.Q.	–	–	–	–	1	
Hd. Qrs. Ambala Bde.	–	–	1	–	–	
9th Horse	–	–	–	5	–	
K. D. Gs.	–	–	2	–	–	
29th Lancers	–	–	–	5	–	
36th Horse	–	–	–	4	–	
Lucknow Bde. Signal Troop	–	–	1	–	–	
C.R.A's. Staff	–	–	1	–	–	
Q. Bty. R.H.A.	–	–	1	–	–	
Field Squadron	–	–	2	–	–	
Divl. Ammn. Column	–	–	1	7	7	
" " Park	–	–	3	–	–	
" Supply Column	–	–	8	–	–	
Total	1	–	26	23	8	

H. Lewis
Captn.
D.A.A. & Q.M.G.

APPENDIX "F"

Deficiencies in establishments – Fighting units – 21-2-1915.

Units	Officers		Other Ranks		offrs Ch.	Horses Riding	Heavy Draught	Light Draught	Pack Horses	Mules	Remarks
	Br.	Ind.	Br.	Ind.							
14th Lancers	3	–	4	–	12	5	–	–	–	–	
5th Cavalry	1	–	–	3	3	–	–	–	–	–	
19th Lancers	–	2	–	3	–	–	–	–	–	–	
8th Hussars	–	–	1	–	1	–	2	–	5	2	
9th Horse	–	1	–	10	4	–	–	–	–	2	
30th Lancers	1	–	–	–	–	–	2	–	–	–	
K.D.G's	–	–	31	–	–	–	–	–	–	–	
29th Lancers	1	–	–	6	1	–	–	–	–	–	
36th Horse	–	1	–	11	3	–	1	–	–	–	
"A" Bty. R.H.A.	–	–	3	–	–	2	–	7	–	–	
"Q" — " —	–	–	4	3	–	–	–	–	–	–	
"U" — " —	–	–	11	–	5	–	1	6	–	–	
Total. –	6	4	54	36	29	7	6	13	5	4	

Hews Capt.
D.A.A. & Q.M.G.

APPENDIX "G"

Weekly Wastage from Sickness - 28-2-1915.

Unit	Officers		Other Ranks		Foll[r]	Remarks
	Br.	Ind.	Br.	Ind.		
17th Lancers	–	–	6	–	–	
6th Cavalry	–	–	–	2	–	
19th Lancers	–	–	–	2	–	
Hd. Qrs Ambala Bde.	–	–	1	2	–	
8th Hussars	–	–	3	–	–	
9th Horse	–	–	–	1	–	
30th Lancers	–	–	–	4	–	
K.D.Gs	–	–	1	–	–	
29th Lancers	–	–	–	3	–	
36th Horse	–	–	–	2	–	
Field Squadron	–	–	2	–	–	
Divl. Ammn Park	–	–	1	–	–	
" Supply Column	–	–	2	–	–	
'A' Bty. R.H.A.	–	–	1	–	–	
'U' " "	–	–	1	–	–	
Sialkot Cavy Fd Amble	–	–	–	–	12	
Total	–	–	18	16	12	

Lewis
Captn
D.A.A. & Q.M.G.

APPENDIX "H"

Deficiencies in establishments - Fighting units - 28-2-1915.

Units	Officers		Other Ranks		Offy. Ch.	Horses Riding	Heavy Draught	Light Draught	Pack Horse	Mules	Remarks
	Br.	Ind.	Br.	Ind.							
14th Lancers	1	-	4	-	-	18	-	-	-	1	
6th Cavalry	1	-	-	2	-	-	-	-	-	-	
19th Lancers	-	2	-	5	-	-	2	-	-	-	
8th Hussars	-	-	-	-	4	-	-	-	-	2	
9th Horse	-	1	-	11	4	-	-	-	-	2	
30th Lancers	1	1	-	-	-	-	2	-	-	-	
K.D.Gs.	-	-	4	-	-	-	-	-	-	-	
29th Lancers	-	1	-	10	1	-	-	-	-	-	
36th Horse	-	1	3	-	-	-	-	-	-	-	
'A' Bty. R.H.A	-	-	5	-	-	-	-	2	-	-	
'Q' " "	-	-	6	3	-	-	-	-	-	-	
'U' " "	-	-	8	-	4	-	-	2	-	-	
Total	3	6	30	31	16	18	4	4	-	5	

H Lewis
Capt.
D.A.A. & Q.M.G.

WAR DIARY OF A & Q

1st INDIAN CAVALRY DIVISION

MARCH - 1915

WAR DIARY
with appendices.
OF
D.A.A. and Q.M.G., 1st Indian Cavalry Division.

From 1st March 1915 to 31st March 1915

Army Form C. 2118.

WAR DIARY
INTELLIGENCE SUMMARY.
(Erase heading not required.)

Instructions regarding War Diaries and Intelligence Summaries are contained in F. S. Regs., Part II, and the Staff Manual respectively. Title pages will be prepared in manuscript.

Hour, Date, Place.		Summary of Events and Information.	Remarks and references to Appendices
1-3-15	NORRENT FONTES.	Revised orders received regarding replacement of deficiencies in personnel. In future, demands to be sent direct to D.A.G. 3rd Echelon Base, and not this A.G. G.H.Q.	
2-3-15 – 3-3-15	"	nil.	
4-3-15	"	Weekly wastage in sickness. Statement showing deficiencies in establishment - fighting units.	APP 'A' " 'B'
6-3-15	"	Reinforcements & Remounts arrived.	
9-3-15 – 10-3-15	"	nil.	
11-3-15	MARLES.	Div. H.Q'rs moved to MARLES – Lee – 3 Bdes to BOIS DE DAMES Field Sect. I.H.A. Section, Div Ammn Col, to AUCHEL Lucknow Fd. Amblce.	APP. 'C & D'
12-3-15	"	SIALKOT Bde moved to MARLES AMBALA " – CAUCHY & FLORINGHEM LUCKNOW " – AUCHEL	
13-3-15	"	nil.	

Army Form C. 2118.

WAR DIARY
INTELLIGENCE SUMMARY.
(Erase heading not required.)

Instructions regarding War Diaries and Intelligence Summaries are contained in F. S. Regs., Part II, and the Staff Manual respectively. Title pages will be prepared in manuscript.

Hour, Date, Place.	Summary of Events and Information.	Remarks and references to Appendices
14-3-15. MARLES.	Weekly wastage in sickness Statement showing deficiencies in establishments - fighting units.	APP "E". "F".
15-3-15 BOURECQ	Division moved to new billets Div. Hd.Qrs BOURECQ Signal Sqdr. " Lucknow Hd Arty " field Sqdn + Sqdn - LESPESSES S.A.H. Section Div Ammn Coln WESTREHEM SIALKOT Bde. - ST HILAIRE - COTTES - LIERES AMBALA " - FONTAIN - LES - HERMANS - NEDONCHELLE - NEDON - AMETTES. LUCKNOW - CUHEM - FLECHIN - BONCOURT - PIPPEMONT - FEBVIN.	
16-3-15 — 17-3-15 "	nil.	
16-3-15 ENQUIN.	Div. Hd.Qrs moved to ENQUIN. Signal Squadron to " field Squadron + Troop to SERNY.	

Army Form C. 2118.

WAR DIARY
or
INTELLIGENCE SUMMARY.

(Erase heading not required.)

Instructions regarding War Diaries and Intelligence Summaries are contained in F. S. Regs., Part II, and the Staff Manual respectively. Title pages will be prepared in manuscript.

Hour, Date, Place.	Summary of Events and Information.	Remarks and references to Appendices
16-3-15 (contd.) ENQUIN	Lucknow Hd. Amb. to RELY with other 2 Ambces. SIALKOT Bde - ERNY ST JULIEN - BONY - RUPIGNY - GREUPPE - BEAUMETZ - LES - AIRE - LAIRES LUCKNOW Bde. - LINGHEM - LIETTRES - LONGHEM - ESTREE BLANCHE - FLECHINELLE - CUHEM FLECHIN - BONCOURT.	
19-3-15 - 20-3-15 "	nil	
21-3-15 "	Weekly Wastage in sickness. Statement deficiencies in establishment fighting unit	APP G " H
22-3-15 "	nil	
23-3-15 "	2 Section Ammn. Col - organised on Home lines - arrived Strength - 16 G. S. Wagons. 6 " Limbered Wagons 132 Light Draught Horses 10 Riding Horses + 3 British Ranks	
24-3-15	51 addl. British Ranks for Ammn Column arrived.	

Army Form C. 2118.

WAR DIARY
or
INTELLIGENCE SUMMARY.

(Erase heading not required.)

Instructions regarding War Diaries and Intelligence Summaries are contained in F. S. Regs., Part II, and the Staff Manual respectively. Title pages will be prepared in manuscript.

Hour, Date, Place.		Summary of Events and Information.	Remarks and references to Appendices
25-3-15	ENQUIN(?)	nil	
26-3-15	"	Remounts arrived.	
27-3-15	"	nil	
28-3-15	"	Weekly wastage in sickness. Deficiencies in establishments of fighting units	APP. I " J
29-3-15	"	nil	
30-3-15	"	106 A.T. Carts with Mules & Personnel, set free from Ammn Column by arrival of Brit. Personnel, entrained at BERGUETTE & returned to Base.	
31-3-15.	"	Nil.	

Henri Capt:
D.A.A.& Q.M.G. 1st Ind. Cav. Dn
31/3/15.

APPENDIX "A"

Weekly wastage from Sickness – 4-3-1915

Unit	Officers		Other Ranks		Follrs	Remarks
	Br.	Ind.	Br.	Ind.		
19th Lancers	-	-	-	2	-	
Hd.Qrs Ambala Bde.	-	-	1	-	-	
9th Horse	-	-	-	3	-	
30th Lancers	-	1	-	1	-	
Ambala Bde Sig. Troop	-	-	1	-	-	
9th Lancers	-	1	-	2	1	
36th Horse	-	5	2	8	-	
Lucknow Bde Mob. Vety Sect	-	-	-	1	-	
Field Squadron	-	-	1	-	-	
Field Troop	-	-	-	3	-	
Divl. Supply Column	-	-	6	-	-	
Total	-	7	11	20	1	

Henri Capt.
D.A.A. & Q.M.G.

APPENDIX B

Deficiencies in Establishments – Fighting units – 7-3-1915.

Unit	Officers Br.	Officers Ind.	Other Ranks Br.	Other Ranks Ind.	offrs Ch.	Horses Riding	Heavy Draught	Light Draught	Horses Pack	Mules	Remarks
17th Lancers	–	–	3	–	–	–	–	–	–	–	
19th Lancers	–	–	–	–	–	2	–	–	–	–	
8th Hussars	–	–	–	–	–	2	–	–	–	–	
9th Horse	–	–	–	3	–	4	–	–	–	–	
30th Lancers	1	1	–	–	–	–	–	–	–	–	
K.D.G.	–	–	4	–	–	–	–	–	–	–	
29th Lancers	–	1	–	3	–	1	–	–	–	–	
36th Horse	–	5	–	10	1	–	–	–	–	–	
Total	1	7	7	16	1	12	–	–	–	–	

Henri Capt.
D.A.A. & Q.M.G.

SECRET app: 'C' DAAG

OPERATION ORDER No 1

By MAJOR GENERAL H.D. FANSHAWE, C.B.,

Commanding 1st Indian Cavalry Division.

Headquarters, 1st Ind: Cav: Division.
10th March 1915.

Reference Map $\frac{1}{80,000}$

1.   The Division will march to BOIS-DES-DAMES as follows :-

Sialkot Brigade Starting point BELLERY at 4.30 a.m., Route FERFAY - CAUCHY - A la TOUR - CAMBLAIN - CHATELAIN - MARLES - LA BEUVRIERE.

Lucknow Brigade. Starting point NEDONCHELLE Church at 4.30 a.m., Route AUMERVAL - PERNES - CAMBLAIN - CHATELAIN - MARLES.-

Ambala Brigade Starting point FEBVIN at 4.30 a.m., Route FEBVIN - FONTAINE - LEZ - HERMANS - NEDON- CHELLE and thereafter as for Lucknow Brigade.

Troops will be in BOIS DES DAMES by 8.0 AM.

2.   Transport. (a) Transport of Sialkot Brigade will follow its brigade along the main AUCHY - AU - BOIS, FERFAY, CAUCHY CAMBLAIN - CHATELAIN road to MARLES and LABEUVRIERE and will park in the BOIS DES DAMES with its Brigade.

(b) Transport of Lucknow and Ambala Brigades will follow in the order mentioned in rear of the Ambala Brigade and will park at MARLES, the Lucknow Brigade transport will turn to the left in MARLES up the LOZINGHEM road and park North of the railway crossing - The Ambala Brigade transport will turn to the right in MARLES and park on the LABUISSIERE road South of the railway.

(c) The Divisional Troops transport will march to MARLES at the same hour and at the head of the Divisional Ammunition Column (See para 3) - Route AMES, BELLERY, AUMERVAL, PERNES, CAMBLAIN - CHATELAIN, MARLES.

3. Divisional Ammunition Column, S.A.A., Section. The Divisional Ammunition Column will march to AUCHEL at 7.30 a.m., Starting point Bridge under LIERES - LILLERS railway on ST HILAIRE - LIERES road. Route AMES, BELLERY, AUMERVAL, PERNES, FLORINGHEM, CAUCHY, AUCHEL.

4. Medical. Lucknow Field Ambulance (Less motor ambulance) only will accompany the Division and will follow the Divisional Ammunition Column to AUCHEL Motor ambulances of the Lucknow Field Ambulance will proceed to AUCHEL at 9.0 a.m.,

Sialkot and Ambala Field Ambulances will remain in billets.

5. Field Squadron. The Field Squadron will remain in its present billets.

6. Reports. Report centre will be opened at MARLES at 7.0 a.m.,

                R.o'B.Taylor
                            Lieut: Colonel,
                   General Staff,
            1st Indian Cavalry Division.

Issued at 7.35 p.m.,

Rendyvous of S.C. at 5 p.m.
Marles at 6. a.m
warn B M's aeroplanes.

APPENDIX "D".

Orders were issued by I.C.C. to move into the BOIS DE DAMES during the night of 10th/11th.

See Appendix "C" for Division Orders.

From BELLERY - MARLES is 7½ miles. The head of SIALKOT Bde arrived at 6.30 a.m.; the head of its 1st Line Transport at 8.45 a.m. Allowing for the length of the Bde it lost quite 2 hours in 7½ miles.

The transport of the other Bdes lost time in about the same proportion.

The only transport that kept up was the pack mules carrying ammunition led by mounted men.

This form of transport was unsatisfactory as the mules having to trot with a load at a horse's pace were much distressed, and it was evident that 2 or 3 average marches would break them down.

The rest of the transport is capable of about 2½ miles an hour unless fitted with light draught horses and limbered wagons. From the above, and previous experience, it is clear that the transport of the Division is very bad. In ordinary cavalry work the bulk of the transport would never be seen after the first day and the pack mules would be dead by about the 3rd day. The native mule drivers, syces, etc, are not very satisfactory. For many miles behind the column they wandered about along in parties of 2 or 3; they are mostly of miserable physique and in boots usually 6 sizes too large. Some wearing 5 flannel shirts apiece, 2 coats and a heavy overcoat, lame and exhausted, unable to ask the way, and presented a pitiable appearance.

H Lewis Capt

WORKING OF SUPPLY COLUMN.

The Corps fixed the preliminary rendezvous at S1 Exit of CHOCQUES on CHOCQUES - MARLES road at nothing

By 1 p.m. the Division with transport was in the BOIS DE DAMES with Divl. Troops at AUCHEL and H.Q. at MARLES.

At 1.30 p.m. an order came from Corps saying that roads between MARLES and CHOCQUES were not to be used by M.T. and no M.T. was to move N. of the MARLES - LABUISSIERE road. The road to be followed was AIRE - LILLERS - BURBURE - RAIMBERT - AUCHEL - MARLES and return via LOZINGHEM and LILLERS; rendezvous to be fixed at 5.p.m. by Division.

The Corps did not inform Supply Column.

The Division at once informed Supply Column and gave rendezvous at S.W. Exit of MARLES at 5 p.m. Bdes were told to refill there with Horse Transport.

It was then considered likely that Division might billet at AUCHEL, MARLES, LABEUVRIERE.

Supply Column was then intercepted between RAIMBERT and AUCHEL and a rendezvous given at AUCHEL.

5 p.m. it was decided that Bdes should pass the night in the BOIS DE DAMES and Supply Column was ordered in to S.W. end of MARLES.

Refilling points were given for each Brigade in 3 different points in MARLES and Brigades informed. Horse Transport then refilled.

APPENDIX E
Weekly Wastage from Sickness 14-3-1915

Unit	Officers Br.	Officers Ind.	Other Rks. Br.	Other Rks. Ind.	Foll⁰	Remarks
17th Lancers	-	-	1	-	-	
6th Cavalry	1	1	-	3	-	
19th Lancers	-	-	-	4	-	
8th Hussars	1	-	-	-	-	
9th Horse	1	1	-	10	-	
30th Lancers	-	-	-	6	-	
Ambala Bde S. & T.	-	-	-	1	-	
K.D.Gs.	-	-	3	-	-	
29th Lancers	-	-	-	6	1	
36th Horse	-	-	-	5	-	
Lucknow Bde S.& T.	-	-	-	-	1	
Divl. Ammn Col.	1	-	-	-	-	
Divl. Supply Col.	-	-	6	-	-	
Field Squadron	-	-	2	-	-	
Field Troop	-	-	-	3	2	
Total	4	2	12	38	4	

Henri Capt
D.A.A. & Q.M.G.

APPENDIX F

Deficiencies in Establishments - Fighting Units - 14-3-1915.

Unit	Officers		Other Ranks		Offrs Ch.	Horses Riding	Heavy Draught	Light Draught	Horse Pack	Mules	Remarks
	Br.	Ind.	Br.	Ind.							
14th Lancers		1									
6th Cavalry				2							
19th Lancers				1	1	6					
8th Hussars						12					
9th Horse	1			11		8					
30th Lancers	1			1							
K.D.Gs.			4			2					
2nd Lancers		1		10							
36th Horse	3			11							
Total	6	8	36	1	28	-	.	.			

Hewis Capt.
D.A.A.&Q.M.G.

APPENDIX G

Weekly Wastage from Sickness - 21-3-1915.

Unit	Officers Br.	Officers Ind.	Other Ranks Br.	Other Ranks Ind.	Follrs	Remarks
Divl. Hd. Qrs	-	-	1	#	1	
17th Lancers	-	-	5	-	-	
6th Cavalry	-	-	-	3	1	
8th Hussars	-	-	2	-	-	
38th Lancers	-	-	-	6	-	
Ambala Bde S. & T.	-	-	-	1	1	
K. D. Gs.	-	-	4	-	-	
29th Lancers	-	-	1	1	5	
36th Horse	-	-	-	4	-	
Lucknow Bde S & T.	-	-	-	-	3	
S.A.A. Sec. Divl. Ammn. Col.	-	-	-	-	1	
Ammn Park	-	-	1	-	-	
Field Squadron	-	-	1	-	-	
Sialkot Cavy Fd. Amb.	-	-	-	-	14	
Lucknow — " —	-	-	1	-	1	
Motor Amblce workshops	-	-	2	-	-	
Divl. Supply Col.	-	-	1	-	-	
Hd.Qrs A. S. C.	-	-	-	-	1	
Total	-	-	19	15	28	

H Lewis Capt.
D.A.A. & Q.M.G.

APPENDIX H

Deficiencies in Establishments - Fighting units - 21-3-1915.

Unit	Officers Br.	Officers Ind.	Other Ranks Br.	Other Ranks Ind.	Offrs. Ch.	Horses Riding	Heavy Draught	Light Draught	Horses Pack	Mule	Remarks
17th Lancers		4									
6th Cavalry				4							
19th Lancers					2	9	1				
8th Hussars		4			1	67					
9th Horse		1		10		30	1				
30th Lancers		1		5	3	20					
K.D.G's.			34			25					
29th Lancers		1		10							
36th Horse		2		12	1	1					
Total	-	5	42	41	7	152	2	-	-	-	

Hewis Captn
D.A.A.&Q.M.G.

APPENDIX I

Weekly Wastage from Sickness.— 28-3-1915.

Unit	Officers		Other Ranks		Foll.	Remarks
	Br.	Ind.	Br.	Ind.		
Divl. Hd. Qrs.	-	-	1	-	-	
14th Lancers	-	-	3	-	1	
6th Cavalry	-	-	-	5	-	
19th Lancers	-	-	-	1	-	
8th Hussars	1	-	1	-	-	
9th Horse	-	-	-	2	-	
30th Lancers	-	1	-	-	-	
29th Lancers	-	-	-	2	-	
36th Horse	-	-	-	11	5	
Lucknow Bde. S. & T.	-	-	-	-	2	
Ammn. Park	-	-	1	-	-	
Field Squadron	-	-	1	-	-	
Divl. Supply Col.	-	-	1	-	-	
Field Troop	-	-	-	2	1	
Signal Squadron	-	-	1	-	-	
Total	1	1	9	23	9	

H Lewis Captn.
D.A.A. & Q.M.G.

APPENDIX J

Deficiencies in Establishments - Fighting Units - 28-3-1915.

Unit	Officers		Other Ranks		Offrs. Ch.	Horses Riding	Heavy Draught	Light Draught	Horses Pack	Mules	Remarks
	Br.	Ind.	Br.	Ind.							
17th Lancers			4		2	4					
6th Cavalry				2		3					
19th Lancers					3	6					
8th Hussars			6		1	47					
9th Horse				10	1	31					
30th Lancers		2		3	3	19					
K.D.Gs.			29			27					
29th Lancers		2		10	2						
36th Horse		2		22	1	1					
A. Bty. R.H.A.	1				3			8			
'Q' — " —	1							9			
'U' — " —					5			6			
Total	2	6	42	47	19	140	3	23	-	-	

H Lewis Capt.
D.A.A.& Q.M.G.

WAR DIARY
OF
A & Q.

1ST INDIAN CAVALRY DIVISION

APRIL - 1915.

121/5504

Serial No. 2.

MUL 5

WAR DIARY.
with appendices.
OF

D.A.A. & Q.M.G.
Administrative Branch, 1st Indian Cavalry Division.

From 1st April 1915 To 30th April 1915

Army Form C. 2118.

WAR DIARY
or
INTELLIGENCE SUMMARY.

(Erase heading not required.)

Instructions regarding War Diaries and Intelligence Summaries are contained in F. S. Regs., Part II, and the Staff Manual respectively. Title pages will be prepared in manuscript.

Hour, Date, Place.		Summary of Events and Information.	Remarks and references to Appendices
1-4-15 ENQUIN	1h	Reinforcements & remounts arrived	
2-4-15	1h	Capt Conlin inspection of all remounts that have arrived since 1st March.	
3-4-15	1h	nil	
4-4-15	1h	Weekly tonnage in sick. Deficiencies in establishments of fighting units	APP "A"
5-4-15	1h	nil	"B"
6-4-15	1h	2/13 Batt Remounts arrived for Divl Ammn Col Column reorganised as Horse Lines now complete as regards Personnel, though horses G.S. wagons still required for 1 Section.	
7-4-15 & 9-4-15	1h	nil	
10-4-15	1h	Remounts arrived	
11-4-15	1h	4 off & Bath off sent to MARSEILLES to superintend training of reinforcements. Weekly tonnage in sickness. Deficiencies in Establishment	APP "C" "D"

Army Form C. 2118.

WAR DIARY
or
INTELLIGENCE SUMMARY.
(Erase heading not required.)

Instructions regarding War Diaries and Intelligence Summaries are contained in F.S. Regs., Part II, and the Staff Manual respectively. Title pages will be prepared in manuscript.

Hour, Date, Place.	Summary of Events and Information.	Remarks and references to Appendices
12-4-15 ENQUIN	22 Ordnance Mules received for each Cavy Regt of the 5th These are for carriage of SAA, & are in replacement of small pack mules hitherto employed for this purpose	
13-4-15 — 14-4-15 — "	nil	
15-4-15 — "	18 Yeomanry Officers arrived. Attached to Ind. Cavy Regts 3 to each Regt.	APP 'E'
16-4-15 — 17-4-15 — "	nil	" F
18-4-15 — "	Weekly wastage in sickness. & fractures in totals of fighting units.	
19-4-15 — "	nil	
20-4-15 — "	Reinforcements arrived for Brit Cavy Regts	
21-4-15 — 23-4-15 — "	nil	
24-4-15 — "	Orders received from Ind Cavy Corps to train NCO. of 26 men per unit in transport duties for scheme of "Ride & Drive"	

Army Form C. 2118.

WAR DIARY
or
INTELLIGENCE SUMMARY.
(Erase heading not required.)

Instructions regarding War Diaries and Intelligence Summaries are contained in F. S. Regs., Part II, and the Staff Manual respectively. Title pages will be prepared in manuscript.

Hour, Date, Place.	Summary of Events and Information.	Remarks and references to Appendices
24-4-15 ENQUIN	Div received orders to not proceed "to front" re march see	APP "G"
25-4-15 ST MARIE CAPPEL	Division under orders to move at 1 hour notice. Div H.Q. at ST MARIE CAPPEL Signal Sqn 3rd Cav Bde (less 4th Hussars) SIALKOT C.Bde — in neighbourhood of BAVINCHOVE AMBALA — STAPLE LUCKNOW — OXELAERE R.H.A Batteries rejoined Bdes from gun Dr camps S.E. of CASSEL. Ambala & Lucknow Bdes endless remained at RELY. Weekly wastage in sickness statement re difference in Estabs of fighting units.	
26-4-15	nil	
27-4-15	Reinforcement & remounts arrived L.D. rides now being withheld for strenght issues. A few rides arrived today	APP "H" "I"

Army Form C. 2118.

WAR DIARY
or
INTELLIGENCE SUMMARY.
(Erase heading not required.)

Instructions regarding War Diaries and Intelligence Summaries are contained in F. S. Regs., Part II, and the Staff Manual respectively. Title pages will be prepared in manuscript.

Hour, Date, Place.	Summary of Events and Information.	Remarks and references to Appendices
28.4.15 ST MARIE CAPPEL	Orders received for Divn to move to WATOU. Troops would parade, but details of Transport rendezvous at ST MARIE CAPPEL & proceed to new billets via BLARINGHEM to march at 12 noon.	
29.4.15 WATOU	Rendezvous & hours were postponed & the new rendezvous was point on road where by-road branches off to by-road... The march of Bde-Lt-Col from ... to WATOU Church (distance about 7 miles) took from noon till 1300. Then we did to 1430 owing to congestion & multiple horse & carts. The Thou shouted the horse for close of 1 hour in every hour, halted to feed. Arrived new camp prepared to fight. The march was tediously + slow 2½ mph.	
30.4.15	Nil	
1-3-15		Hewo Capt. D.A.A.Q.M.G. 1st Can Div

APPENDIX 'A'

Weekly Wastage from Sickness - 4-4-1915

Unit	Officers		Other Rks		Fol	Remarks
	Br.	Ind.	Br.	Ind.		
Divl. Head Qrs	-	-	-	-	1	
6th Cavalry	-	-	-	2	-	
19th Lancers	-	-	-	2	-	
Ambala Bde. S & T Hd Qrs	-	-	1	-	-	
29th Lancers	-	-	-	8	-	
36th Horse	-	-	-	1	-	
30th Lancers	-	-	-	2	-	
Lucknow Bde. S & T Hd Qrs	-	-	1	-	-	
Ammunition Park	-	-	1	-	-	
Total	-	-	3	15	1	

H Lewis Capt.
D.A.A & Q.M.G.

APPENDIX "B"

Deficiencies in Establishments Fighting units – 4-4-1915.

Unit	Officers Brit	Officers Ind	Other Ranks Brit	Other Ranks Ind	offrs. Chr.	Horses Riding	Heavy Draught	Light Draught	Mules L.D.	Mules Ord	Remarks
17th Lancers	-	-	7	-	2	13	-	-	-	-	
6th Cavalry	-	-	-	1	-	-	1	-	-	-	
19th Lancers	-	-	-	3	1	8	1	-	-	-	
8th Hussars	-	-	1	-	-	34	-	-	-	-	
9th Horse	-	-	-	-	-	9	-	-	-	-	
30th Lancers	-	1	-	-	-	-	-	-	-	-	
K.D.Gs.	-	-	4	-	-	6	-	-	-	-	
29th Lancers	-	2	-	13	-	-	-	-	-	-	
36th Horse	-	2	-	10	-	2	-	-	-	-	
Total	-	5	12	27	3	72	2	-	-	-	

H Lewis
Capt.
D.a.a.&Q.M.G.

APPENDIX "C"

Weekly Wastage in Sickness - 11-4-1915.

Unit.	Officers Br.	Officers Ind.	Other Ranks Br.	Other Ranks Ind.	Follrs	Remarks.
14th Lancers.	-	-	1	-	-	
6th Cavalry	-	-	-	1	-	
19th Lancers.	-	-	-	6	-	
8th Hussars.	1	-	3	-	-	
9th Horse	-	-	-	5	-	
30th Lancers.	-	-	-	1	-	
K.D.G.	-	-	3	-	-	
36th Horse.	-	1	-	-	-	
Lucknow Mob. Vety. Sect.	-	-	1	-	-	
Divl. Ammn Column	-	-	2	-	-	
Divl. Supply Column	-	-	3	-	-	
Field Squadron	-	-	1	-	-	
29th Lancers.	-	1	-	3	-	
Total.	1	2	14	16	-	

Henri Capt̄
D.A.A.& Q.M.G.

APPENDIX "D"

Deficiencies in Establishments, Fighting units. — 11-4-1915.

Unit	Officers		Other Ranks		Offrs Chr.	Horses Riding	Heavy Draught	Light Draught	Mules		Remarks
	Brit.	Ind.	Brit.	Ind.					L.D.	Ord.	
17th Lancers.	—	—	22	—	—	2	—	—	—	—	
6th Cavalry.	—	—	—	10	1	11	—	—	—	—	
19th Lancers.	—	—	—	23	2	—	—	—	—	—	
8th Hussars.	—	—	16	—	—	—	—	—	—	—	
9th Horse.	—	—	—	17	3	—	—	—	—	—	
30th Lancers.	—	—	—	14	2	—	—	—	—	—	
K.D.Gs.	—	—	19	—	—	—	—	—	—	—	
29th Lancers.	—	2	—	26	—	—	1	—	—	—	
36th Horse.	—	3	—	15	—	—	—	—	—	—	
Total.	—	5	57	108	8	13	1	—	—	—	

H. Lewis Capt.
D.A.A.&Q.M.G.

APPENDIX 'E'

Weekly Wastage in Sickness — 18-4-1915.

Unit	Officers Br.	Officers Ind.	Other Ranks Br.	Other Ranks Ind.	Follrs	Remarks
Divl. Head Qrs	-	-	1	-	-	
14th Lancers	-	-	1	-	-	
6th Cavalry	-	-	-	2	-	
8th Hussars	-	-	2	-	-	
9th Horse	-	-	-	3	-	
Ambala Bde. S & T. Ha Qrs	-	-	-	-	1	
Lucknow Bde Hd. Qrs	-	-	1	-	-	
29th Lancers	1	-	-	4	-	
36th Horse	-	1	-	2	1	
Lucknow Bde S & T. Hd Qrs	-	-	-	-	1	
" " Vety. Section	-	-	-	-	1	
Divl. Ammn Column	-	-	4	-	1	
Divl. Supply Column	-	-	4	-	-	
Field Troop	-	-	-	-	1	
Signal Squadron	-	-	1	-	-	
Total	1	1	14	11	6	

Lewis
Capt.
D.A.A.Q.M.G.

APPENDIX "F"

Deficiencies in Establishments - Fighting units - 18-4-1915.

Unit	Officers		Other Ranks		Offrs Ch.	Horses Riding	Heavy Draught	Light Draught	Mules		Remarks
	Brit.	Ind.	Brit.	Ind.					R.D.	Ord.	
14th Lancers	-	-	22	-	1	7	-	-	4	-	
6th Cavalry	-	-	-	11	-	20	-	-	-	-	
19th Lancers	-	-	-	22	2	-	-	-	4	-	
8th Hussars	-	-	21	-	-	-	-	-	-	-	
9th Horse	-	-	-	15	3	6	-	-	-	-	
30th Lancers	-	1	-	10	3	-	-	-	-	-	
K.D.Gs.	-	-	17	-	-	-	-	-	-	-	
29th Lancers	-	2	-	26	-	-	-	-	4	-	
36th Horse	-	4	-	6	-	-	-	-	-	-	
Total	-	7	60	90	9	33	-	-	12	-	

Lewis
Capt.
D.A.A & Q.M.G.

APPENDIX "G"

On receipt of I.C.C. G.A.332, Operation Order No.3 and Administrative Instructions were issued.

As no time was given by the Corps for the march of 1st Division, the 2nd Division was asked when they would be clear of WARDRECQUES STATION. The reply was at first 7.30 p.m., afterwards altered to 8 p.m.

This enabled 1st Division to give time, but owing to delay in getting this information orders could not be got out till 5 p.m. and so did not reach Brigades sufficiently soon to enable them to be up to time.

The 2nd Division was not clear of WARDRECQUES STATION till at least 11 p.m. This was due to transport difficulties, owing to steep inclines and also to the fact that the Level Crossing at EBBLINGHEM was repeatedly closed owing to a large number of troops trains passing: this delay could not be foreseen or allowed for.

The Sialkote Brigade arrived at Cross Roads ½ mile North of D in QUIESTEDE at about 9.00 p.m.

Lucknow Brigade at about 9.10; the latter joining in at the tail of the Sialkote Bde, and both passing the 2nd Division transport.

Passing transport at night should be avoided if possible except on 1st class roads.

The metalled part of the road is not more than sufficient for the vehicles.

The unmetalled part very often bounded by a deep ditch is very often rotten, especially after the heavy winter rains, and under a heavy wagon the whole thing is apt to subside.

It is obvious that very careful timing is necessary and that it would be best to send the transport on a separate road, or if that is impossible not to start the transport till the fighting troops are clear, unless the road is a 1st class one.

Harris Capt
D.A.A. & Q.M.G.

Copy No.

1st Indian Cavalry Division Order No. 3.

Reference $\frac{1}{80,000}$

1. The Division will move on the area South East of the ST OMER - CASSEL road and billet within the limits MAISON BLANCHE, STAPLE, inclusive ST MARIE CAPPEL inclusive - OXELAERE exclusive BAVINCHOVE Station exclusive.

2. Division will march as follows :-

Lucknow Brigade. Railway arch ESTREE BLANCHE at 5.30 p.m., Route BASSEE BOULOGNE, MARTHES, MAMETZ, ROQUETOIRE, forked road ½ mile North of D in QUISTEDE, BELLECROIX, WARDRECQUES, ERB-LINGHEM, STAPLES, cross roads just west of L in LONGUECROIX where the Staff Captain will meet it.

Sialkot Brigade. Starting point - THEROUANNE 6.20 p.m., Route THEROUANNE, CLARQUES, QUIESTEDE, BELLE CROIX, WARDRECQUES, EBBLINGHEM, LE NIEPPE to MAISON BLANCHE where the Staff Captain will meet it.

Ambala Brigade. Starting point - Church at LIERES at 5.30 p.m., Route ST HILAIRE, Cross raods East of ESTRACELLE, thence via MISSISSIPI, NEUFPRE, PECQUER, M of BOESEGHEM, WALLON CAPPEL to STAPLES.

3. Transport of Lucknow and Sialkot Brigades will follow their Brigades - Starting point as for Brigades at the following times.

LUCKNOW Bde Transport....... 6.0 p.m.,

SIALKOT Brigade Transport,...7.0 p.m.,

Divisional Headquarters Transport will march at head of Lucknow Brigade Transport.

Transport of AMBALA Brigade will follow Brigade.

4. Divisional Ammunition Column will follow the Ambala Brigade and proceed via LONGUECROIX to ST MARIE CAPELLE.

5. Medical Sialkot Field Ambulance will follow the Divisional Ammunition Column to ST MARIE CAPELLE.
The remainder of F.E Ambulance will remain in billets

6. Report Centre will close at ENQUIN at 6.0 p.m., and open at ST MARIE CAPELLE at same time.

Norway-Enden Major,
General Staff,
1st Indian Cavalry Division.

Headquarters 1st Indian Cavalry Division,
24th April 1915.

No. 1.

Administrative Instructions based on 1st Indian Cavalry Division Order No. 3

1. The billeting areas will be as follows :-
   Corps Headquarters -- OXE LAERE.
   Corps Troops   -- BAVINCHOVE
   Divl. Headquarters.   ⎫
   Field Squadron.   ⎪
   Signal Squadron.   ⎬ STE. MARIE CAPELLE.
   O.C., A.S.C.   ⎪
   Field Ambulance-Sialkot- ⎪
   S.A.A. Section.   ⎭
   Ambala Brigade - STAPLE.
   Sialkot Brigade - Area - STAPLE (exclusive) MAISON BLANCHE CASSEL-ST OMER road inclusive to S.W. Corner of BAVINCHOVE, thence S.E. by road to Roman road ½ mile North of L in LONGUE CROIX - STAPLE exclusive.
   Lucknow Brigade - Area - N.E. of Sialkot Brigade. Western limit Sialkot Brigade, Northern limit the line joining BAVINCHOVE, OXE LAERE, ST. MARIE CAPELLE, excluding all these villages. South Eastern limit a line running from South East corner of St. MARIE CAPELLE to X roads ½ mile North of L in LONGUE-CROIX.

2. Supply Column and Ammunition Park will become Corps Troops.

W K Bourne

Lieut-Colonel,
A.A. & Q.M.G., 1st Indian Cavalry Division.

APPENDIX "H"

Weekly wastage in sickness – 25-4-1915

Units	Officers Br	Officers Ind.	Other Ranks Br	Other Ranks Ind	Folls	Remarks
Divl. Head Qrs.	–	–	–	–	1	
14th Lancers	–	–	1	–	–	
19th Lancers	–	–	–	1	–	
8th Hussars	1	–	2	–	–	
9th Horse	–	–	–	3	–	
30th Lancers	1	–	–	1	–	
K.D.Gs.	–	–	4	–	–	
29th Lancers	1	–	–	5	–	
Lucknow Mob. Vety. Sect.	–	–	–	1	–	
Divl Ammn Park	–	–	1	–	–	
Divl Supply Column	–	–	2	–	–	
Lucknow Cavy Fd Amblce	–	–	1	–	–	
Total	3	–	11	11	1	

Henri
Capt.
D.A.A.&Q.M.G.

APPENDIX "I"

Deficiencies in Establishments, Fighting units, 25-4-1915.

Unit	Officers Brit	Officers Ind.	Other Rank Brit	Other Rank Ind.	offrs Ch.	Horses Riding	Heavy Draught	Light Draught	Mules L.D.	Mules Ord.	Remarks
14th Lancers	1	-	27	-	1	2	-	-	4	1	
6th Cavalry	-	-	-	21	-	17	-	-	-	-	
19th Lancers	-	-	-	36	2	-	-	-	4	-	
8th Hussars	-	-	22	-	-	-	-	-	-	-	
9th Horse	-	-	-	28	6	13	-	-	-	1	
30th Lancers	-	1	-	23	4	-	-	-	-	-	
K.D.Cp.	-	-	21	-	-	13	-	-	-	-	
29th Lancers	-	3	-	44	-	-	-	-	4	-	
36th Horse	-	4	-	17	-	9	-	-	-	-	
'A' Bty. R.H.A.	-	-	5	-	-	2	-	13	-	-	
'Q' — " —	-	-	12	-	3	-	-	11	-	-	
'U' — " —	-	-	14	-	-	1	-	10	-	-	
Divl. Ammn. Col.	1	-	5	-	-	-	-	14	-	-	
Total	2	8	106	169	16	57	-	48	12	2	

Hewis Capt.
D.A.A.&Q.M.G.

Serial No 2.

12/5799

WAR DIARY
with appendices.
OF
Administrative Branch, 1st Indian Cavalry Division.

From 1st May 1915 To 31st May 1915.

Army Form C. 2118.

WAR DIARY

INTELLIGENCE SUMMARY.

(Erase heading not required.)

Instructions regarding War Diaries and Intelligence Summaries are contained in F. S. Regs., Part II, and the Staff Manual respectively. Title pages will be prepared in manuscript.

Hour, Date, Place.		Summary of Events and Information.	Remarks and references to Appendices.
WATOU.	1-5-15	nil.	
ST. MARIE CAPPEL.	2-5-15	The Div. moved to ST. MARIE CAPPEL neighbourhood at 6 a.m. Weekly wastage in sickness deficiencies in establishments & fighting units.	App'x "B"
	3-5-15	nil.	
ROQUETOIRE.	3/4-5-15	The Corps marched to billets in THEROUANNE area. Starting point of Div. at LONGUE CROIX at 12 midnight. Billeting area was as follows.— Div. Troops. QUIESTEDE - ST. VINOQ - LIGNE - ROQUETOIRE. GRANDEQUIESTEDE. Head Q'rs at ROQUETOIRE CHATEAU. Sialkot Bde. - ECQUES - INGHEM - THEROUANNE - ENQUINGATTE - CRECQUES - REBECQ - CAUCHIE - D'ECQUES. H.Q'rs CLARQUES - CHATEAU. Ambala Bde. - CAMPAGNE - HEURINGHEM - COUBRONNE - LERONS - LAPIERRE - RACQUINGHEM - WARDRECQUES Ch.H.Q. Lucknow Bde. - CRECQUES - MARTHE - MAM - BLESSY - ST. MARTIN - LAPIERRE - ROCQUETOIRE - WARNE - QLOMENGHEM - MAMETZ. Bde H.Q'rs MAMETZ.	

Army Form C. 2118.

WAR DIARY
or
INTELLIGENCE SUMMARY.
(Erase heading not required.)

Instructions regarding War Diaries and Intelligence Summaries are contained in F. S. Regs., Part II, and the Staff Manual respectively. Title pages will be prepared in manuscript.

Hour, Date, Place.	Summary of Events and Information.	Remarks and references to Appendices.
ROQUETOIRE 6-5-15.	Reinforcements arrived.	
" 7 + 8-5-15	nil.	
" 9-5-15.	Weekly wastage in sickness. Deficiencies in establishments of fighting units. French Bridging Train passed through Div. Area & our field Ambs & M.A. Sect. Div. Ammn Col. moved to WITTES & ST VENANT. ROQUETOIRE WEST & LIGNE being temporarily evacuated.	APP C. " D.
" 10 & 11-5-15.	nil.	
" 12-5-15.	Reinforcements & remounts arrived.	
" 13 - 15-5-15	nil.	
" 16-5-15	Remounts arrived. Weekly wastage in sickness. Deficiencies in establishments of fighting units. Limbered g.l. wagons for units (Bde & Div H.Q.) & 4a. Ambces complete with men & horses, arrived to replace A.T. Carts.	APP 'E' " F.

Army Form C. 2118.

WAR DIARY
or
INTELLIGENCE SUMMARY.
(Erase heading not required.)

Instructions regarding War Diaries and Intelligence Summaries are contained in F. S. Regs., Part II, and the Staff Manual respectively. Title pages will be prepared in manuscript.

Hour, Date, Place.	Summary of Events and Information.	Remarks and references to Appendices.
ROQUETOIRE 17-5-15. ALLOUAGNE.	Orders to proceed to area ALLOUAGNE. Report centre closed 5 p.m. Arrived. Report centre opened 5 p.m. Reinforcements arrived for Field Squadron.	
" 18-5-15.	G.S. Wagons & personnel for 3rd Sect. Sub. Ammn. Col. arrived. Column now complete. A.T. Carts set free from Col., units &c. returned to Base with mules & drivers.	
" 19-5-15.	Moved back to original billets - THEROUANNE Area.	
ROQUETOIRE 20-22-5-15.	Nil.	
" 23-5-15.	Weekly wastage in sickness. Deficiencies in establishments of fighting units	APP'G'
" 24-26-5-15.	Nil	" H.
ROQUETOIRE STAPLE 27-5-15.	Div. temporarily transferred to 5th Corps, 2nd Army, & left ROQUETOIRE for RUBROUCK, billeting at STAPLE	
STAPLE RUBROUCK. 28-5-15.	Arrived RUBROUCK. Probation of troops sent up to trenches.	

Army Form O. 2118.

WAR DIARY
or
INTELLIGENCE SUMMARY.
(Erase heading not required.)

Instructions regarding War Diaries and Intelligence Summaries are contained in F. S. Regs., Part II, and the Staff Manual respectively. Title pages will be prepared in manuscript.

Hour, Date, Place.	Summary of Events and Information.	Remarks and references to Appendices.
ROUBROUCK. 29-5-15.	Reinforcements arrived for 4th Squadron. Squadron now complete, except in matter of Riding Horses.	
" 30-5-15.	Arrival of 66 H.D., in part replacement of H.D. Horses. All H.D. Horses in S⁰ are to be replaced by L.D. Weekly wastage in sickness. Deficiencies in establishments of fighting units.	APP "1" "J"
" 31-5-15.	H.D. horses set free by arrival of L.D. returned to Base.	

Mervin Capt.
D.A.A. + Q.M.G. H.Q. C.C.

APPENDIX "A"

Weekly Wastage from Sickness 2-5-15

Unit	Officers		Other Ranks		Foll^{rs}
	Br.	Ind.	Br.	Ind.	
17th Lancers	-	-	1	-	-
6th Cavalry	-	-	-	1	-
19th Lancers	-	-	-	2	-
8th Hussars	1	-	1	-	-
9th Horse	-	-	-	4	-
30th Lancers	-	-	-	1	-
K. d. Ga.	-	-	5	*	-
29th Lancers	2	-	*	5	-
36th Horse	-	1	-	5	-
Lucknow Bde. S.T. HQ.	-	-	1	-	1
"A" B^{ty} R.H.A.	-	-	2	-	-
"U" " "	-	-	5	-	-
Ammunition Col.	-	-	3	-	-
Supply Col.	-	-	1	-	-
Field Troop	-	-	-	4	-
Signal Sqdn.	-	-	2	-	-
Total	3	1	21	22	1

Harris
Captⁿ
D.A.A. & Q.M.G.

APPENDIX 'B'

Deficiencies in Establishments Fighting units – 2-5-1915.

Unit	Officers		Other Ranks		Offrs Ch.	Horses Riding	Heavy Draught	Light Draught	Mules R.D.	Mules Ind.	Remarks
	Brit.	Ind.	Brit.	Ind.							
17th Lancers	-	-	13	-	-	4	-	-	-	2	
6th Cavalry	-	-	-	14	-	25	-	-	-	-	
19th Lancers	-	-	-	11	4	20	-	-	-	-	
8th Hussars	-	-	6	-	-	18	-	-	-	-	
9th Horse	-	-	-	16	5	20	-	-	1	2	
30th Lancers	-	-	-	9	7	-	-	-	-	-	
K.D. Gds	-	-	11	-	-	28	-	-	-	-	
29th Lancers	-	2	-	18	-	-	-	-	4	-	
36th Horse	-	2	-	4	4	26	-	-	-	-	
B&y. R.H.A.	-	-	5	-	-	-	-	13	-	-	
'Q' - " -	-	-	12	-	-	-	-	4	-	-	
'U' - " -	-	-	14	-	-	-	-	8	-	-	
Divl. Ammn. Col.	-	-	19	-	-	-	-	14	-	-	
Total		4	80	75	20	141		39	5	2	

Henri
Captn
D.A.A. & Q.M.G.

APPENDIX "C"

Weekly Wastage from Sickness 9-5-15

Unit	Officers		Other Ranks		Foll'rs	Remarks
	Br.	Ind	Br.	Ind		
17th Lancers	-	-	7	-	-	
19th Lancers	-	-	-	1	-	
8th Hussars	1	-	1	×	-	
9th Horse	-	-	-	2	-	
30th Lancers	1	-	-	1	-	
R.H.A.	-	-	4	-	-	
Amm" Col.	-	-	-	-	1	
Supply Col.	-	-	6	-	-	
Field Troop	-	-	-	2	-	
Field Sqdn	-	-	-	2	-	
Signal Sqdn	-	-	1	-	-	
Total	2	-	19	8	1	

Hearn Capt
D.A.A.Q.M.G

APPENDIX "D"

Deficiencies in Establishments – Fighting Units – 9-5-15

Unit	Officers		Other Ranks		Horses Riding	Heavy Draught	Light Draught	Officers Chargers	Mules L.D.	Mules A.T.	Remarks
	Br.	Ind.	Br.	Ind.							
14th Lancers				2	4			2		3	
6th Cavalry				5	28			1			
19th Lancers					34			4			
8th Hussars					31						
9th Horse				3	33			6	1	2	
30th Lancers					13			4	4		
K.D. Gds.					38						
29th Lancers		2		6	34						
36th Horse		1			54			4			
A Bty. R.H.A.					2		6				
" "							5				
" "							10				
Div. Ammn. Col.							14				
Total		3	2	14	277		35	24	5	5	

Henri Captn
D.A.A. & Q.M.G.

APPENDIX "E"

Weekly Wastage from Sickness 16-5-1915

Unit	Officers		Other Ranks			Remarks
	B⁺	2nd	B⁺	2nd	Foll⁺	
17th Lancers	-	-	4	-	-	
6th Cavalry	-	-	-	1	-	
8th Hussars	-	-	1	-	-	
9th Horse	-	-	-	5	-	
30th Lancers	-	-	-	1	-	
Ambala Sig Troop	-	-	-	1	-	
Ambala S&T HQ	-	-	-	1	-	
K H Co	-	-	3	-	-	
29th Lancers	-	-	-	4	-	
36th Horse	-	-	-	1	-	
Field Sqn	-	-	1	-	-	
Supply Col	-	-	5	-	-	
Ammunition Park	-	-	3	-	-	
Div H Q⁺	-	-	1	-	-	
Total	-	-	18	14	-	

Henn
Capt
D.A.A. & Q.M.G.

APPENDIX "F"

Deficiencies in establishments - Fighting units - 16-5-15.

Unit	Officers		Other Rank		Officers Chargers	Horses Riding	Heavy Draught	Light Draught	Mules L.D.	Mules Ord.	Remarks
	Br.	Ind.	Br.	Ind.							
14th Lancers					4						
6th Cavalry				4							
19th Lancers					2	10					
8th Hussars	2										
9th Horse					8	3				2	
30th Lancers					3						
K.D. Gds.											
29th Lancers		3		9							
36th Horse		3			10				1		
'A' Bty. R.H.A.											
'Q' — " —									4		
'U' — " —					1				2		
Div. Ammn Col.			2	2							
Total	2	6	2	23	23	10		6		3	

Harris Captn
D.A.A. & Q.M.G.

APPENDIX "G"

Weekly Wastage from Sickness 23-5-15

Unit	Officer Br	Officer Ind	Other Ranks Br	Other Ranks Ind	Foll'd	Remarks
17th Lancers	-	-	3	-	-	
6th Cavalry	1	1	-	-	-	
19th Lancers	-	-	-	2	-	
8th Hussars	-	-	1	-	-	
9th Horse	-	-	-	6	-	
30th Lancers	-	-	-	2	-	
Ambala S. Troop	-	-	1	-	-	
Div Amm'n Col.	-	-	4	-	-	
Div Supply Col.	-	-	1	-	-	
Field Troop	-	-	-	1	-	
Signal Sqd'n	-	-	3	-	-	
K. D. Coy	-	-	1	-	-	
20th Lancers	-	-	-	5	-	
36th Horse	-	-	-	4	-	
Total	1	1	14	20	-	

Hewis Capt
D.A.A. & Q.M.G

APPENDIX "H"

Deficiencies in Establishments - Fighting Units - 28-5-15

Unit	Officers Br.	Officers Ind.	Other Ranks Br.	Other Ranks Ind.	Officers Chargers	Horses Riding	Heavy Draught	Light Draught	Mules L.D.	Mules Pack	Remarks
17th Lancers	.	.	.	.	4	11	1	.	.	3	
6th Cavalry	.	.	.	4	.	.	1	.	.	.	
19th Lancers	.	.	.	.	2	10	.	.	.	.	
8th Hussars	.	.	.	.	.	7	.	.	.	.	
9th Horse	.	.	.	13	3	6	.	.	.	3	
30th Lancers	.	.	.	.	3	.	1	.	.	.	
K. D. Gds.	.	.	.	.	.	7	.	.	.	.	
29th Lancers	.	3	.	13	.	1	.	.	.	.	
26th Horse	.	2	.	.	10	8	.	.	.	1	
A Bty. R.H.A.	.	.	.	.	.	.	.	10	.	.	
"Q" — "	.	.	.	.	.	.	.	4	.	.	
"U" — "	.	.	.	.	2	.	.	.	.	.	
Div. Ammn Col.	.	.	2	.	2	7	.	5	.	.	
Total	.	5	2	30	26	54	3	19	.	7	

Henrs Capt.
D.A.A. & Q.M.G.

APPENDIX "I"

Weekly Wastage from Sickness - 30-5-15

Unit	Officers		Other Ranks		Foll.	Remarks
	Br.	Ind.	Br.	Ind.		
Sialkot Bde. Hd. Qrs.	.	.	2	.	.	
17th Lancers	.	.	5	.	.	
6th Cavalry	.	.	.	3	.	
19th Lancers	.	.	.	4	.	
8th Hussars	.	.	3	.	.	
9th Horse	.	.	1	5	.	
30th Lancers	.	.	.	1	.	
Ambala Bde. S. & T. Estab.	.	.	1	.	.	
'O' Bty. R.H.A.	.	.	2	.	.	
'Q' " " "	.	.	4	.	.	
'U' " " "	.	.	5	.	.	
Div. Ammn. Col.	.	.	6	.	.	
" Supply Col.	.	.	2	.	.	
Field Squadron	.	.	4	.	.	
Field Troop	.	.	1	.	.	
Total	-	-	36	13	-	

Hewi Capt.
D.A.A. & Q.M.G.

APPENDIX "J"

Deficiencies in Establishments of Fighting units. 30-5-15

Unit	Officers Br.	Officers Ind.	Other Ranks Br.	Other Ranks Ind.	Officers Chargers	Horses Riding	Heavy Draught	Light Draught	Mules L.D.	Mules Dri.	Remarks
17th Lancers	.	.	.	.	4	13	.	.	.	.	
6th Cavalry	.	.	.	.	6	18	.	.	.	.	
19th Lancers	.	.	.	3	4	10	.	.	.	.	
8th Hussars	.	.	.	.	2	24	.	.	.	.	
9th Horse	.	.	.	18	5	21	1	.	.	3	
30th Lancers	.	.	.	.	3	.	.	.	.	2	
K.D. Gds.	.	.	9	.	.	13	.	.	.	.	
29th Lancers	.	2	.	8	.	.	.	.	.	1	
36th Horse	.	1	.	10	10	7	.	.	.	1	
"A" Bty. R.H.A	.	.	.	.	.	.	.	21	.	.	
"Q" — "	.	.	.	.	2	.	.	15	.	.	
"U" — "	.	.	.	.	2	.	.	16	.	.	
Div. Ammn. Col.	.	.	.	2	10	.	9	.	.	.	
Total	.	3	9	38	31	116	1	61	.	7	

Hewi Capt.
D.A.A. & Q.M.G.

WAR DIARY

OF

A & Q

1ST INDIAN CAVALRY DIVISION

JUNE - 1915

Serial No. 2.

121/6/28

WAR DIARY
OF
Administrative Branch, 1st Indian Cavalry Division

From 1st June 1915. To 30th June 1915.

Army Form O. 2118.

WAR DIARY
INTELLIGENCE SUMMARY.
(Erase heading not required.)

Hour, Date, Place.	Summary of Events and Information.	Remarks and references to Appendices.
RENINGHELST 28/5/15. ROUBROUCK	The Dn moved up from billeting area in 170 buses to huts S. of VLAMERTINGHE. "A" Echelon transport moved independently. SIALKOT & AMBALA Bdes were accommodated in huts, also 2 regiments of LUCKNOW Bde - The 3rd regt - 29th Lancers - Bivouaced in some brickfields Divl. Hd. Qrs Advanced report bentre at RENINGHELST. Divl. Hd. Qrs remained at RUBROUCK Each unit left Depot in neighbourhood of RUBROUCK with certain number of men to look after horses. Supply Column delivered direct to troops as usual Troops asked for following returns:— "A" Effective strength up to noon - to be in by 9.0.a.m following morning "B" Casualties up to noon, to be in by 9.0.a.m following morning "C" Rough estimate of casualties if over 50 in one unit.	
29/5/15.	Field troops moved up to VLAMERTINGHE. Respirators collected from DMS 2nd Army, D.D.M.S. 6th Corps 2nd Ind Cav D: - from billeting area of own Dn - All men of dismounted troops provided with Respirator.	

Army Form C. 2118.

WAR DIARY
INTELLIGENCE SUMMARY.
(Erase heading not required.)

Instructions regarding War Diaries and Intelligence Summaries are contained in F. S. Regs., Part II, and the Staff Manual respectively. Title pages will be prepared in manuscript.

Hour, Date, Place.		Summary of Events and Information.	Remarks and references to Appendices.
RENINGHELST RUBROUCK	29/5/15	One Lorry of Ammn Park ordered up to "Advance" to complete the chain from Ammn Railhead, to be attached to 5th Corps.	
	30/5/15	Pack animals sent up to "Advance", as being useful for taking up rations & stores to trenches.	
		Remarks of Corps Commander on excellent inspection report of M.T. units.	APP. I
		Impossible to buy fuel near VLAMERTINGHE. Coal therefore ordered to be brought up daily in supply lorries.	
		Application made to 5th Corps for armoured motor cars for Staff, similarly to British Army Corps.	
		Liaison Officer sent to PARIS to buy sprayers for trenches.	
	31/5/15	"B" Echelon & remaining Stretcher bearers of LUCKNOW Fd Amb[ce] ordered up to "Advance".	
		4 500 Smoke Helmets arrived at "Advance". Every man in the Dn (dismounted force) now complete with respirator, in bag, & smoke helmet.	
		K.D.Gs moved up to trenches, attached to 3rd Dn.	
		Rations sent up chiefly on pack, also hand grenades & very pistols. Ammn.	

Army Form C. 2118.

WAR DIARY
or
INTELLIGENCE SUMMARY.
(Erase heading not required.)

Instructions regarding War Diaries and Intelligence Summaries are contained in F. S. Regs., Part II, and the Staff Manual respectively. Title pages will be prepared in manuscript.

Hour, Date, Place.	Summary of Events and Information.	Remarks and references to Appendices.
RENINGHELST RUBROUCK. 1/6/15.	One Lorry from Amm: Park ordered up to "Advance" to act as Amm: Park, as 5th Corps ordered it to draw direct from STRAZEELE Railhead, & not from 5th Corps Park.	
	300 Esbavations brought up & sent to trenches for K.D.Gp, as unit might be cut off from communication for a time.	
2/6/15.	Men sprayers sent up to K.D.Gp. K.D.Gp. informed where to place wounded for evacuation. Time 10 p.m. daily.	
	Capt. Tyrrell, Staff Capt. AMBALA Bde. to succeed Major Cheyne as Bde Major, AMBALA Bde.	
	Capt. Mills, 18th Lancers to be Staff Captain AMBALA Bde	
	Ordnance Warrant officer of Lucknow Bde. placed in Ordnance charge of all dismounted troops.	
	Sialkot 4d Amb. ordered up to 'Advance'.	
	Divl. Sanitary Section arrived RUBROUCK strength:– 1 Brit Offr. 11 Brit. Ranks. 2 & Ind. Ranks.	
	Instructions issued re provision of chemicals for gas. Lucknow 4d Amb.ce to draw the lot, & issue ready for use to troops as required.	APP. II

WAR DIARY or INTELLIGENCE SUMMARY.

Army Form C. 2118.

(Erase heading not required.)

Place	Hour, Date.	Summary of Events and Information	Remarks and references to Appendices.
RENINGHELST RUBROUCK	3/6/15	5th forty asked for a Lorry for Field Squadron to bring up stores to the front, as allowed to other Bde. K.D.Cys casualties filled up by reinforcements from fulfilling area. 3 Buses sent to fetch them. Daily rendezvous changed from 4 p.m. to 2 p.m. to allow more time before rations are brought up to the trenches. K.D.Cys returned from trenches. One M.Gun damaged by shell. Replacement asked for. Casualties of K.D.Cys:- 1 Off. Killed, 4 wounded. 21 Other Ranks killed, 43 wounded, 13 missing. K.D.Cys. respirators filled up from reserves of other Bdes.	
	4/6/15	L.D. Mules arrived at RUBROUCK in replacement of H.D. horses. 29th Lancers & 28th Horse ordered up to trenches with 3rd Cav Bde. Very Pistol Ammn + Hand Grenades drawn from STRAZEELE. Army Commander visited K.D.Cys.	

Army Form C. 2118.

WAR DIARY
INTELLIGENCE SUMMARY.
(Erase heading not required.)

Instructions regarding War Diaries and Intelligence Summaries are contained in F. S. Regs., Part II, and the Staff Manual respectively. Title pages will be prepared in manuscript.

Hour, Date, Place.	Summary of Events and Information.	Remarks and references to Appendices.
RENING HELST RUBROUCK 5/6/15	Remainder of S.A.A. Section, Ammn Park, ordered up to Advance. Instructions issued for taking over new Ammn Pack saddles. Respirators placed in supply Column daily & always available for issue. Heavy Draught horses set free by arrival of L.D. on counted. Divl. Sanitary Section ordered up to "Advance". 29th Lancers & 34th Horse returned from trenches.	
6/6/15	Machine Guns of K.D.G. replaced. 29th Lancers & 34th Horse respirators replaced. Instructions issued to troops re mode of drawing hand grenades, Very Pistol Ammn, R.E. stores &c. Remaining Sprayers handed over to R.E. Park, as they now become trench stores. Weekly wastage in sickness. deficiencies in establishments of fighting units	APP III APP IV V

Army Form O. 2118.

WAR DIARY
INTELLIGENCE SUMMARY.
(Erase heading not required.)

Instructions regarding War Diaries and Intelligence Summaries are contained in F.S. Regs., Part II, and the Staff Manual respectively. Title pages will be prepared in manuscript.

Hour, Date, Place.	Summary of Events and Information.	Remarks and references to Appendices.
RENINGHELST/RUBROUCK 7-6-15.	Difficulty experienced in washing of clothes, & obtaining clean clothes.	APP VI
" 8-6-15	Reinforcements arrived RUBROUCK from Base 15 K.D.G.	
" 9-6-15 } " 12-6-15 }	nil.	
" 13-6-15.	Additional reinforcements for K.D.G. arrived from Base.	
	Troops returned from trenches to billeting area around RUBROUCK	APP VII
	Weekly wastage in sickness	APP VIII
	Deficiencies in establishments of fighting units	
RUBROUCK " 14-6-15	nil.	
RUBROUCK/ROQUETOIRE " 15-6-15.	Divn returned to billeting area. Billeted as follows:—	
	DIVL. HD. QRS.— ROQUETOIRE	
	DIVL. TROOPS.— ROQUETOIRE — LA SABLON — OUIESTEDE — ECQUES — REBECQ — ST. MARTIN — CAUCHY D'ECQUES — QUIESTEDE.	
	SIALKOT Bde.— CLARQUES — THEROUANNE — NIELLES — INGHEM — BIENTQUES — HERBELLE — UPON D'AMONT — UPON D'AVEL WESTREHEM — REMILLY — WIRQUIN.	
	LUCKNOW Bde.— MAMETZ — RINCQ — GLOMENGHEM — WARNE — LA JUMELLE CRECQUES — MARTHES — BLESSY — HAM.	
ROQUETOIRE " 16-6-15.	nil.	
" 17-6-15.	Remounts arrived.	
" 18-19-6-15.	nil.	

Army Form C. 2118.

WAR DIARY
INTELLIGENCE SUMMARY.
(Erase heading not required.)

Instructions regarding War Diaries and Intelligence Summaries are contained in F.S. Regs., Part II, and the Staff Manual respectively. Title pages will be prepared in manuscript.

Hour, Date, Place.	Summary of Events and Information.	Remarks and references to Appendices.
ROCQUETOIRE 20/6/15.	Weekly wastage in sickness. Deficiencies in establishments of fighting units	APP IX / APP X
" " 21st to 26/6/15	nil.	
" " 27/6/15	Weekly wastage in sickness. Deficiencies in establishments of fighting units	APP XI / APP XII
" " 28/6/15	Capt. Muspratt-Bell Major Lucknow Bde appointed G.S.O. 2nd Grade, 2nd Cav Dn. Maitland, Staff Capt. Lucknow Cav Bde appointed Bde. Major, vice Capt. Muspratt. MacLeod. Orderly off. Lucknow Bde appointed Staff Captn., vice Capt. Maitland	
" " 29th. 30/6/15	nil.	

Henn Capt.
D.A.A & Q.M.G. 1st Ind. Cav Dn

APP. I

Copy of

Report on 1st Indian Cavalry Division Supply Column,

Inspected on 12/13th May 1915.

	Motor Cars.	Motor Cycles	LORRIES			
			3 Ton.	30cwt.	Workshop.	Store.
Establishment.	5	9	6	136	3	3
Strength.	5	9	6	136	3	3

Officer Commanding: Major Blunt.

" The vehicles of this Column were found to be in remarkably
" good order and reflect great credit on all ranks.
       The workshops are well organized and equipped, careful
" records are kept of all work etc.,
       The painting of the vehicles is now well in hand.
       Superstructures of approved pattern will be fitted as
" opportunity occurs.   Arrangements are now being made for a
" quantity of unserviceable stores to be returned to the Base.
       The importance of training Officers and other personnel
" was discussed with a view to providing instruction for all
" positions.
       Total number of vehicles inspected: 117.

(Signed) J.M.Hutchinson. Major.
A.S.C.,

Copy of Corps Commanders' remarks on inspection of M.T. units.

___

"The Corps Commander is much gratified by the attached reports on the M.T. units of the Corps which reflect credit on all concerned.   He is particularly pleased with the effer efforts that are being made to make the unit self contained and to obviate the evacuation of lorries; and I am to direct that you will convey his appreciation to the Os C.,

He would like to see every man put through a short course of musketry.   Small schemes for the defence of echelons of the Supply Columns should be carried out on the return runs to accustom the men to be quick and handy with their rifles on emergency.   He would like all men instructed, when asked on the road what they belong to, to reply at once what they serve i.e. " 1st Indian Cavalry Division Supply Column" 2nd Indian Cav. Division Supply Column", and so on, as this is more illuminating than if they merely say the number of the M.T. unit which conveys nothing th the uninitiated."

(Signed)   W.B.James.   Brigadier-General

23-5-1915.   D.A. & Q.M.G. Indian Cavalry Corps.

A.P.P. II

Headquarters,
1st Indian Cavalry Division.

No. Q b 188.   2nd June 1915.

MEMORANDUM.

Dry chemicals will not be issued to units. The solution will be made up in bulk by Officer Commanding Lucknow Cavalry Field Ambulance, and drawn by units as required. Units will give 24 hours' notice of the amount they require, and will send their own tins to draw it. When troops are in the trenches demands will be made through "A" Echelon, and the solution will be drawn in time to be taken up with the rations next day; two tins per squadron should suffice for spraying and dipping.

X The solution as issued by the Ambulance is full strength, and two parts of water should be added for use in spraying or in dipping respirators.

The position of the Lucknow Cavalry Field Ambulance is in VLAMERTINGHE, square H 9 b.

2. The following instructions are issued for guidance if the division takes over part of the line.

   1. Each man should carry up two sand bags in case these are wanted at once. These can be drawn from the R.E., dump, ½ mile East of VLAMERTINGHE on an indent countersigned by the senior R.E., officer present.

   2. Brigades will inform Divisional Headquarters daily by noon what R.E., stores, explosives, bombs, handgrenades, very pistols or very pistol ammunition they require. These will be sent up with the rations each night.

   3. A useful method of carrying up kit for an officer is to put the blanket into a sack, and use the sack as a sleeping bag in the trenches.

   4. Petrol tins will be carried up by the men for storage of water in the trenches.

W K Browne
Lieutenant Colonel,
A.A. and Q.M.G.,
1st Indian Cavalry Division.

A. P. P. / 3.

Extract from Divisional Orders No. 149. dated 6th June 1915

4.-- STORES--INDENTS FOR.

The following stores will be/ obtained by the troops by direct application to the O.C., S.A.A., Section, Divisional Ammunition Column.

        S.A. Ammunition.
        Grenades, Hand, Friction, Time, Heavy.
        Grenades, Hand, Mills' (when obtainable)
        Very pistol ammunition,

(2) All other R.E. Stores, explosives, sandbags, tools, &c., will be obtained on application to the S.R.E.O.,

(3.) Deficiencies in Machine Guns, Very Pistols, Rifles and all Ordnance Stores will be made good by the D.A.D.O.S.,

(4) It is of the first importance that steps should be taken immediately to make good deficiencies as they occur. When troops are in the trenches, information of deficiences should be given to the A.A.,and Q.M.G., daily by 12 noon, in order that replacements may be sent up with the ration party the same night.

(5) When troops return to billets from the trenches, the Ordnance warrant officer has orders to visit units at once, and obtain a list of deficiencies.

(6) A brigade ordered up to the trenches should take with it 100 hand grenades.

(7) Sandbags at the rate of two per man will be taken up daily with the rations, unless information is given that these are not required.

(8) Sprayers and trench Stores, and will be taken over in the trenches.

APPENDIX IV

Weekly Wastage from Sickness – 6-6-15.

Unit	Officers		Other Ranks		Folls	Remarks
	Br.	Ind.	Br.	Ind.		
Sialkot Bde. Hd. Qrs.	–	–	1	–	–	
14th Lancers	–	–	3	–	–	
6th Cavalry	–	1	–	4	–	
19th Lancers	–	–	–	4	–	
8th Hussars	–	–	1	–	–	
9th Horse	1	–	–	–	–	
30th Lancers	–	–	–	2	–	
36th Horse	–	1	–	3	–	
'Q' Bty. R.H.A.	–	–	7	–	–	
'U' — .. —	–	–	4	–	–	
Divl. Ammn. Col.	–	–	4	1	–	
Supply Column	–	–	1	–	–	
Field Squadron	–	–	1	–	–	
Field Troop	–	–	–	3	–	
Signal Squadron	–	–	1	–	–	
	1	2	23	17	–	

Hewit Capt.
D.A.A. & Q.M.G.

APPENDIX V

Deficiencies in Establishments of Fighting units – 6-6-15

Unit	Officers		Other Ranks		Offrs. Ch.	Horses Rdg.	L.D. Horses	L.D. Mules	Ord. Mules	Remarks
	Br.	Ind.	Br.	Ind.						
14th Lancers	–	–	–	–	4	21	–	–	3	
6th Cavy.	–	–	–	6	–	22	–	–	2	
19th Lancers	–	–	–	6	4	15	2	–	–	
8th Hussars	–	–	–	–	2	28	–	–	–	
9th Horse	1	–	–	18	4	18	–	–	3	
30th Lancers	–	–	–	–	3	3	–	–	2	
K.D.G's.	5	–	89	–	–	13	–	–	–	
29th Lancers	–	2	–	2	–	–	–	–	–	
6th Horse	–	2	–	–	10	10	–	–	1	
'A' Bty. R.H.A	–	–	–	–	–	–	1	–	–	
'Q' – " –	–	–	–	7	–	–	4	–	–	
'U' – " –	–	–	–	11	–	–	2	–	–	
Div. Ammn. Col.	–	–	–	4	–	–	3	–	–	
Total	6	4	111	32	27	130	12	–	11	

Henri Capt.
D.A.A. & Q.M.G.

APP VI

Some difficulty occurred re washing of men and clothes. The huts were very lousey, and being up for a short time only and every available building being occupied, it was difficult to do much.

However, the 5th Division allotted this Division hours for the men to bathe at RENINGHELST. They could not supply clean clothing. Divisions who are permanently in an area have a comprehensive scheme of washing, disinfecting, and mending clothes.

A large number of women are hired to wash and mend clothes after disinfection; so much a piece is charged. Clothes are disinfected by a Thresh disenfector. Men as soon as they have bathed are given fresh clothing - their old taken over-.

This Division could not obtain the women at short notice, as all available were already employed. Consequently the following arrangements were made:-

Clothes were collected and taken to AIRE where they were disinfected at the Meerut Casualty Clearing Hospital, and contracts placed for washing.

Clean clothes would have then been brought and issued to men as they bathed, but Division was ordered back before this took effect.

APPENDIX VII

Weekly Wastage in Sickness – 13-6-1915.

Unit	Officers		Other Ranks		Folls	Remarks
	Br.	Ind.	Br.	Ind.		
17th Lancers	–	–	3	–		
6th Cavalry	–	–	1	2	–	
19th Lancers	–	–	1	1	–	
8th Hussars	–	–	5	–		
9th Horse	2	–	–	2	–	
K.D.G.	–	–	4	–	–	
29th Lancers	–	–	–	3	–	
36th Horse	–	–	–	5		
Lucknow Bde. S.&T. Estab.	–	–	–	–	1	
" " Mob. Vety. Sect.			1			
'A' Bty. R.H.A.	–	–	1	–	–	
'Q' " "	–	–	1	–	–	
'U' " "	–	–	4	–	–	
Divl. Ammn. Col.	–	–	6	–	–	
Supply Column	–	–	1	–	–	
Field Squadron	–	–	2	–	–	
Field Troop	–	–	–	1	–	
Total	2	–	33	14	1	

Mani Capt.
D.A.A. & Q.M.G.

APPENDIX VIII

Deficiencies in Establishments of Fighting units – 13-6-15.

Unit	Officers		Other Ranks		Ops. Ch.	Horses Rdg.	L.D. Horses	L.D. Mules	Ord. Mules	Remarks
	Br.	Ind.	Br.	Ind.						
14th Lancers	–	–	3	–	4	20	–	–	–	
6th Cavy.	–	–	–	6	7	14	–	–	2	
19th Lancers	–	–	–	1	5	15	–	–	–	
8th Hussars	–	–	–	–	5	24	–	–	–	
9th Horse	–	–	–	10	3	14	–	–	3	
30th Lancers	–	–	–	–	4	6	–	–	2	
K.D. Gs.	3	–	23	–	–	25	–	–	–	
29th Lancers	–	1	–	–	–	–	1	–	3	
36th Horse	–	2	–	–	10	12	–	–	1	
'A' By. R.H.A.	–	–	4	–	4	–	6	–	–	
'Q' – . –	–	–	3	–	–	–	–	–	–	
'U' – . –	–	–	7	–	–	–	22	–	–	
Div. Ammn. Col.	–	–	1	–	–	4	5	–	–	
Total	3	3	41	17	42	134	32	–	11	

Reni Captn.
D.A.A. & Q.M.G.

APPENDIX IX

Weekly Wastage from Sickness - 20-6-15

Unit.	Officers Br.	Officers Ind.	Other Ranks Br.	Other Ranks Ind.	Holls	Remarks.
14th Lancers.	-	-	16	-	-	
6th Cavalry.	-	1	-	8	-	
19th Lancers.	-	-	-	4	-	
8th Hussars.	1	-	-	-	-	
9th Horse.	1	-	-	4	-	
30th Lancers.	-	-	-	2	-	
Ambala Bde. Sig. Troop.	-	-	1	-	-	
K.D.Gs.	-	-	10	-	-	
'A' Bty. R.H.A.	-	-	2	-	-	
'Q' " "	-	-	4	-	-	
'W' " "	-	-	2	-	-	
Divl. Ammn. Col.	-	-	5	1	-	
" " Park	-	-	1	-	-	
Supply Column	-	-	6	-	-	
Field Squadron	-	-	2	-	-	
Field Troop.	-	-	-	1	-	
Signal Squadron	-	-	1	-	-	
Total.	2	1	50	20	-	

Meux Captn.
D.A.A.& Q.M.G.

APPENDIX X

Deficiencies in Establishments of Fighting units - 20-6-15.

Unit	Officers		Other Ranks		Officers Chargers	Horses Riding	L.D. Horses	L.D. Mules	Ord. Mules	Remarks
	Br.	Ind.	Br.	Ind.						
17th Lancers	–	–	17	–	–	2	–	–	1	
6th Cavy.	–	–	–	18	–	–	–	–	–	
19th Lancers	–	–	–	5	3	–	–	–	–	
8th Hussars	–	–	–	–	–	8	–	–	–	
9th Horse	–	–	–	10	2	6	–	–	–	
30th Lancers	–	–	–	1	–	–	–	–	–	
K.D.Gs	3	–	26	–	–	1	–	–	1	
9th Lancers	–	1	–	6	–	1	–	–	–	
36th Horse	–	2	–	4	–	–	–	–	1	
'A' Bty. R.H.A.	–	–	1	–	–	–	8	–	–	
'Q' " "	–	–	5	–	–	–	8	–	–	
'U' " "	–	–	1	–	–	–	4	–	–	
Divl. Amm. Col.	–	–	–	–	2	–	25	–	–	
Total	3	3	50	44	7	19	46	–	3	

Meuri Capt.
D.A.A. & Q.M.G.

APPENDIX XI

Weekly Wastage in Sickness – 27-6-15

Unit	Officers Br.	Officers Ind.	Other Ranks Br.	Other Ranks Ind.	Fol.	Remarks
14th Lancers	–	–	10	–	–	
6th Cavalry	–	–	–	3	–	
19th Lancers	–	–	–	4	–	
Ambala Bde. Hd. Qrs.	–	–	1	–	–	
8th Hussars	–	–	3	–	–	
9th Horse	–	–	–	1	–	
30th Lancers	–	–	–	2	–	
K.D.Gs.	–	–	4	4	–	
29th Lancers	–	–	1	2	–	
36th Horse	–	–	–	3	–	
'A' Bty. R.H.A.	–	–	3	–	–	
'Q' " "	–	–	1	–	–	
'U' " "	–	–	1	–	–	
Divl. Ammn. Col.	–	–	5	–	–	
Ammn. Park	–	–	2	–	–	
Supply Column	–	–	4	–	–	
Total	–	–	35	15	–	

H Lewis Capt.
D.A.A. & Q.M.G.

APPENDIX XII

Deficiencies in Establishments of fighting units – 27-6-15.

Unit	Officers Br.	Officers Ind.	Other Ranks Br.	Other Ranks Ind.	Officers Chargers	Horses Riding	L.D. Horses	L.D. Mules	Ord. Mules	Remarks
14th Lancers	–	–	26	–	–	11	–	–	1	
6th Cavy.	–	–	–	18	–	–	1	–	–	
19th Lancers	–	–	–	9	–	–	–	–	1	
8th Hussars	1	–	2	–	–	12	–	1	–	
9th Horse	–	–	–	–	2	6	–	–	–	
30th Lancers	–	–	–	3	–	6	–	1	–	
K.D.Gs.	3	–	40	–	–	6	–	1	–	
29th Lancers	–	1	–	4	–	1	1	–	–	
6th Horse	–	2	–	5	–	5	–	–	1	
A. Bty. R.H.A.	–	–	–	–	–	–	9	–	–	
Q. " "	–	–	5	–	–	–	8	–	–	
U. " "	–	–	–	1	–	–	4	–	–	
Divl. Ammn. Col.	–	–	–	–	–	2	25	–	–	
Total	4	3	73	40	2	49	47	4	3	

Meuri Captn.
D.A.A. & Q.M.G.

WAR DIARY
OF
A & Q.

1ST INDIAN CAVALRY DIVISION

JULY - 1915

Serial No. 2

131/6502

WAR DIARY
with Appendices

OF
Administrative Branch, 1st Indian Cavalry Division

FROM — 1st July — 1915. TO — 31st July — 1915

Army Form C. 2118.

WAR DIARY
or
INTELLIGENCE SUMMARY.
(Erase heading not required.)

Instructions regarding War Diaries and Intelligence Summaries are contained in F. S. Regs., Part II, and the Staff Manual respectively. Title pages will be prepared in manuscript.

Hour, Date, Place.	Summary of Events and Information.	Remarks and references to Appendices
ROQUETOIRE 1-7-15	Representation to Controller of complaints re non-payment of Indian family remittances, & charges of Commission on money orders.	
	Capt. D.Y. WATT, 14th Lancers, Staff Captain SIALKOT Cavy. Bde. left D.S. on appointment to Bde Major, SEELY's Bde.	App I
4-7-15	Weekly wastage in sickness Deficiencies in establishments of fighting units	App II
5-7-15	Capt. H. ALLARDICE, 36th Horse, appointed Staff Capt. SIALKOT Bde vice Capt. WATT	
6-7-15	Capt. H. LEWIS, D.A.A. & Q.M.G. left D.S. on appointment to Leicester yeomanry. Provisioned that a weekly return to be rendered giving applicants for Munition work at Home.	App III, IV
11-7-15	Weekly wastage in sickness Deficiencies in establishments of fighting units	
	Capt. G. de la P. BERESFORD, 18th Lancers, attached to 9th Horse, appointed A.D.C. to G.O.C. LUCKNOW Bde, vice Capt. McLEOD appointed Staff Captain.	

Army Form C. 2118.

WAR DIARY
or
INTELLIGENCE SUMMARY.
(Erase heading not required.)

Hour, Date, Place.	Summary of Events and Information.	Remarks and references to Appendices
ROQUETOIRE 12-4-15	Increased issue of newspapers to admit of a 10% distribution. Stock taking of Boots.	F/1 F/2
14-4-15	Reduction of meat ration to 1 lb. fresh or ¾ lb. preserved meat.	F/3
15-4-15	Exchange to be carried out between officers of the I.A.R. & officers serving at MARSEILLES & those serving in the List, in order to complete the training of the former.	F/4
	Orders issued that Billeting certificate for period prior to 1st March to be submitted by units direct to Branch Requisitioning Officer.	F/5
	Withdrawal of short Lee Enfield Rifles & longer Rifles which have been re-sighted for Mark VII Ammn. from :— Hd. Qrs R.H.A. Btties. + Bakeries — except 10 per Bty to be retained for Guards, &c. Ammn. Column A.S.C. Personnel of Cavy. Fd. Amblces. } To be rearmed with Carbines or rifles not re-sighted for Mark VII Ammn. Officers' Servants & Grooms.	F/6
17-4-15	Census taken of Motor Cars	F/7

Army Form C. 2118.

WAR DIARY
or
INTELLIGENCE SUMMARY.
(Erase heading not required.)

Instructions regarding War Diaries and Intelligence Summaries are contained in F. S. Regs., Part II, and the Staff Manual respectively. Title pages will be prepared in manuscript.

Hour, Date, Place.	Summary of Events and Information.	Remarks and references to Appendices
ROQUETOIRE 14-4-15.	Revised scale of H.E. & Shrapnel fixed for Batteries. H.E. increased to 50%. Shrapnel reduced to 50%.	Appx
	Units warned that complaints have been received of Indian detachments returning to India from Field Service having been found in possession of ammunition concealed in their bedding.	Appx
18-4-15.	Weekly wastage in sickness. Deficiencies in establishments of fighting units	Appx I " II Appx
19-4-15.	Decision received that each man to be in possession of 2 smoke Helmets. 1 Helmet to be carried in pocket sewn in the inside of the coat. 2nd Helmet to be carried in a satchel carried on the man.	Appx
21-4-15	Capt. G.R. MAITLAND, Bde Major, LUCKNOW Bde, appointed D.A.A.&Q.M.G. of the 5th vice Capt. H.LEWIS	Appx
	Major A.M.TURNER, K.D.G., appointed Bde Major, LUCKNOW Bde, vice Capt. MAITLAND.	Appx
22-4-15.	Circular memo from H.H. the Rajah Sahib of BILASPORE re the duties & loyalty of men of his state serving in the war. Copies issued to Indian Units.	Appx
	Report received from LUCKNOW Bde that Pistol Ammr dated 30-1-15 defective. Pistols examined & found correct. Corps notified.	Appx

Army Form C. 2118.

WAR DIARY
INTELLIGENCE SUMMARY.

(Erase heading not required.)

Instructions regarding War Diaries and Intelligence Summaries are contained in F.S. Regs., Part II, and the Staff Manual respectively. Title pages will be prepared in manuscript.

Hour, Date, Place.	Summary of Events and Information.	Remarks and references to Appendices
ROQUETOIRE 23-4-15	Horse rations readjusted in the 5". Oat ration of horses of Ind. Cavy. units reduced by 1 lb. per diem, & that of Australian horses of Batteries increased by 2 lbs. per diem.	
	Rajah of AKALKOT to be attached to G.O.C. Staff.	
	Circular issued re chargers. During a shortage, no future chargers only to be demanded for General & Senior Staff officers.	
25/28-4-15	Official photographs taken of 5" Bdes, &c, as ordered by Gov.t of India.	App VII / VIII
28-4-15	Weekly wastage in sickness. Deficiencies in establishments of fighting units.	
	Reserve of cartridges to be carried by Ind. Armd. Col. increased by 25%.	
29.4.15	Recommendation re braziers for use in trenches during winter months, & amount of fuel considered necessary :—	
	No. of braziers recommended — 20 per Regt.	
	Type — Iron drum, Iron buckets & biscuit tins	
	Fuel — Charcoal 80 lbs ¾ per brazier	
	Coke 160 lbs S ∫ per 24 hours	

Army Form C. 2118.

WAR DIARY

INTELLIGENCE SUMMARY.

(Erase heading not required.)

Instructions regarding War Diaries and Intelligence Summaries are contained in F.S. Regs., Part II, and the Staff Manual respectively. Title pages will be prepared in manuscript.

Hour, Date, Place.	Summary of Events and Information.	Remarks and references to Appendices
ROQUETOIRE 29-7-15.	Representation made to Corps re scale of hay & certain cereal fodders fixed by Controller not being in all cases the most favourable rate.	
30-7-15.	Lt-Col. R.O'B TAYLOR, G.S.O.1, vacated his appointment, & proceeded home to report to War Office.	
	Major A.N. BARRON, D.A.D.O.S. transferred to 3rd Cavy. Dn.	
	B.P.S. ROOKE assumed duties of D.A.D.O.S.	
31-7-15.	Instructions received that Divn. is to march on 1st August to join 3rd Army.	

D.P. Martin
Capt. for Lt-Col.
A.A. & Q.M.G. 1st Div.

APPENDIX I.

Wastage from Sickness – 4th July 1915.

Unit	Officers Brit.	Officers Ind.	Other Ranks Br.	Other Ranks Ind.	Other Ranks Foll.	Remarks
17th Lancers	–	–	5	–	–	
6th Cavalry	–	–	–	2	–	
19th Lancers	–	–	–	2	–	
Sialkot Bde Signal Troop	–	–	1	–	–	
8th Hussars	–	–	2	–	–	
9th Horse	–	–	–	2	–	
30th Lancers	–	1	–	–	–	
K.D.Gs.	–	–	4	–	–	
29th Lancers	–	–	–	2	–	
36th Horse	–	–	–	2	–	
A Bty. R.H.A.	–	–	1	–	–	
Q	–	–	1	–	–	
Div. Ammn Column	–	–	11	1	–	
Signal Squadron	–	–	1	–	–	
Ammn Park	–	–	1	–	–	
Supply Column	–	–	2	–	–	
Total	–	1	28	12	–	

C.R. Maitland
Capt. for Lt-Col.
A.A.Q.M.G.
1st.I.C.D.

APPENDIX II.

Deficiencies in Establishments of Fighting units — 4.7.1915.

Units	Officers		Other Ranks			Chargers	Horses Riding	L.D. Horses	L.D. Mules	Ord. Mules	Remarks
	Br.	Ind.	Br.	Ind.	Foll.						
17th Lancers	.	.	2	.	.	.	9	.	.	1	
6th Cavalry	1	-	-	16	-	-	5	.	2	.	
19th Lancers	-	-	-	11	.	-	25	.	3	.	
8th Hussars	2	.	4	.	.	.	13	.	1	1	
9th Horse	1	.	.	1	.	.	11	.	.	.	
30th Lancers	2	1	.	3	.	.	3	.	.	.	
K.D.Gs	2	.	2	.	.	.	.	.	1	.	
29th Lancers	.	1	.	10	.	.	2	.	.	.	
36th Horse	.	2	.	7	.	.	5	.	1	1	
Bty. R.H.A.	.	.	.	.	.	.	8	.	.	.	
Q — —	.	.	.	.	.	.	8	.	.	.	
U — —	.	.	.	.	.	.	8	.	.	.	
Divl. Ammn. Col.	.	.	.	.	.	.	25	.	.	.	
Total	8	4	8	48	.	.	73	49	8	3	

Lt. Col.
A.A. & Q.M.G. 1st C.D.

APPENDIX III

Wastage in Sickness for week ended 11th July 1915.

Unit	Officers		Other Ranks			Remarks
	Brit.	Ind.	Br.	Ind.	Foll.	
14th Lancers	-	-	4	-	-	
6th Cavalry	1	-	-	2	-	
19th Lancers	-	1	-	1	-	
Ambala Bde. Hd. Qrs.	-	-	1	-	-	
8th Hussars	1	-	2	-	-	
9th Horse	-	-	-	4	-	
30th Lancers	-	-	-	2	-	
36th Horse	-	-	-	1	-	
A Bty. R.H.A.	-	-	-	1	-	
Q " "	-	-	1	-	-	
Divl. Ammn. Column	1	-	4	-	-	
Supply Column	-	-	1	-	-	
Field Squadron	-	-	1	-	-	
Field Troop	-	-	-	5	-	
Total	3	1	14	16	-	

G. R. Markland
Capt. for
Lt-Col
A.A. & Q.M.G.
1st I.C.Dn.

APPENDIX IV

Deficiencies in Establishments of Fighting units – 11-7-1915.

Unit	Officers		Other Ranks			Chargers	Horses Riding	L.D. Horses	L.D. Mules	Ord. Mules	Remarks
	Br.	Ind.	Br.	Ind.	Folls						
17th Lancers	.	.	.	.	.	.	1	.	.	.	
6th Cavalry	2	.	.	6	1	.	4	.	2	.	
19th Lancers	.	.	.	8	.	.	10	1	.	.	
8th Hussars	1	.	3	.	.	.	2	.	.	.	
9th Horse	1	.	.	4	.	.	.	.	.	.	
30th Lancers	2	1	.	5	1	.	3	.	.	.	
K.D.Gs	2	.	.	.	.	.	.	.	1	.	
29th Lancers	.	1	.	1	2	.	.	.	.	.	
36th Horse	.	1	.	5	1	.	10	.	1	.	
Q.Bty.R.H.A.	.	.	2	.	.	.	.	.	.	.	
Divl Amm.Col.	.	.	1	.	.	.	.	7	.	.	
Total	8	3	6	29	5	.	30	8	2	2	

G R Maitland
Capt for Lt Col.
A.A. & QMG 1st C.D.

APPENDIX V

Wastage in Sickness — 18th July 1915.

Unit	Officers		Other Ranks			Remarks
	Br.	Ind.	Br.	Ind.	Foll.	
17th Lancers	–	–	4	–	–	
6th Cavalry	–	–	–	5	–	
19th Lancers	–	–	–	1	–	
8th Hussars	–	–	2	–	–	
9th Horse	–	–	–	2	–	
30th Lancers	–	–	–	2	–	
29th Lancers	–	–	–	1	–	
36th Horse	–	–	–	1	–	
A Bty. R.H.A.	–	–	1	–	–	
Q " " "	–	–	3	–	–	
U " " "	–	–	1	–	–	
Div. Ammn. Column	–	–	1	–	–	
Ammn. Park	–	–	1	–	–	
Field Troop	–	–	–	–	2	
Signal Squadron	–	–	1	–	–	
Supply Column	–	–	1	–	–	
Total	–	–	15	12	2	

G.P. Maitland
Lt. Col.
A.A. & Q.M.G.
1st I.C. Div.

APPENDIX VI

Deficiencies in establishments of Fighting units – 18-7-1915.

Unit	Officers Br.	Officers Ind.	Other Ranks Br.	Other Ranks Ind.	Folls.	Chargers	Horses Riding	L.D. Horses	L.D. Mules	Pack Mules	Remarks
17th Lancers							3				
6th Cavalry		2		11	1	1	12			2	
19th Lancers				6			1				
8th Hussars	1		7				3				
30th Lancers	2	1		4			7				
9th Horse	3			9							
K.D.Gs	2						12				
29th Lancers	1	1		3	1						
36th Horse		1		6	1		11				
Q Bty. R.H.A			2								
Total	9	5	9	42	3	1	48	1		2	

APPENDIX VII

Wastage in Sickness - 25th July 1915.

Unit.	Officers		Other Ranks			Remarks
	Br.	Ind.	Br.	Ind.	Foll.	
Divl. Hd. Qrs.	1	-	1	-	-	
14th Lancers.	-	-	4	-	-	
6th Cavalry	-	-	-	3	-	
19th Lancers.	-	-	-	2	-	
8th Hussars	-	-	1	-	-	
9th Horse.	-	1	-	2	-	
30th Lancers	-	-	-	2	-	
K.D.Gs.	-	-	4	-	-	
36th Horse.	-	-	-	3	-	
Lucknow Bde. Signal Troop	-	-	2	-	-	
" Mob. Vety Sect	-	-	1	-	-	
Q Bty, R.H.A.	-	-	1	-	-	
U " "	-	-	1	-	-	
Supply Column	-	-	4	-	-	
Ammn. Park	-	-	1	-	-	
Signal Squadron	-	-	2	-	-	
Total	1	1	22	12	-	

TR Maitland
Capt / Lt. Col.
A.A. & Q.M.G. 1st C.D.

WAR DIARY
with appendices

OF

Administrative Branch - 1st Indian Cavalry Division.

FROM 1st August 1915 TO 31st August 1915.

Army Form C. 2118.

WAR DIARY
or
INTELLIGENCE SUMMARY.
(Erase heading not required.)

Instructions regarding War Diaries and Intelligence Summaries are contained in F. S. Regs., Part II. and the Staff Manual respectively. Title pages will be prepared in manuscript.

Hour, Date, Place	Summary of Events and Information	Remarks and references to Appendices
1st to 4th Aug 1915	Division on the March.	
	Weekly wastage in sickness	App. I
	Deficiencies in Establishments of fighting units	" II
3-8-15	Lt. Col. C.A.C GODWIN, Bde Major MHOW Bde, assumed duties of G.S.O.I, vice Lt. Col. TAYLOR	
DOMART 4-8-15	Div. arrived in new area -	
	Detailed list of billets attached	" III
	Points brought to notice in connection with the march.	" IV
" 4-8-15	Method of carrying Pioneer Equipment & Explosives by Pack Transport.	
	1 lb of total explosives to be carried by each Sqdn. One extra pull bore of Gun Cotton to be drawn from Ammnt Column by each Regt, so that there will be 1 box for each Sqdn. When pack animals not available, the 2 lead mules of the Limbered G.S. Wagon will be used	
8-8-15	Weekly wastage in sickness	" V
	Deficiencies in establishments of fighting units	" VI
	"A" & "Q" Batteries R.H.A. proceeded to 3rd Div.	

Army Form C. 2118.

WAR DIARY
or
INTELLIGENCE SUMMARY.
(Erase heading not required.)

Instructions regarding War Diaries and Intelligence Summaries are contained in F. S. Regs., Part II. and the Staff Manual respectively. Title pages will be prepared in manuscript.

Hour, Date, Place		Summary of Events and Information	Remarks and references to Appendices
DOMART	9-8-15	Capt F. R. TEESDALE G.S.O. 3, departed to take up appointment of G.S.O. 3, Indian Cavalry Corps Head Qrs	
"		All 13 Mr. H.E. Coy'd killed from k 20.7.1915 sent to Railhead for inspection, after which it was ordered to be returned to Armourers.	
"	12.8.15	SIALKOT Bde – dismounted – strength 300 Rifles per Regiment moved to front with 2nd Ind Cavy Dn & held in Reserve. Under command of 51st Divn – II Corps. Bde moved up by Gus. ⅔ of A.A. Section Divl Ammn Column accompanied the Bde.	
"	13.8.15	In order to allow the inhabitants sufficient farm accommodation for the storage of their harvest, Censuses taken showing the number of men & horses who cannot be accommodated - for whom later provision must be made. Result 1600 men & 16 so horses	
"	14.8.15	Capt H. E. MACFARLANE, 19th Hussars, assumed the duties of G.S.O. 3, vice Capt TEESDALE	
"		Report regarding number of schools occupied by nipts. Theory occupied in the Divn but only for period of School Holidays	
"	15.8.15	Weekly wastage in horses	APP VII
"		Deficiencies in establishments of fighting units	VIII

Forms/C. 2418/10

Army Form C. 2118.

WAR DIARY
INTELLIGENCE SUMMARY.
(Erase heading not required.)

Instructions regarding War Diaries and Intelligence Summaries are contained in F. S. Regs., Part II. and the Staff Manual respectively. Title pages will be prepared in manuscript.

Hour, Date, Place	Summary of Events and Information	Remarks and references to Appendices
DOMART 15-8-15	All No 5. Mills Hand Grenades on charge returned to Railhead	
19-8-15	Major Genl H.D. FANSHAWE, C.B., Comdg the 2nd, departed to take command of 5th Cavy Corps	
	Orders received that all Mark G.14 & G.15. S.A.A. to be returned to Railhead. Rounds returned Mark G.14 – 229,085 " G.15 22,160	APP IX / X
22-8-15	AMBALA & LUCKNOW Bdes. dismounted moved up to front, joined SIALKOT Bde., & the 9th went into the trenches	
	Weekly wastage in sickness Deficiencies in establishments of fighting units	
23-8-15	Major Genl G. des BARROW, C.B., assumed command of the 2nd vice Major Genl FANSHAWE	
24-8-15	"U" Bty R.H.A. proceeded to front.	
29-8-15	100 reinforcement for each Ind. Cavy Regt. arrived from Base. Strength of these units increased from 471 Rank & File to 545.	APP XI / XII
	Weekly wastage in sickness Deficiencies in establishments of fighting units.	

J.R.A.T? Lt. Col.
A.A.Q.M.G. 1st Ind Cav 2
19/15

APPENDIX I

Weekly Wastage from Sickness — 1-8-1916

Unit	Officers		Other Ranks			Remarks
	Brit	Ind	Brit	Ind	Foll'r	
Head Qrs Divn				1		
6th Cavalry				6		
19th Lancers				1		
8th Hussars			3			
9th Horse				1		
Ambala Cde & St Extel					1	
K.D.G.			1			
29th Lancers				5		
36th Horse	1			3		
Q Bty R H A			1			
R — "			3			
U — "			2			
Div Amm Column			2	2		
Amm Park			2			
Supply Column			2			
Field Squadron			3			
Ambala Cav Fd Aml					1	
Total	1		19	17	2	

Capt
D.A.A. & Q.M.G. 1st C.D.

APPENDIX II

Deficiencies in Establishment of Fighting Units. 1-2-1918

Unit	Officers Br.	Ind.	Other Rk. Br.	Ind.	Horses Riding	Horses Draught	Mules Draught	Mules ord	Remarks
19th Lancers	1		4		6			1	
6th Cavalry	1			12	8				
19th Lancers				12					
8th Hussars	1		16		6				
9th Horse	2			10	2				
38th Lancers	2	1		4	2	2			
K D G	3		13		20				
29th Lancers	2	1		2	8				
38th Horse			1	5	6				
Q Bty RHA			2						
9 L			2						
No Amm Cl			3						
Total	12	3	40	45	58	2		1	

Headquarters.
1st Indian Cavalry Division.

App. III

Billeting areas - 1st Indian Cavalry Division.

Units.	Where billeted.
Divl. Headquarters	DOMART-EN-PENTHIEU.
A.D.M.S.	" "
A.D.V.S.	LONGPRE-LES-CORPS-SAINTS.
D.A.D.O.S.	DOMART-EN-PENTHIEU.
A.P.M.	" "
O.C., A.S.C.	" "
Field Squadron	" "
Hq: 1st Ind: R.H.A., Brigade	SURCAMPS.
"A" Battery R.H.A.	detached
"U" Battery R.H.A.	ST HILAIRES.
"Q" Battery R.H.A.	detached
Divl Ammunition Column	GORENFLOS.
Divl Ammunition Park	LONG.
Divl Supply Column	LONGPRE-LES-CORPS-SAINTS.
Sialkot Cav: Fd Ambulance	DOMART-EN-PENTHIEU.
Ambala Cav: Fd Ambulance	" "
Lucknow Cav: Fd Ambulance	" "

SIALKOT BRIGADE.
Headquarters	ST LEGER.
Signal Troop	" "
Mobile Vet: Section	ST OUEN.
17th Lancers	" "
6th Cavalry	BETHENCOURT+ST OUEN.
19th Lancers	" "

AMBALA BRIGADE
Headquarters	VILLIERS-SOUS-AILLY
Signal Troop	" "
Mobile Vet: Section	L'ETOILE.
8th Hussars	BOUCHON.- L'ETOILE.
9th Horse	LONG.
30th Lancers	AILLY.

LUCKNOW BRIGADE.
Headquarters	HALLOYS.
Signal Troop	"
Mobile Vet: Section	BERTEAUCOURT
1st K.D.Gds	HALLOYS.- PERNOIS.
29th Lancers	MONTRELET.- FIEFFES.
36th Horse	BERTEAUCOURT.

W K Bourne
Lieutenant Colonel.
A.A., and Q.M.G.,
1st Indian Cavalry Division.

9th August 1915.

No Q-2305

Headquarters.
1st Indian Cavalry Division.
7th August 1915.

App IV

MEMORANDUM.

The following points, noted during the march from the ROQUETOIRE area, are forwarded for guidance :-

(1)   Some Mess Carts were too heavily laden. There is great danger of this with some of the hooded carts which are in possession of units.   The removal of these hoods would in many cases considerably lighten the load, and a total weight of 5 cwt behind the horse should not be exceeded.

(2)   Watercarts should travel empty.

(3)   Roads should be reconnoitred.   One road marked good on the map turned out to be a track through the fields, and its use involved a heavy strain on the transp

(4)   In one case a loaded wagon of "B" echelon was moving away from its destination en route to a regimental rendezvous.   All rendezvous should be fixed sufficiently in advance to insure that no troops or transport have to move back to reach them.

(5)   The regulation paces were exceeded both in the case of troops and transport.   The result was an undue number of galls among the mules of "A" echelon.

A K Bourne
Lieutenant Colonel.
A.A., and Q.M.G.,
1st Indian Cavalry Division.

APPENDIX V

Weekly Wastage from Sickness - 8-8-1915

Unit	Officers		Other Ranks			Remarks
	Br	Ind	Br	Ind	Foll'rs	
17th Lancers			5			
6th Cavalry				4		
19th Lancers				4		
8th Hussars	1		1			
9th Horse				5		
30th Lancers		1		5		
Ambala Bde S&T ExtKt			1			
29th Lancers	1			4		
36th Horse				1	1	
A Bty R H A			2			
Q —			1			
U — —			2			
Xid Ammn Col			10			
Supply Column			1			
Lucknow Cavy Fd Amb			2			
Total	2	1	25	23	1	

Capt
D A A + Q M G : 1st C D

APPENDIX VI

Deficiencies in Establishments of Fighting units. 8-8-1915

Unit	Officers Br	Officers Ind	Other Ranks Br	Other Ranks Ind	Horses Riding	Horses Draught	Mules Draught	Mules Other	Remarks
17th Lancers	1		10		8			1	
6th Cavalry	1			11	7				
19th Lancers				16	10				
8th Hussars	1		19		6				
9th Horse				7					
3rd Lancers		1		6	5				
K D G	2		13		21				
29th Lancers	2	1		7	13				
36th Horse		1		6	3				
A Bty R H A			2						
Q —			5						
U —			6		1				
2nd Ammn Col			3		1	2			
Total	7	3	58	53	75	2		1	

Capt
D.a.a.& Q.M.G, 1SCD

APPENDIX VII

Weekly wastage in sickness - 15-8-1915.

Unit	Officers		Other Ranks			Remarks
	Br	Ind.	Br	Ind	Fol	
14th Lancers			1			
6th Cavalry			1	3		
19th Lancers				2		
8th Hussars			1			
9th Horse				3		
29th Lancers	1			6		
Lucknow Bde B. & T. Estb	1					
— Inf. Vety Sect			1			
U. Bty R.H.A.			3	1		
Div. Ammn Col			6			
Supply Column			3			
Field Squadron			2			
Total	2		18	15		

Capt
DAA&QMG

APPENDIX VIII

Deficiencies in Establishments of Fighting units - 15-8-1915

Unit	Officers		Other Ranks		Horses Riding	Horses Draught	M.G. Draught	Mules Others	Remarks
	Br.	Ind.	Br.	Ind.					
17th Lancers					1				
6th Cavy	3			8	11				
19th Lancers	1	1		5	10				
8th Hussars	1		1		3	3			
9th Horse					11	4			
30th Lancers	2	1			4	3			
K.E.O.	2								
29th Lancers	3	1			10				
36th Horse		1			5	1			
U Bty RHA			5	1		2			
Div Amm Col			12		2	6			
Total	12	4	18	44	55	8	3		

Capt
D.A.A. & Q.M.G

APPENDIX IX

Weekly Wastage in Sickness – 22.8.1915

Units	Officers		Other Ranks			Remarks
	Br	Ind	Br	Ind	Foll	
17th Lancers			1			
6th Cavalry				2		
19th Lancers			1			
9th Horse				6		
38th Lancers				2		
36th Horse					1	
U Bty RHA			2			
Supply Column			3			
Field Sqn			1			
K D Gs			4			
29th Lancers				2		
Total			11	13	1	

Capt.
D.A.A. & Q.M.G.

APPENDIX X

Deficiencies in Establishments of Fighting units - 22-8-1916

Unit	Officers		Other Ranks		Horses Riding	Horses Draught	Mules	Donkeys	M.T. A.T.	Remarks
	Br.	Ind.	Br.	Ind.						
14th Lancers	1		4		11					
6th Cavy	2			9	9					
19th Lancers		1			10					
8th Hussars	2		3		6	1				
9th Horse				10	5					
30th Lancers	1									
K.D.Gs.	1									
29th Lancers	2	1		3		1				
"U" Bty R.H.A				1						
Total	9	2	7	23	41	2				

Capt
D.A.A.Q.M.G

APPENDIX XI

Weekly Wastage in Sickness. 29-8-1915

Unit	Officers		Other Ranks			Remarks
	Br	Ind	Br	Ind	Foll'r	
Sialkot Bde Hd Qrs			1			
17th Lancers			1			
6th Cavalry				3		
8th Hussars			1			
9th Horse				2		
5th Lancers				1		
K D G			1			
29 L Lancers				4		
Supply Column			2			
Field Squadron			1			
Sialkot Cavy Fd Amb			1			
No 399 M T Coy ASC	1					
Signal Squadron			1			
Total	1		9	10		

Capt
D A A & Q M G

APPENDIX XII

Deficiencies in Establishments of Fighting Units. 29-8-15

Unit	Officers		Other Ranks		Horses Riding	Horses Draught	M. Ley Draught	M. Ley Mule	Remarks
	Br	Ind	Br	Ind					
17th Lancers	1		6		11				
6th Cavalry	2			20	11				
19th Lancers				15	6				
8th Hussars	2		5	10		1			
9th Horse				20	1		1		
30th Lancers	1	1		6					
K D Y	1								
29th Lancers	1	2		10	1				
36th Horse				6					
1st Ammn Col					2	2			
Total	8	3	11	77	32	2	1	1	

Capt
D.A.A & Q.M.G

WAR DIARY

OF

A & Q.

1ST INDIAN CAVALRY DIVISION

SEPTEMBER - 1915

Serial No. 2.

121/7226

WAR DIARY
with appendices

OF

Administrative Branch, 1st Indian Cavalry Division.

From 1st September 1915 TO 30th September 1915

Army Form C. 2118.

WAR DIARY
or
INTELLIGENCE SUMMARY.
(Erase heading not required.)

Instructions regarding War Diaries and Intelligence Summaries are contained in F.S. Regs., Part II. and the Staff Manual respectively. Title pages will be prepared in manuscript.

Hour, Date, Place	Summary of Events and Information	Remarks and references to Appendices
DOMART 3-9-15	Troops relieved from trenches & employed in digging Reserve Trenches. Statement of casualties for period Div was in trenches.	APP "A" all
5-9-15	Weekly wastage in sickness. Deficiencies in establishments of fighting units	B all C
6-9-15	Divl Bathing Establishment opened at M Saints jute factory at ST OUEN. Capacity 1,80 men per diem. Each man has a hot bath and exchanges his dirty linen for clean. Washing of linen carried out by a laundry at AMIENS, connected by a lorry service.	all
10-9-15	Redistribution of billets.	APP "D" E F all
12-9-15	Weekly wastage in sickness. Deficiencies in establishments of fighting units	all
13-9-15	Divsn went into trenches night of 14/15th	all
15-9-15	AMBALA Bde transferred to 2nd Ind Cav Dn MHOW ,, ,, ,, ,, 1st Ind Cav Dn	all
17-9-15	Div relieved from trenches on night of 16/17th & R 16/17th APP "G" B Statement of casualties for period night 14/15	APP "G" B

(9 29 6) W 4141—463   100,000   9/14   H W V   Forms/C. 2418/10

Army Form C. 2118.

WAR DIARY
or
INTELLIGENCE SUMMARY.
(Erase heading not required.)

Instructions regarding War Diaries and Intelligence Summaries are contained in F.S. Regs., Part II. and the Staff Manual respectively. Title pages will be prepared in manuscript.

Hour, Date, Place		Summary of Events and Information	Remarks and references to Appendices
DOMART	19.9.15	Weekly wastage in Lichness. Deficiencies in Establishments of fighting units	App "H" I A.
DOMART LE MILLARD	22.9.15	Division moved to new billeting area. Detailed list of billets	" J A
LE MILLARD	25.9.15	All kits were dumped & stores in Central Dept in billets. "B" Echelon wagons thus set free sent to Ruckless & horses sent 2 days rations in men and horses. 2 days iron rations for Brit: units & 2 days emergency rations for Indian troops drawn. That for mounted units carried by Coys. That for wheeled units on existing Transport. Scale of Machine Guns changed from 2 Maxims to 4 Vickers per unit. Brit: units now in possession of 4 Vickers. Indian " — " 2 maxims or 2 Vickers. 17th Lancers to have 4 Vickers. The 2 maxims with Ind: units will be withdrawn & replaced by 2 Vickers, when latter become available. 4 Officers' G.S. horses + 4 L.D. horses received per unit, for	A

Army Form C. 2118.

WAR DIARY
or
INTELLIGENCE SUMMARY.
(Erase heading not required.)

Instructions regarding War Diaries and Intelligence Summaries are contained in F.S. Regs., Part II. and the Staff Manual respectively. Title pages will be prepared in manuscript.

Hour, Date, Place	Summary of Events and Information	Remarks and references to Appendices
LE MILLARD		
26-9-15	For transport of the 2 additional guns, 1 of the Limbered G.S. wagons now with units to be set aside for this purpose, the Limbered G.S. being replaced by the G.S. wagon now received.	APP "K" R.
	Weekly wastage from sickness. Statement showing deficiencies in fighting units.	L R.
28-9-15	Auxiliary Transport Coy. A.S.C. joined the Div. Strength – 2 Officers 102 Other Ranks 41 Vehicles 146 Horses	

30/9/15

R.R.Maitland Capt.
D.A.A. & Q.M.G. 1st Cav Div.

APPENDIX A

STATEMENT OF CASUALTIES FOR THE PERIOD 20TH AUGUST 1915 TO 3RD SEPTEMBER 1915.

1ST INDIAN CAVALRY DIVISION.

UNIT.	KILLED.				WOUNDED.				MISSING.				REMARKS.
	B.Os.	I.Os.	B. Rks.	I. Rks.	B. Os.	I. Os.	B. Rks.	I. Rks.	B. Os.	I. Os.	B. Rks.	I. Rks.	
17th Lancers.							2.						
6th Cavalry.								15.					
19th Lancers.			1.					10.					
8th Hussars.							9.@						@ 1 since died of wounds.
9th Horse.			1.					16.					
30th Lancers.			1.					11.					
K.D.G's.							2.						
29th Lancers.								1.					
36th Horse.		1.	1.					2.					
TOTAL.	1.	-	4.				13.	55.					

G.R. Maitland
Capt.
D.A.A.Q.M.G.

APP. B

Weekly wastage from sickness – 5-9-15

Unit	Officers		Other Ranks			Remarks
	Brit	Ind	Br	Ind	Foll	
17th Lancers	–	–	5	–	–	
19th Lancers	–	–	–	2	–	
8th Hussars	–	–	3	–	–	
9th Horse	–	–	1	7	–	
30th Lancers	–	–	–	4	–	
Lucknow Bde Hd Qrs	–	–	2	–	–	
K D Gp	–	–	5	–	–	
29th Lancers	–	–	–	3	–	
36th Horse	–	–	–	2	–	
Lucknow Bde Signal Troop	–	–	1	–	–	
Divl Ammn Col	–	–	1	–	–	
Ammn Park	–	–	2	–	–	
Supply Column	–	–	3	–	–	
Field Sqdr	–	–	1	–	–	
Signal Sqdr	–	–	2	–	–	
Divl Santy Section	–	–	–	–	1	
Total	–	–	26	18	1	

G R Maitland Capt
D.A.A. & Q.M.G

APP "C"

Deficiencies in Establishments of Fighting units. 5-9-15

Unit	Officers		Other Ranks		Horses Riding	Horses L.P.	Mules L.P.	M.L.s N.I.	Remarks
	Br.	Ind.	Br.	Ind.					
14th Lancers	-	-	10	-	7	-	-	-	
6th Cavalry	1	-	-	27	-	-	-	-	
19th Lancers	-	-	-	18	-	-	-	-	
8th Hussars	1	-	14	-	14	-	-	-	
2nd Horse	-	-	-	39	9	-	-	-	
30th Lancers	1	-	-	20	2	-	-	-	
29th Lancers	-	2	-	10	-	-	-	1	
36th Horse	-	1	-	8	4	-	-	-	
Total	3	3	24	122	36	-	-	1	

C.R. Maitland
Capt
D.A.A. & Q.M.G

No.Q-4164.　　　　　　Headquarters 1st Indian Cavalry Division,

　　　　　　　　　　　　　　　　18th September 1915.

This Division No.Q-3845, dated 11th September 1915 is cancelled and the following substituted.-

BILLETING AREAS - 1ST INDIAN CAVALRY DIVISION.

Nuit.	Where billeted.
Divl. Headquarters	DOMART en PENTHIEU.
A.D.M.S.	" " "
A.D.V.S.	" " "
A.P.M.	" " "
O.C., A.S.C.	" " "
Field Squadron	" " "
D.A.D.O.S.	LONGPRE.
Head Qrs. 1st Indian R.H.A.Bde.	LA HAIE (SURCAMPS).
"A" Battery, R.H.A.	ST.OUEN.
"Q" Battery, R.H.A.	LANCHES.
"U" Battery, R.H.A.	ST.HILAIRE.
Divl. Ammunition Column	BETHENCOURT.
Divl. Ammunition Park	FRANQUEVILLE.
Divl. Supply Column	LONGPRE.
Sialkot Cavalry Field Amblce.	} DOMART en PENTHIEU.
Motor Amblce. Workshop.	
Ambala Cavalry Field Amblce.	" " "
Lucknow Cavalry Field Amblce.	BERNEUIL.
Sanitary Section	FRANQUEVILLE.

Sialkot Bde.
　Headquarters .... GORENFLOS.
　Signal Troop .... "
　Mobile Vety. Section .... "
　17th Lancers .... FRANSU (1 Sqdn) DOMQUEUR (2 Sqdns
　　　　　　　　　　　　　　　& HdQrs) LE PLOUY (1 Sqdn)
　19th Lancers .... ERGNIES (HdQrs. M.G. & 2 Sqdns)
　　　　　　　　　　　　　　　BRUCAMPS (2 Sqdns).
　6th Cavalry .... MOUFFLERS-LA FOLIE AUBERGE (HdQrs
　　　　　　　　　　　　　　　M.G. & 1 Sqdn).
　　　　　　　　　　　　　　　SURCAMPS (2 Sqdns) VAUCHELLE (1
　　　　　　　　　　　　　　　　　　Sqdn).

Mhow Bde.
　Headquarters .... VILLERS-SOUS-AILLY.
　Signal Troop .... " " "
　Mobile Vety. Section .... COCQUEREL.
　6th Innis. Dragoons .... L'ETOILE, BOUCHON.
　2nd Lancers .... LONG, LONGUET, COCQUEREL.
　38th C.I. Horse .... BUSSUS, YAUCOURT BUSSUS.

Lucknow Bde.
　Headquarters .... ST.LEGER.
　Signal Troop .... "
　Mobile Vety. Section .... "
　1st K.D. Guards .... PERNOIS, HALLOY.
　29th Lancers .... MONTRELET, FIEFFES (3 Sqdns. &
　　　　　　　　　　　　　　　Headqrs) BERNEUIL (1 Sqdn).
　36th Horse .... BERTEAUCOURT-LES-DAMES.

　　　　　　　　　　　　W K Brown
　　　　　　　　　　　　　　　　Lieut-Colonel,
　　　　　　A.A. & Q.M.G., 1st Indian Cavalry Division.

APP. E

Weekly Wastage from Sickness - 12-9-1915.

Unit	Officers		Other Ranks			Remarks
	Brit.	Ind.	Br.	Ind.	Fol'rs	
17th Lancers	-	-	14	-	-	
6th Cavy	-	-	-	2	-	
19th Lancers	2	-	-	1	-	
8th Hussars	-	-	3	-	-	
30th Lancers	-	-	-	5	-	
K.D.G.	1	-	10	-	-	
36th Horse	1	-	-	6	1	
Divl Ammn Col.	-	-	1	-	-	
Ammn Park	-	-	1	-	-	
Supply Column	-	-	2	-	-	
1st Ind. Fd Sqdn	-	-	2	-	-	
Total	4	-	36	14	1	

E.R.Maitland
Capt.
D.A.A. & Q.M.G.

APP F

Deficiencies in Establishments of Fighting units - 12·9·15

Unit	Officers		Other Ranks		Horses Riding	Horses L.D.	Mules L.D.	Mules A.T.	Remarks
	Br	Ind	Br	Ind					
17th Lancers	-	-	28	-	8	-	-	1	
6th Cavy	1	-	-	34	-	-	-	-	
19th Lancers	-	-	-	17	2	-	-	-	
8th Hussars	1	-	17	-	6	-	2	1	
9th Horse	-	-	-	35	8	-	-	-	
30th Lancers	-	-	-	24	5	-	-	-	
K) Gs	-	-	11	-	-	-	-	-	
29th Lancers	-	2	-	14	6	-	1	-	
36th Horse	-	1	-	13	-	-	-	-	
Total	2	3	56	139	35	-	3	2	

W.R. Maitland
Capt
D.A.A. & Q.M.G.

APP 'G'

No. A-4195.

Headquarters.
1st Indian Cavalry Division.
19th September 1915.

STATEMENT OF CASUALTIES FOR THE PERIOD NIGHT OF 12/13TH TO NIGHT OF 16/17TH SEPTEMBER 1915.

	KILLED.				WOUNDED.				MISSING.				REMARKS.
	B. Os.	I. Os.	B. Rks.	I. Rks.	B. Os.	I. Os.	B. Rks.	I. Rks.	B. Os.	I. Os.	B. Rks.	I. Rks.	
6th Cavalry.				1.	@1.	1.		10.					@ Slightly. At duty.
19th Lancers.						1.		2.					
K.D.Gds.							1.						
29th Lancers.				3.				13.					Also 1 Fell'n wounded.
36th Horse.								@5.					@ 1 slightly at duty.
TOTAL.				4.	1.	2.	1.	30.					Plus 1 Fell'n wounded.

G.R. Maitland
Capt
DAA-QMG.

APP 'H'

Weekly wastage from sickness - 19-9-15

Unit	Officers		Other Ranks			Remarks
	Br	Ind	Br	Ind	Foll	
17th Lancers	-	-	3	-	-	
6th Cavalry	-	-	1	8	-	
19th Lancers	-	-	-	1	-	
6th Dragoons	-	-	3	-	-	
2nd Lancers	-	-	-	5	-	
38th Horse	-	-	1	2	-	
K's G'	-	-	1	-	-	
29th Lancers	-	-	-	3	-	
36th Horse	-	-	-	1	-	
Q Bty R H A	1	-	1	-	-	
Divl. Ammn. Col	-	-	1	-	-	
No.6 G H Q Ammn Park	-	-	8	-	-	
1st Ind. Fd. Sqdr	-	-	3	-	-	
Sialkot Cavy Fd Amb	-	-	2	-	-	
Supply Column	-	-	1	-	-	
Total	1	-	25	20	-	

G.R. Maitland
Capt.
D.A.A. & Q.M.G.

APP I

Deficiencies in Establishments of Fighting Units. 19-9-1915

Unit	Officers		Other Ranks		Horses Riding	Horses L.D.	Mules L.D.	Mules Pack	Remarks
	Br.	Ind.	Br.	Ind.					
17th Lancers	-	-	7	-	-				
6th Cavy	-	1	-	37	-				
19th Lancers	-	1	-	11	10				
6th Dragoons	-	-	9	-	11				
2nd Lancers	-	-	-	24					
38th Horse	-	-	-	26					
K.D.G.	-	-	8	-					
29th Lancers	-	2	-	21					
34th Horse	-	-	-	20					
A Bty RHA	-	-	-	-		8			
Q —	-	-	6	-		4			
D.A. Amm.Col.	-	-	4	-		1			
Total	-	4	34	139	21	13			

G.C. Maitland
Capt.
D.A.A. & Q.M.G.

No. Q-4430.   Headquarters 1st Indian Cavalry Division,
                              23rd September 1915.

BILLETING AREA - 1ST INDIAN CAVALRY DIVISION.

Unit.	Where billeted.
Divl. Headquarters	LEMEILLARD.
A.D.M.S.	"
A.D.V.S.	"
A.P.M.	"
O.C.A.S.C.	"
Signal Squadron	"
D.A.D.O.S.	LONGPRE.
R.H.A. Bde	HEUZECOURT.
Field Squadron	OUTRE BOIS.
Ambala Cavalry Field Amblce	"
Sialkot " " "	BOIS BERGUES.
Lucknow " " "	"
Motor Amblce. Workshop	"
Sanitary Section	"
Sialkot Bde.	
Headquarters	PROUVILLE.
Mobile Vety. Section	"
17th Lancers	"
6th Cavalry	BEAUMETZ.
19th Lancers	"
Mhow Brigade	BERNAVILLE.
Headquarters	"
Mobile Vety. Section	"
6th Inniskilling Dragoons	"
2nd Lancers	"
38th Horse	"
Lucknow Brigade.	
Headquarters	MONT PLAISIR, MACFER.
Mobile Vety. Section	FERME DE GUESNEL.
1st K.D.G's.	AUTHIEUX.
29th Lancers	OCCOCHES. HARDINVAL.
36th Horse	LONGUEVILLETTE.

[signature]

                              Lieut-Colonel,
            A.A. & Q.M.G., 1st Indian Cavalry Division.

APP "K"

Weekly Wastage from Sickness – 26-9-1915

Unit	Officers		Other Ranks			Remarks
	Br.	Ind.	Br.	Ind.	Foll.	
Divl Head Qrs	–	–	1	–	–	
Sialkot Bde Hd Qrs	2	–	1	–	–	
17th Lancers	–	–	10	–	–	
6th Cavalry	–	–	–	6	–	
19th Lancers	–	–	–	4	–	
6th Dragoons	–	–	3	–	–	
2nd Lancers	–	–	–	3	–	
38th Horse	–	–	–	9	–	
K.D.G.	–	–	4	–	–	
29th Lancers	–	–	–	1	–	
36th Horse	–	1	–	5	–	
A Bty R H A	–	–	1	–	–	
Q	–	–	1	–	–	
U	–	–	2	–	–	
Divl Ammn Col	–	–	6	–	–	
Supply Column	–	–	5	–	–	
Ind. Fd Sqn	–	–	5	–	–	
Total	2	1	39	28	–	

G.R. Maitland
Capt
DAA & QMG

APP. L

Deficiencies in Establishments of Fighting Units. 26-9-15

Unit	Officers		Other Ranks		Horses Riding	Horses LD	Mules LD	Mules Pack	Remarks
	Br	Ind	Br	Ind					
17th Lancers	-	-	57	-	-	-	1	1	Regt. to replace men
6th Cavy	1	1	-	30	4	-	-	2	sent as Batmen to
19th Lancers	1	1	-	11	10	-	-	1	Ind Cavy Regts
6th Dragoons	-	-	28	-	4	-	-	2	men for transport
2nd Lancers	1	-	-	27	10	-	1	-	for Horse Rugs &
38th Horse	1	-	-	31	3	-	-	1	men gone sick
K D Gs	1	-	23	-	22	-	2	-	
29th Lancers	-	2	-	24	10	-	-	-	
36th Horse	-	1	-	23	18	-	-	-	
Q Bty R H A	-	-	13	-	-	-	-	-	
Div Ammn Col	-	-	-	-	-	2	19	-	
Total	5	5	121	146	83	2	23	4	7

G.P. Maitland
Capt
D.A.A. & Q.M.G

WAR DIARY

OF

A & Q

1st INDIAN CAVALRY DIVISION

OCTOBER - 1915

Serial No. 2.

Confidential

121/7601

War Diary

with appendices.

of

Q.A.A. and Q.M.G. 1st Indian Cavalry Division

FROM 1st October 1915 TO 31st October 1915.

WAR DIARY
OR
INTELLIGENCE SUMMARY.
(Erase heading not required.)

Army Form C. 2118.

Instructions regarding War Diaries and Intelligence Summaries are contained in F. S. Regs., Part II. and the Staff Manual respectively. Title pages will be prepared in manuscript.

Hour, Date, Place		Summary of Events and Information	Remarks and references to Appendices
LE MEILLARD.	2/10/15.	Redistribution of billets on account of shortage of water in certain villages. Revised lists of billets attached.	APP "A" "B" "C" } Q
" "	3/10/15.	Weekly wastage in sickness. Deficiencies in establishments of fighting units. Machine Gun detachments of Regiments increased by 2 N.C.O.s & 18 men per regiment consequent on increase of 2 Machine Guns.	
" "	10/10/15.	Weekly wastage in sickness. Deficiencies in establishments of fighting units.	APP "D" "E" } Q
DOMART.	13/10/15.	Division moved to new billeting area. Lists of Billets attached.	" "F" Q
" "	14/10/15.	Weekly wastage in sickness. Deficiencies in establishments of fighting units.	" "G" "H" } Q
LE QUESNOY.	27/10/15.	Division moved to new billeting area. List of Billets attached.	" "I" Q

Army Form C. 2118.

WAR DIARY

INTELLIGENCE SUMMARY.

(Erase heading not required.)

Instructions regarding War Diaries and Intelligence Summaries are contained in F. S. Regs., Part II, and the Staff Manual respectively. Title pages will be prepared in manuscript.

Hour, Date, Place.		Summary of Events and Information.	Remarks and references to Appendices
LE QUESNOY.	24/10/15.	Weekly wastage in Sickness. Deficiencies in establishments of Fighting units.	App "J", "K".
"	27/10/15.	All Cavalry Regts. now complete with 4 Vickers Guns each, & provided with Mules & Pack Saddlery for carrying same.	
"	31/10/15.	Weekly wastage in Sickness. Deficiencies in establishments of Fighting units.	App "L", "M".

3/XI/1915.

E.R. Maitland.
Capt.
D.A.A. & Q.M.G., 1st Ind Cav. Dr.

APP. 'A'

No. Q-4970.

Headquarters,
1st Indian Cavalry Division.
2nd October 1915.

BILLETING AREA 1ST INDIAN CAVALRY DIVISION.

Unit.	Where billeted.
Divisional Headquarters	LE MEILLARD.
A.D.M.S.	"
A.D.V.S.	"
A.P.M.	"
O.C. A.S.C.	"
Signal Squadron	"
D.A.D.O.S.	DOULLENS.
R.H.A. Brigade	HEUZECOURT.
Divnl Ammunition Column	ST. ACHEUL.
Field Squadron	OUTRE BOIS
Ambala Cavalry Field Amblce	VILLERS L'HOPITAL.
Sialkot " " "	" "
Lucknow " " "	" "
Motor Ambulance Workshop	" "
Sanitary Section	" "
Auxiliary Horse Transport Co	BOIS BERGUES.

Sialkot Brigade.
    Headquarters .... REMAISNIL.
    Mobile Vety Section .... "
    17th Lancers .... BARLY.
    6th Cavalry .... OUTRE BOIS.
    19th Lancers .... OUTRE BOIS & MEZEROLLES.

Mhow Brigade.
    Headquarters .... Chateau de BEAUVOIN.
    Mobile Vety Section .... " "
    6th Inniskilling Dragoons .... FROHEN LE GRAND.
    2nd Lancers .... VILLERS L'HOPITAL
    38th Horse .... WAVANS.

Lucknow Brigade.
    Headquarters .... MONT PLAISIR. MACFER.
    Mobile Vety Section .... FERME DE GUESNEL.
    1st K.D.Gds .... AUTHEUX.
    29th Lancers .... OCCOCHES. MARDINVAL.
    36th Horse .... LONGUEVILLETTE.

Lieutenant Colonel,

A. A., and Q. M. G.,
1st Indian Cavalry Division.

APPENDIX 'B'

Weekly Wastage in Sickness — 3-X-1915.

Unit	Officers		Other Ranks		Folls	Remarks
	Br.	Ind.	Br.	Ind.		
17th Lancers.	–	–	4	–	–	
6th Cavalry	–	1	–	8	–	
19th Lancers.	–	–	–	1	–	
Mhow Bde. Hd. Qrs.	–	–	1	–	–	
6th Dragoons.	–	–	9	–	–	
2nd Lancers.	–	–	–	7	–	
38th Horse.	–	–	–	3	–	
K. D. G.	–	–	3	–	–	
29th Lancers.	–	–	–	4	–	
36th Horse.	–	1	–	5	–	
Hd.Qrs. 1st Ind. R.H.A Bde	–	–	1	–	–	
"A". Bty. R.H.A	–	–	4	–	–	
"Q" " "	–	–	2	–	–	
"U" " "	–	–	1	–	–	
Dvl. Ammn. Park	–	–	3	–	–	
1st Ind. Fd. Sqdn.	–	–	1	–	–	
Total.	–	2	29	28	–	

G.R.Maitland
Capt.
D.A.A. & Q.M.G.

APPENDIX "C"

Deficiencies in establishments of Fighting units — 3-X-1915

Unit	Officers Br.	Officers Ind.	Other Ranks Br.	Other Ranks Ind.	Horses Riding	Horses Draught	Mules Draught	Mules Adrift	Remarks
17th Lancers	-	-	74	-	20	-	-	-	
6th Cavalry	1	2	-	54	29	-	1	-	
19th Lancers	-	2	-	30	24	-	-	-	
6th Dragoons	-	-	42	-	23	1	-	-	
2nd Lancers	-	-	-	41	20	-	-	-	
38th Horse	-	-	-	52	37	-	-	-	
1st K.D.Gs	1	-	47	-	20	-	-	-	
29th Lancers	-	3	-	36	32	-	-	-	
36th Horse	-	1	-	43	20	-	1	-	
Q Bty R.H.A.	-	-	2	-	-	-	-	-	
U " "	-	-	3	-	-	5	-	-	
Divl. Ammn. Col.	-	-	14	-	1	3	-	-	
Total	2	8	182	256	226	9	2	-	

G.R. Maitland
Capt
D.A.A. & Q.M.G.

APPENDIX 'E'

Deficiencies in Establishments of Fighting units - 10 x 1915.

Unit	Officers		Other Rks		Horses Riding	Horses Draught	Mules Draught	Mules Orince	Remarks
	Br.	Ind.	Br.	Ind.					
14th Lancers	-	-	16	-	20	-	1	-	
6th Cavalry	-	2	-	54	-	-	1	-	
19th Lancers	-	1	-	28	1	-	-	-	
6th Dragoons	1	-	18	-	33	-	-	-	
2nd Lancers	-	-	-	48	26	-	-	-	
38th Horse	-	-	-	53	28	-	-	-	
1st K.D.Gs.	2	-	16	-	20	2	-	-	
29th Lancers	-	3	-	30	2	-	-	-	
36th Horse	-	1	-	31	3	2	-	-	
'A' Bty. R.H.A.	-	-	-	-	-	2	-	-	
'Q' " "	-	-	6	-	-	-	-	-	
'U' " "	-	-	7	-	-	1	-	-	
Divl. Amm. Col.	-	-	4	-	-	2	-	-	
Total	3	7	67	244	133	9	2	-	

G.R. Maitland
Capt
D.A.A. & Q.M.G.

APP. F

No. Q-5485.   Headquarters.

1st Indian Cavalry Division.

14th October 1915.

BILLETING AREA - 1ST INDIAN CAVALRY DIVISION.

Unit.	Where billeted.
Divisional Headquarters	DOMART
A.D.M.S.	"
A.D.V.S.	"
A.P.M.	"
O.C.A.S.C.	"
Signal Squadron	"
D.A.D.O.S.	DOULLENS
R.H.A. Bde Headquarters	MOUFFLERS.
Divisional Ammunition Column	MOUFFLERS, VAUCHELLES
Field Squadron	DOMART
Ambala Cavalry Field Ambulance	DOMART
Sialkot " " "	DOMART
Lucknow " " "	FIENVILLERS.
Motor Ambulance Workshop	DOMART.
Sanitary Section	DOMART.
Auxilary Horse Transport Co.	FIENVILLERS.

Sialkot Brigade.
```
    Headquarters.....................LE MEILLARD.
    Mobile Vety Section..............     "
    17th Lancers.....................(1) BARLY.
6th Cavalry..........................OUTRE BOIS.
    19th Lancers.....................(1) REMAISNIL. MEZEROLLES, OUTRE-
    "Q" Battery R.H.A................LE MEILLARD.                 BOIS.
```

Mhow Brigade.
```
    Headquarters.....................BERNEUIL.
    Mobile Vety Section..............     "
    6th Inniskilling Dragoons........(1) SURCAMPS. FRANQUEVILLE.
    2nd Lancers......................(1) BERNEUIL. FIENVILLERS.
    38th Horse.......................(1) VACQUERIE. GORGES. LANCHES.
                                             EPECAMPS. DOMESMONT.
    "A" Battery......................ST. HILAIRE.
```

Lucknow Brigade.
```
    Headquarters.....................MONT PLAISIR.
    Mobile Vety Section..............FERME DE GUESNEL.
    1st K.D.Gds......................BERNAVILLE.
    29th Lancers.....................(1) BOIS BERGUES. AUTHEUX.
    36th Horse.......................BERNAVILLE.
    "U" Battery......................AUTHEUX.
    Brigade Supply & S.V.O.          BERNAVILLE.
```

(1) - Regimental Headquarters.

W.K.Brown

Lieutenant Colonel,

A. A., and Q. M. G.,

1st Indian Cavalry Division.

APPENDIX "G"

Weekly Wastage in Sickness — 14-X-1915.

Unit	Officers		Other Rks		Fol^{rs}	Remarks
	Br.	Ind.	Br.	Ind.		
14th Lancers.	—	—	7	—	—	
6th Cavalry.	—	—	—	3	—	
19th Lancers.	—	—	—	2	1	
6th Dragoons.	—	—	7	—	—	
2nd Lancers.	—	—	—	1	—	
38th Horse.	—	—	—	4	—	
K. D. Gs.	1	—	2	—	—	
29th Lancers.	—	—	—	5	—	
36th Horse.	—	—	—	2	—	
Lucknow Mob. Vety Sect.	—	—	1	—	—	
Hd.Qrs 1st Ind. R.H.A. Bde	—	—	1	—	—	
A. Bty. R.H.A.	—	—	3	—	—	
Div. Ammn Col	—	—	13	—	—	
Ammn Park.	—	—	2	—	—	
Supply Column	—	—	5	—	—	
Field Sqdn	—	—	4	—	—	
Aux. H.T. Coy. A.S.C.	—	—	2	—	—	
Total	1	—	48	17	1	

G.R. Maitland
Capt.
D.A.A. & Q.M.G.

APPENDIX "H"

Deficiencies in Establishments of Fighting Units - 14-10-15

Unit	Officers		Other Rks		Horses Riding	Horses Draught	Mules Draught	Mules Ordnance	Remarks
	Br	Ind	Br	Ind					
14th Lancers	-	-	24	-	23	-	1	-	
6th Cavalry	-	2	-	58	13	-	1	-	
19th Lancers	-	1	-	33	15	-	1	-	
6th Dragoons	-	-	25	-	39	-	-	-	
9th Lancers	-	-	-	51	-	-	-	-	
34th Horse	-	-	-	55	2	-	-	1	
1st K.D.Gs	2	-	20	-	34	2	1	-	
29th Lancers	2	3	-	36	10	-	-	-	
36th Horse	-	-	-	30	14	-	1	-	
A Bty R.H.A.	-	-	6	-	-	-	-	-	
Q " "	-	-	4	-	-	14	-	-	
U " "	-	-	6	-	-	-	-	-	
2. Ammn. Col.	-	-	17	-	-	2	-	-	
Total	4	6	103	263	153	18	5	1	

G.R. Maitland
Capt
D.A.A.&Q.M.G.

No. 5802/2.

APP. "I"

Headquarters,
1st Indian Cavalry Division.
28th October 1915.

REVISED BILLETING AREA – 1ST INDIAN CAVALRY DIVISION.

UNIT.	WHERE BILLETED.
Divisional Headquarters	LE QUESNOY.
Signal Squadron	" "
O.C., A.S.C.	" "
A.D.M.S.	RICHECOURT Fme.
A.D.V.S.	" "
D.A.D.O.S.	LONGPRE.
Supply Column	CONDE FOLIE.
Divnl Troops Supply Officer	St. MAZIS.
R.H.A. Bde Headquarters	SOUES.
Divisional Ammunition Column	(@) LE MAZIS – LE QUESNE – ARGUEL.
Divisional Ammunition Park	LPAUMESNIL.
Field Squadron	LIOMER.
Sialkot Field Ambulance	ST. MAULVIS.
Ambala do	ANDAINVILLE.
Lucknow do	PICQUIGNY.
Sanitary Section	ANDAINVILLE.
Motor Ambulance Workshop	CONDE FOLIE.
Auxiliary Horse Transport Co	AIRAINES.
Inspector Ordnance Machinery	

Sialkot Brigade.	
Headquarters	BELLOY ST LEONARD.
17th Lancers	(@) HANGEST – CROUY.
6th Cavalry	(@) TAILLY – WARLUS – AVELESGES – MONTAGNE – ARBRE-A-MOUCHES.
19th Lancers	(@) VERGIES – HEUCORT – CROQUOISON.
"Q" Battery	ALTIGNY – LALEU.
Mobile Veterinary Section	TAILLY.

Lucknow Brigade.	
Headquarters	CAVILLON.
"U" Battery	FOURDRINOY.
1st K.D.Gds	(@) MOLLIENS VIDAME – CAMPS.
29th Lancers	(@) PICQUIGNY – ST PIERRE-A-GOUY – MONASTERY LE GARD.
36th Jacob's Horse	LIMEUGE-RIENCOURT – (@) OISSY.
Mobile Veterinary Section	RICHECOURT Fme.

Mhow Brigade.	
Headquarters	SELINCOURT.
"A" Battery	AVESNE.
6th Inniskilling Dragoons	(@) HORNOY – BLEINCOURT.
2nd Lancers	(@) AUMONT-MERICOURT-LROMESNIL.
38th C.I.Horse	FRESNEVILLE-VILLERS CAMPSART – BROCOURT.
Mobile Veterinary Section	SELINCOURT.

G. Craster
Captain for
Lieutenant Colonel,
A. A., and Q. M. G.,
1st Indian Cavalry Division.

(@) Denotes Hdqrs.

APPENDIX 'J'

Weekly Wastage in Sickness - 24-x-1915.

Unit.	Officers		Other Rks		Follrs	Remarks.
	Br.	Ind.	Br.	Ind.		
14th Lancers.	-	-	1	-	-	
6th Cavalry.	-	-	-	6	-	
19th Lancers.	-	-	-	1	-	
6th Dragoons.	-	-	9	-	-	
2nd Lancers.	-	-	-	5	-	
38th Horse.	-	-	-	2	-	
K.D.Gs.	-	-	3	-	-	
29th Lancers	-	-	-	2	-	
36th Horse	-	-	-	1	-	
Lucknow Mob. Vty. Sect.	-	-	1	-	-	
"A" Bty. R.H.A.	-	-	1	-	-	
"Q" " "	-	-	1	-	-	
Divl. Ammn. Col.	-	-	3	-	-	
" Supply Col.	-	-	3	-	-	
Mec. M.T. Coy A.S.C	-	-	1	-	-	
Signal Sqdn.	-	-	1	-	-	
Field Sqdn.	-	-	1	-	-	
Mhow Bde. Hd Qrs.	1	-	-	-	-	
Total	1	-	25	17	-	

G.R. Maitland
Capt.
D.A.A & Q.M.G.

APPENDIX "K"

Deficiencies in Establishments of Fighting units - 24-10-1915

Unit	Officers		Other Rks		Horses Riding	Horses Draught	Mules Draught	Mules (other)	Remarks
	Br.	Ind.	Br.	Ind.					
14th Lancers	-	-	35	-	22	-	-	-	
6th Cavalry	-	1	-	61	15	-	-	-	
19th Lancers	-	1	-	32	41	-	1	-	
6th Dragoons	-	-	35	-	53	-	-	-	
2nd Lancers	-	-	-	53	-	-	-	-	
38th Horse	-	-	-	52	8	-	-	1	
1st K.D.Gs.	2	-	23	-	36	-	-	1	
29th Lancers	2	3	-	36	14	-	-	-	
36th Horse	-	-	-	31	23	-	4	-	
'A' Bty R.H.A.	-	-	9	-	-	8	-	-	
'Q' " "	-	-	1	-	-	9	-	-	
'U' " "	-	-	6	-	-	-	-	-	
D.l. Ammt. Col.	-	-	10	-	-	6	-	-	
Total	4	4	119	265	212	23	5	2	

G R Maitland
Capt.
D.A.A.&Q.M.G

APPENDIX "L"

Weekly Wastage in Sickness – 31-X-1915.

Unit	Officers		Other Ranks		Followers
	Br.	Ind.	Br.	Ind.	
17th Lancers	–	–	4	–	–
6th Cavalry	–	–	–	2	–
19th Lancers	–	–	–	1	–
6th Dragoons	1	–	4	–	–
2nd Lancers	–	1	–	–	–
38th Horse	–	–	–	2	–
Lucknow Bde. S. & T.	1	–	–	–	–
K.D.Go	–	–	4	–	–
36th Horse	–	–	–	4	1
Hd. Qrs. 1st Ind. R.H.A.Bde	–	–	1	–	–
Q. Bty. R.H.A.	–	–	1	–	–
Div. Ammn. Col.	–	–	3	–	–
Supply Col.	–	–	2	–	–
Field Amb.	–	–	–	–	–
Aux. H.T. Coy. A.S.C.	–	–	5	–	–
Total	2	1	26	9	1

G.R. Maitland
Capt.
D.A.A. & Q.M.G.

APPENDIX "M"

Deficiencies in Establishments of Fighting Units - 31-10-15.

Unit	Officers Br.	Officers Ind.	Other Ranks Br.	Other Ranks Ind.	Horses Riding	Horses Draught	Mules Draught	Mules Orderly	Remarks
17th Lancers	-	-	9	-	-	-	-	-	
6th Cavalry	-	-	-	53	5	-	-	-	
19th Lancers	-	-	-	17	-	-	-	-	
6th Dragoons	-	-	9	-	-	-	-	-	
2nd Lancers	-	-	-	49	4	-	-	1	
38th Horse	-	-	-	50	-	-	-	-	
1st K.D.G.	-	-	13	-	6	-	-	-	
29th Lancers	2	2	-	29	10	-	-	-	
36th Horse	-	-	-	20	-	-	-	-	
"A" Bty. R.H.A.	-	-	9	-	-	1	-	-	
"Q" "	1	-	6	-	-	3	-	-	
"U" "	1	-	4	-	-	3	-	-	
Div. Ammn. Col.	-	-	11	-	2	4	-	-	
Total	4	2	61	218	27	12	-	1	

G.R. Maitland
Capt.
D.A.A. & Q.M.G.

WAR DIARY
OF
A & Q

1st INDIAN CAVALRY DIVISION

NOVEMBER - 1915

Serial No. 2. 12/7780

Confidential

War Diary

of

Administrative Branch, 1st Indian Cavalry Division

FROM 1st November 1915 **TO** 30th November 1915

WAR DIARY
INTELLIGENCE SUMMARY.

(Erase heading not required.)

Army Form C. 2118.

Instructions regarding War Diaries and Intelligence Summaries are contained in F. S. Regs., Part II. and the Staff Manual respectively. Title pages will be prepared in manuscript.

Hour, Date, Place	Summary of Events and Information	Remarks and references to Appendices
LE QUESNOY. 1-11-1915	100 Dismounted men arrived for each British Cavy. Regt.	
" 4-11-1915	Weekly Wastage in sickness.	app. I } II
" — " —	Deficiencies in Establishments of Fighting units.	
" 9-11-15.	Inspection of Division by Corps Commander, & presentation of French Decorations.	
" 11-11-15	Inspection of Corps by 3rd Army Commander.	
" 14-11-15.	Weekly Wastage in sickness.	app. III } IV
" — " —	Deficiencies in Establishments of Fighting units.	
" 19-11-15.	Div¹ Area curtailed & redistribution of Billets. Revise billeting Net attached.	app. X
" 21-11-15.	Weekly Wastage in sickness.	app. V } VI
" — " —	Deficiencies in Establishments of Fighting units.	
" 23-11-15.	Inspection by Corps Commander of all remounts received since 1-9-1915.	
" 28-11-15.	Weekly Wastage in sickness.	app. VIII } IX
" — " —	Deficiencies in Establishments of Fighting units.	

Army Form C. 2118.

WAR DIARY
INTELLIGENCE SUMMARY.
(Erase heading not required.)

Instructions regarding War Diaries and Intelligence Summaries are contained in F.S. Regs., Part II and the Staff Manual respectively. Title pages will be prepared in manuscript.

Hour, Date, Place	Summary of Events and Information	Remarks and references to Appendices
LE QUESNOY.	Division of Dismounted Men organized. 1 Brigade furnished from this Div. Portion of Staff. Equipment not to be indented for until Div actually required.	a/

G.P. Wartant Capt.
D.A.A.& Q.M.G.
1st Ind Cavy. Dr.

APPENDIX I

Weekly Wastage in Sickness — 7-XI-1915.

Unit	Officers		Other Ranks			Remarks
	Br.	Ind.	Br.	Ind.	Fol.	
17th Lancers.	-	-	1	-	-	
6th Cavalry.	-	-	-	1	-	
19th Lancers.	-	-	-	1	-	
6th Dragoons.	-	-	1	-	-	
2nd Lancers.	2	-	-	1	-	
38th Horse.	-	-	1	-	-	
1st K.D.Gs.	-	-	1	-	-	
29th Lancers.	-	-	-	3	-	
36th Horse	-	-	-	2	1	
'A' Bty. R.H.A.	-	-	1	-	-	
'U' " "	-	-	1	-	-	
Divl. Ammn. Col.	-	-	2	-	-	
Supply Column	-	-	4	-	-	
Auxiliary H.T. Coy.	-	-	4	-	-	
Total	2	-	16	8	1	

CRMaitland
Capt.
D.A.A. & Q.M.G.

Deficiencies in Establishments of Fighting Units. - 4-XI-1915.

APPENDIX II

Unit	Officers Br.	Officers Ind.	Other Ranks Br.	Other Ranks Ind.	Riding Horses	Draught Horses	Draught Mules	Ordnance Mules	Remarks
17th Lancers.	1	-	-	-	1	-	-	-	
6th Cavalry	-	-	-	49	2	1	-	-	
19th Lancers.	-	-	-	12	11	-	-	-	
6th Dragoons.	1	-	2	-	3	-	-	-	
2nd Lancers.	-	-	-	48	6	1	-	2	
38th Horse.	-	-	-	49	2	-	-	-	
1st K.D.Gs.	-	-	4	-	-	-	-	-	
9th Lancers.	-	-	-	46	4	-	-	-	
36th Horse.	-	-	-	4	-	1	-	-	
'A' Bty. R.H.A.	-	-	3	-	2	-	-	-	
'Q' " "	-	-	4	-	-	5	-	-	
Divl. Ammn. Col.	-	-	-	-	2	3	-	-	
Total	2	-	19	208	33	11	-	2	

R. Maitland
Captn.
D.A.A.&Q.M.G.

APPENDIX III

Weekly Wastage in Sickness — 14-XI-1915.

Unit	Officers		Other Ranks			Remarks
	Br.	Ind.	Br.	Ind.	Fol=.	
17th Lancers.	-	-	2	-	-	
6th Cavalry.	-	-	1	-	-	
19th Lancers.	-	-	-	3	1	
6th Dragoons.	-	-	5	-	-	
2nd Lancers.	-	-	-	6	-	
38th Horse.	1	-	-	3	-	
Lucknow Bde Hd. Qrs	-	-	2	-	-	
1st K.D.Gs.	1	-	-	-	-	
29th Lancers.	-	-	-	6	-	
36th Horse.	-	-	-	3	-	
'U' Bty. R.H.A.	-	-	1	-	-	
Divl. Ammn. Col.	-	-	2	-	-	
Ammn. Park	-	-	1	-	-	
Supply Column	-	-	2	-	-	
Field Squadron	-	-	6	-	-	
Auxiliary H.T. Coy	-	-	1	-	-	
Total	2	-	23	21	1	

C.P. Maitland
Capt.
D.A.A.& Q.M.G.

APPENDIX IV

Deficiencies in Establishments of Fighting Units – 14-XI-1915

Unit	Officers		Other Ranks		Horses Riding	Horses Draught	Mules Draught	Mules Ordnance	Remarks
	Br.	Ind.	Br.	Ind.					
14th Lancers	1	–	–	–	3	–	–	–	
6th Cavalry	–	–	–	2	4	–	–	–	
19th Lancers	1	–	–	14	8	–	–	–	
6th Dragoons	2	–	9	–	6	–	–	–	
2nd Lancers	–	–	–	4	3	1	–	2	
38th Horse	1	–	–	9	2	–	–	–	
1st K.D.Gs	–	–	–	–	8	–	1	–	
29th Lancers	–	–	–	14	9	–	–	–	
36th Horse	1	–	–	4	–	–	–	–	
'A' Bty. R.H.A	–	–	–	4	–	8	–	–	
'Q' – " –	–	–	–	12	–	5	–	–	
'U' – " –	–	–	–	3	–	–	–	–	
Div. Ammn. Col.	–	–	–	1	3	6	–	–	
Total	6	–	9	73	46	20	1	2	

C.E. Maitland
Capt.
D.A.A. & Q.M.G.

No. Q-240.

Headquarters,
1st Indian Cavalry Division.
19th November 1915.

BILLETING AREA - 1ST INDIAN CAVALRY DIVISION.

UNIT.	WHERE BILLETED.
Divisional Headquarters	LE QUESNOY.
Signal Squadron	" "
O.C. A.S.C.	" "
A.D.M.S.	" "
A.D.V.S.	" "
D.A.D.O.S.	LONGPRE
Supply Column	AIRAINES
Divnl Troops Supply Officer	LIOMER
R.H.A. Bde Headquarters	CROQUOISON
Divisional Ammunition Column	LE MAZIS-LE QUESNE-ARGUEL
Divisional Ammunition Park	AIRAINES.
Field Squadron	LIOMER
Sialkot Field Ambulance	INVAL BOIRON.
Ambala Field Ambulance	FRESNOY
Lucknow Field Ambulance	PICQUIGNY. (Moving to Lucknow Bde area)
Sanitary Section	FRESNOY
Motor Ambulance Workshop	"
Auxiliary Horse Transport Co	METIGNY-LALEU
Inspector Ordnance Machinery	AIRAINES.

Sialkot Brigade.

Headquarters	BELLOY ST LEONARD
17th Lancers	(@) ST MAULVIS - VANDAINVILLE
6th Cavalry	(@) TAILLY - L'ARBRE-A-MOUCHES -- WARLUS AVELESGES - MERICOURT.
19th Lancers	(@) VERGIES - HEUCOURT - LA FAY.
"Q" Battery	EPAUMESNIL.
Mobile Veterinary Section	TAILLY.

Lucknow Brigade.

Headquarters	VIEULAINE.
"U" Battery	BETTENCOURT
1st K.D.Gds	LONGPRE.
29th Lancers	CONDE FOLIE.
36th Horse	(@) FONTAINE - SOREL - WANEL.
Mobile Veterinary Section	CATELET.

Mhow Brigade.

Headquarters	SELINCOURT.
"A" Battery	AVESNE.
6th Inniskilling Dragoons	HORNOY
2nd Lancers	(@) AUMONT - HALLIVILLERS - DROMESNIL.
38th C.I.Horse	(@) VILLERS CAMPSART - FRESNEVILLE - BROCOURT.
Mobile Veterinary Section	SELINCOURT.

(@) Denotes Headquarters.

G.H.C.Bourne
Lieutenant Colonel,
A. A., and Q. M. G.,
1st Indian Cavalry Division.

APPENDIX VI

Weekly Wastage in Sickness – 21-XI-1915

Unit	Officers		Other Ranks			Remarks
	Br.	Ind.	Br.	Ind.	Foll'rs	
17th Lancers.	–	–	2	–	–	
6th Cavalry.	–	–	–	2	–	
19th Lancers.	–	–	–	2	–	
Mhow Bde. Hd. Qrs.	–	–	1	–	–	
6th Dragoons.	–	–	1	–	–	
2nd Lancers.	–	–	–	5	–	
38th Horse.	–	–	–	1	–	
29th Lancers.	–	–	–	5	–	
36th Horse.	–	–	–	3	–	
Hd. Qrs. 1st Ind. R.H.A. Bde.	–	–	1	–	–	
'A' Bty. R.H.A.	–	–	1	–	–	
Div. Amm. Col.	–	–	6	–	–	
Auxiliary H.T. Coy.	–	–	3	–	–	
Supply Column	–	–	1	–	–	
Total	–	–	16	18	–	

C.P. Maitland
Capt'n
D.A.A. & Q.M.G.

APPENDIX VII

Deficiencies in Establishments of Fighting Units - 21-XI-1915

Unit	Officers Br.	Officers Ind.	Other Ranks Br.	Other Ranks Ind.	Horses Riding	Horses Draught	Mules Draught	Mules Ordnance	Remarks
14th Lancers	–	–	1	–	–	–	–	–	
6th Cavalry	–	–	–	2	12	–	–	–	
19th Lancers	1	–	–	15	–	–	–	–	
6th Dragoons	1	–	5	–	5	–	–	–	
2nd Lancers	–	–	–	6	–	–	–	–	
38th Horse	1	–	–	3	2	–	–	–	
1st K.D.Gs.	–	–	3	–	4	–	–	–	
29th Lancers	–	–	–	13	3	–	–	–	
36th Horse	1	–	–	4	3	–	–	–	
A Bty. R.H.A.	–	–	4	–	–	–	–	–	
Q " "	–	–	13	–	–	5	–	–	
U " "	–	–	6	–	–	4	–	–	
Divl. Ammn. Col.	–	–	1	–	2	6	–	–	
Total	4	–	33	43	31	15	–	–	

G. Markham
Capt.
D.A.A. & Q.M.G.

APPENDIX VIII

Weekly Wastage in Sickness — 28-xi-1915

Unit	Officers		Other Ranks			Remarks
	Br.	Ind.	Br.	Ind.	Flrs	
17th Lancers	–	–	3	–	–	
6th Cavalry	–	–	–	2	–	
19th Lancers	1	–	–	3	–	
Signal Troop, Sialkot Bde.	–	–	1	–	–	
6th Dragoons	–	–	5	–	–	
2nd Lancers	–	–	–	2	–	
38th Horse	–	–	–	3	–	
Mobile Vety. Sect. Mhow Bde	–	–	–	1	–	
Lucknow Bde. Hd Qrs.	–	–	1	–	–	
K.D.Gs.	–	–	3	–	–	
29th Lancers	–	–	–	2	–	
36th Horse	1	–	–	–	–	
Head Qrs. 1st Ind. R.H.A. Bde	–	–	1	–	–	
"N" Bty. R.H.A.	–	–	2	–	–	
Divl. Ammn. Col.	–	–	5	–	–	
Supply Column	–	–	1	–	–	
Field Squadron	–	–	1	–	–	
Auxiliary H.T. Coy	–	–	1	–	–	
Total	2	–	24	13	–	

G.D. Maitland
Capt.
D.A.A. & Q.M.G.

APPENDIX IX

Deficiencies in Establishments of Fighting Units - 28-XI-1915.

Unit	Officers		Other Ranks		Riding Horses	Draught Horses	Draught Mules	Riding Mules	Remarks
	Br.	Ind.	Br.	Ind.					
14th Lancers	-	-	12	-	-	-	-	1	
6th Cavalry	-	-	-	4	12	-	-	-	
19th Lancers	1	-	-	9	-	-	-	-	
6th Dragoons	1	-	11	-	-	-	-	-	
2nd Lancers	-	-	-	4	-	-	1	2	
38th Horse	-	-	-	6	3	-	-	-	
1st K.D.Cp.	1	-	4	-	4	-	-	-	
29th Lancers	-	-	-	2	6	-	-	-	
36th Horse	-	-	-	4	7	-	-	-	
"Q" Bty. R.H.A.	-	-	12	-	1	-	-	-	
"U" " "	-	-	6	-	-	9	-	-	
Divl. Ammn. Col.	-	-	-	-	2	7	-	-	
Total	3	-	45	29	35	16	1	2	

R. Maitland
Capt.
D.A.A. & Q.M.G.

War Diary

of

A & Q

1st Indian Cavalry Division

December - 1915

SERIAL NO. 2.

Confidential

War Diary

of

D.A. & Q.M.G., 1st Indian Cavalry Division.

FROM 1st December 1915 TO 31st December 1915.

WAR DIARY
INTELLIGENCE SUMMARY.
(Erase heading not required.)

Army Form C. 2118.

Instructions regarding War Diaries and Intelligence Summaries are contained in F.S. Regs., Part II. and the Staff Manual respectively. Title pages will be prepared in manuscript.

Hour, Date, Place		Summary of Events and Information	Remarks and references to Appendices
LE QUESNOY.	5-12-15.	Weekly wastage in sickness.	APP. I /A.
		Deficiencies in Establishment of fighting units.	" II /A.
" "	12-12-15.	Weekly wastage in sickness.	" III /A.
" "	15-12-15.	Deficiencies in Establishment of fighting units.	" IV /A.
		20 Sappers & 12 Drs received as Dismounted Reinforcement for 7th Sqdr.	
DARGNIES.	16-12-15.	Division moved 15 miles new billeting area.	APP. V /A.
		Administrative Instruction for the march.	" VI /A.
		List of Billets.	
" "	19-12-15.	Weekly wastage in sickness.	" VII /A.
		Deficiencies in Establishment of fighting units.	" VIII /A.
" "	20-24-12-15.	Inspection of all transport of Dn. by Corps Comdt.	
" "	26-12-15.	Weekly wastage in sickness.	" IX /A.
		Deficiencies in Establishment of fighting units.	" X /A.

G.P. Whittam, Capt.
D.A.A. & Q.M.G. 2nd C.D.

APPENDIX I

Weekly Wastage in Sickness — 5-XII-1915.

Unit	Officers Br.	Officers Ind.	Other Ranks Br.	Other Ranks Ind.	Foll'rs	Remarks
17th Lancers	—	—	2	—	—	
6th Cavalry	—	—	—	2	—	
19th Lancers	—	—	—	4	—	
6th Dragoons	—	—	4	—	—	
2nd Lancers	—	—	—	2	—	
38th Horse	—	—	—	8	—	
29th Lancers	—	—	—	4	—	
'A' Bty. R.H.A.	—	—	1	—	—	
'U' — , —	—	—	2	—	—	
Div. Ammn Col.	1	—	11	—	—	
Supply Col.	—	—	3	—	—	
Field Sqdr.	—	—	2	—	—	
Auxy. H.T. Coy.	—	—	1	—	—	
Total	1	—	26	23	—	

G.R. Maitland
Capt.
D.A.A. & Q.M.G.

APPENDIX II

Deficiencies in Establishments of Fighting Units – 5-XII-1915.

Unit	Officers		Other Ranks		Horses Riding	Horses Draught	Mules Draught	Mules ordnance	Remarks
	Br.	Ind.	Br.	Ind.					
17th Lancers	.	.	14	.	4	.	.	1	
6th Cavalry	.	.	.	5	3	.	.	.	
19th Lancers	1	.	.	8	1	.	.	.	
6th Dragoons	1	.	19	.	3	.	.	1	
2nd Lancers	.	.	.	4	6	.	3	2	
38th Horse	.	.	.	12	1	.	.	.	
1st K.D.Gs.	1	.	3	.	3	.	.	.	
29th Lancers	.	.	.	4	.	.	.	.	
36th Horse	.	.	.	3	1	.	.	.	
"A" Bty. R.H.A.	.	.	.	.	.	3	.	.	
"Q" " "	.	.	1	.	.	.	.	.	
" " "	.	.	4	.	.	1	.	.	
Divl. Ammn. Col.	.	.	.	.	2	.	.	.	
Total	3	.	41	36	24	4	3	4	

G.R. Maitland
Capt.
D.A.A. & Q.M.G.

APPENDIX III

Weekly Wastage in Sickness — 12-XII-1915.

Unit	Officers		Other Rks		Hollis	Remarks
	Br.	Ind	Br.	Ind		
Div'l Hd. Qrs	-	-	2	-	-	
17th Lancers	-	-	4	-	-	
6th Cavalry	-	-	-	3	-	
19th Lancers	-	-	-	2	-	
6th Dragoons	-	-	3	-	-	
2nd Lancers	1	-	-	3	-	
38th Horse	-	-	-	12	-	
1st K.D.Gs.	-	-	5	-	-	
29th Lancers	-	-	-	1	-	
36th Horse	-	-	-	2	-	
Q. Bty. R.H.A.	-	-	-	1	-	
Div. Ammn. Col.	-	-	1	-	-	
Ammn. Park	-	-	1	-	-	
Supply Column	-	-	9	-	-	
Field Sqdn	-	-	-	-	-	
Signal Sqdn	-	-	-	-	-	
Total	1	-	25	24	-	

G.R. Maitland
Capt,
D.A.A. & Q.M.G.

APPENDIX IV

Deficiencies in Establishments of Fighting Units – 12-XII-1915

Unit	Officers Br.	Officers Ind.	Other Rks Br.	Other Rks Ind.	Riding Horses	Draught Horses	L.D. Mules	Pack Mules	Remarks
14th Lancers	.	.	13	.	2	.	.	.	
6th Cavalry	.	.	.	2	9	.	.	.	
19th Lancers	1	.	.	9	3	.	.	.	
6th Dragoons	1	.	19	.	6	.	.	1	
2nd Lancers	.	.	.	5	6	.	3	1	
38th Horse	.	.	.	19	1	.	.	3	
1st K.D.Gp.	1	.	6	.	5	.	.	.	
29th Lancers	.	.	.	.	9	.	.	.	
36th Horse	.	.	.	4	2	.	.	.	
Q Bty. R.H.A.	.	.	16	.	.	4	.	.	
Divl. Ammn. Col.	.	.	8	.	.	.	.	.	
Total	3	.	62	39	43	4	3	5	

G.R. Maitland
Capt,
D.A. & Q.M.G.

APP V

SECRET.   Headquarters 1st Indian Cavalry Division,

14th December 1915.

No.Q-593.   ADMINISTRATIVE INSTRUCTIONS.

Reference Indian Cavalry Corps Administrative Orders, No.Q-3215, dated 13th December 1915.

Billeting Areas are as follows :-

Divl. Headquarters.	.. DARGNIES.
1st Indian R.H.A.Bde.)	.. BEAUCHAMPS.
Divl. Ammn. Column.)	
Divl. Ammn. Park.	.. BOUILLANCOURT (billeted by Corps H.Q)
Field Squadron.	.. EMDRLVILLE.
Supply Column.	.. BOUVAINCOURT.
Sialkot Field Ambulance.	.. TOEUFLES. (billeted by Sialkot Bde).
Lucknow Field Ambulance.)	
Ambala Field Ambulance.)	
Sanitary Section.)	BUIGNY.
Motor Ambulance Workshop.)	
Auxiliary Horse Transport Coy.-	VALINES or CHEPY. (To be billeted by Mhow Bde).

Sialkot Bde.	.. LAMBERCOURT - BILNFAY - Route 28 to BAINAST - TRINQUIS exclusive - ACHEUX - FRIERES.
Lucknow Bde.	.. SAIGNEVILLE - CAHON - MIANNAY (exclusive) - HAVRE - LILLE Route to St.MERC (exclusive) - FRANLEU.
Mhow Bde.	.. SAUCOURT - MONCHAUX - CHEPY - FEUQUIERES - FRESSENNEVILLE.

2. D.M. of the Lucknow Brigade will move by train from LONGPRE on 16th : time and station of destination will be notified later.

3. D.M. of Sialkot and Mhow Brigades will be conveyed to the new area in lorries on 15th. 5 lorries per unit will rendezvous at a regimental H.Q. at 9.0.a.m. on that date.

4. D.M. will take with them their kit, rations for consumption on the 15th and 16th, and also the extra day's ration which is in regimental charge for these men.

5. In order to set free lorries for this purpose, rations for all units for consumption on the 16th will be delivered about noon on the 14th to the extent to which units can carry them. Units should take as much of the ration for the 16th as they can, that is, all the mens' ration, all the grain except the evening feed, and enough hay to last them till the hour of marching.

6. G.O.C.Mhow Bde. will billet the Auxiliary Horse Transport Coy. either at the South East end of VALINES or the North West end of CHEPY, as their work will be chiefly at the railway station between those villages.

7. The Lucknow Casualty Clearing Station is billeted in FRESSENNEVILLE in two empty chateaux on the North side of the

main

main HAVRE - LILLE road. The remainder of that street to the East of the Chateaux and Usine opposite has been allotted for billeting accommodation.

8. G.O.C. Sialkot Bde. will reserve for the Sialkot Fd. Ambulance an old farm Chateau on the Western side of TOEUFLES, which will be used as a hospital, and also sufficient billets for that Field Ambulance, i.e., 5 Officers, 60 British, 110 Indian and 70 horses.

9. Sialkot Field Ambulance will move on 15th: and Ambala Field Ambulance on 17th. Times of movement will be notified later.

10. The road leading from DARGNIES to FEUQUIERES is impassable for motor traffic.

WK Bowne

Lieut-Colonel,

A.A. & Q.M.G., 1st Indian Cavalry Division.

Q - 626.

Headquarters,

1st: Indian Cavalry Division.

17th December 1915

APP VI

BILLETING AREA - 1st INDIAN CAVALRY DIVISION.

UNIT.	Where BILLETED.
Divisional H.Q.	DARGNIES.
Signal Squadron	- do -
O.C. A.S.C.	- do -
A.D.M.S.	- do -
A.D.V.S.	- do -
D.A.D.O.S.	BOUTTENCOURT.
Supply Column	DARGNIES-BOUVAINCOURT-BEAUCHAMPS.
R.H.A. Bde Headquarters	BEAUCHAMPS.
Div. Ammn. Column	- do -
Div. Ammn Park	BOUILLANCOURT - EN - SERY.
Field Squadron	EMBREVILLE.
SIALKOT F. Ambulance	TOUUFLES.
AMBALA F. Ambulance	BUIGNY.
LUCKNOW F. Ambulance	-do -
Sanitary Section	- do -
Motor Ambn Workshop	- do -
Aux. H.T. Co.	ST. MARC

SIALKOT Bde.
    Headquarters.........................ACHEUX
    "Q" Battery..........................- do -
    17th Lancers.........................MIANNAY-LAMBERCOURT-BOUILLANCOURT.
    6th Cavalry..........................BEHEN-BOENCOURT-BAINAST-ZALLEUX.
    19th Lancers.........................MOYEMMEVILLE-BIENFAY.
    Mob. Vet. Sect.......................CHAUSSOY.

LUCKNOW Brigade.
    Headquarters........................FRANLEU.
    1st K.D.G's.........................LEMONTANT-QUESNOY-CAHON.
    29th Lancers........................SAIGNEVILLE-GOUY-CHAON.
    36th J. Horse.......................FRANLEU-CAMPAGNE-NYEMEVILLE-FRIREULLES
    Mob Vet Sect........................FRIREULLES.

MHOW Brigade.
    Headquarters........................SAUCOURT.
    6th Dragoons........................FEUQUIERES-HOCQUELUS.
    2nd Lancers.........................CHEPY.
    38th Horse..........................FRESSENNEVILLE - FEUQUIRES.
    Mob. Vet Section....................VALINES.

Headquarters underlined.

Lieut: Colonel,
A.A. & Q.M.G.
1st Indian Cavalry Division.

APPENDIX VII

Weekly Wastage in Sickness - 19-XII-1915.

Unit	Officers		Other Rks		Foll.	Remarks
	Br.	Ind.	Br.	Ind.		
Sialkot Bde. Hd Qrs.	-	-	1			
17th Lancers.	-	-	3			
6th Cavy.	-	-	1	1		
19th Lancers.	1	-	-	2		
6th Dragoons			6			
2nd Lancers.				4		
38th Horse.				3		
1st K.D.Gs.			6			
Supply Column			3			
Field Sqdn.			2			
Total	1	-	22	10		

G.R. Maitland
Capt.
D.A.A. & Q.M.G.

APPENDIX VIII

Deficiencies in Establishments of Fighting Units – 19-XII-1915

Unit	Officers		Other Rks		Riding Horses	Draught Horses	L.D. Mules	Ord. Mules	Remarks
	Br.	Ind.	Br.	Ind.					
14th Lancers	.	.	13	.	.	.	.	.	
6th Cavalry	.	.	.	2	9	.	.	.	
19th Lancers	.	.	.	10	4	.	.	.	
6th Dragoons	1	.	20	.	.	.	.	.	
2nd Lancers	.	.	.	7	1	.	.	.	
38th Horse	.	.	.	15	3	.	.	.	
1st K.D.G.	.	.	10	–	1	.	.	.	
29th Lancers	.	.	.	4	3	.	.	.	
36th Horse	.	.	.	4	3	.	.	.	
D. Ammn. Col.	.	.	6	.	.	.	.	.	
Total	1	.	49	42	24	.	.	.	

G.R. Maitland
Capt.
D.A.A. & Q.M.G.

APPENDIX IX

Weekly wastage in sickness - 26-XII-1915.

Unit	Officers		Other Ranks		Folls	Remarks
	Br.	Ind.	Br.	Ind.		
17th Lancers	-	-	1	-	-	
6th Cavy.	-	-	-	1	-	
38th Horse	-	-	-	2	-	
1st K.D.Gs.	-	-	6	-	-	
29th Lancers	-	-	-	2	-	
36th Horse	-	-	-	2	-	
Lucknow Bde.Sig.Troop	-	-	-	3	-	
Supply Col.	-	-	1	-	-	
Div. Ammn. Col.	-	-	2	-	-	
Cavy. H.T. Coy.	-	-	5	-	-	
Total	-	-	15	10	-	

G.R.Maitland
Capt
D.A.A.&Q.M.G.

APPENDIX X

Deficiencies in Establishments of Fighting Units - 26-x-15

Unit	Officers		Other Rks		Riding Horses	Draught Horses	L.D. Mules	Ord Mules	Remarks
	Br.	Ind.	Br.	Ind.					
14th Lancers			10		4				
6th Cavy			2		11				
19th Lancers	1		2		5				
6th Dragoons	1		23	-	6		3	2	
2nd Lancers				6	4				
38th Horse			-	2	6				
1st K.O.			17		2				
29th Lancers				7	2				
36th Horse			-	6	4		2		
d Amm Col			10						
Total	2		60	25	47		5	2	

E.L. Maitland
Capt
D.a.a.Q.M.G.

SERIAL NO. 2.

Confidential

War Diary

of

G.O.C. Gp. 1st Indian Cavalry Division

FROM 1st January 1916 TO 31st January 1916

Army Form C. 2118.

WAR DIARY
or
INTELLIGENCE SUMMARY.
(Erase heading not required.)

Hour, Date, Place	Summary of Events and Information	Remarks and references to Appendices
DARGNIES. 9.1.16.	Weekly wastage in sickness. Deficiencies in Establishment of fighting units	APP. I " — II } A.
— 10.1.16.	Major General H.P. Leach, C.B., assumed command of the Division, vice Major-General J. de S. Barrow, C.B., with effect from 26.12.15.	A.
— 15.1.16.	Weekly wastage in sickness.	
— 16.1.16.	Deficiencies in Establishment of fighting units.	APP. III " — IV } A.
— 19.1.16.	Mules for Machine Guns having been severed unsuitable for the purpose their replacement by cobs was completed today.	
— 22.1.16.	Weekly wastage in sickness.	
— 23.1.16.	Deficiencies in Establishment of fighting units.	APP. V " — VI } A.
— 27.1.16.	The Canadian Cavalry Brigade having joined the Corps is attached to the 1st Indian Cavy Divn for training and Administration.	
— 29.1.16	Weekly wastage in sickness.	APP. VII " — VIII } A.
— 30.1.16	Deficiencies in Establishment of fighting units.	

G.M. Maitland Capt.
1st I.C. Divn. G. Staff.

APPENDIX I

Weekly wastage in Sickness. 8.1.16.

Unit	Officers		Other Ranks		Remarks
	Kr.	Died	Kr.	Died	
17th Lancers	2		6		
6th Cavy				2	
19th Lancers				3	
6th Dragoons	1		2		
38th C.I. Horse				6	
1st K.D.G.			4		
29th Lancers				4	
36th Horse				1	
Divnl Ammn. Col.			1		
Divnl Supply Col.			3		
Total	3	–	16	16	

C.R. Maitland
Captain
D.A.A. & Q.M.G.

APPENDIX II

Deficiencies in Establishments of Fighting Units. 9.1.16.

Unit	Officers		Other Ranks		Horses Riding	Horses Draught	Mules Draught	Mules Detronance	Remarks
	Br.	Ind.	Br.	Ind.					
17th Lancers			10		10		1		
6th Cavalry				2	3	1	1		
19th Lancers				3			1		
6th Dragoons	3				15		1		
2nd Lancers					9	5			
38th C.I. Horse						6			
1st K.D.G.			21		14				
29th Lancers				6	4	7			
36th Horse				6	5	1			
"Q" Bty. R.H.A.	1		3			4			
Divl. Ammn. Col.			10			6			
Total	4	·	44	26	58	12	4	·	

G.R. Maitland
Captain
D.A.A. & Q.M.G.

APPENDIX III

Weekly Wastage in Sickness. 15. 1. 16.

Unit	Officers		Other Ranks		Remarks
	Br.	Ind.	Br.	Ind.	
17th Lancers			3		
6th Cavy				5	
6th Dragoons			1		
2nd Lancers				4	
38th Horse				7	
1st K. D. G.	1		4		
29th Lancers				2	
3rd Horse				2	
Divnl Supply Col.			1		
Auxy. H.T. Coy			3		
Total	1	–	12	20	

G. R. Maitland
Capt.
D.A.A. & Q.M.G.

APPENDIX IV

Deficiencies in Establishments of Fighting Units. 16.1.16.

Unit.	Officers		Other Ranks		Horses Riding	Horses Draught	Mules Draught	Mules Ordnance	Remarks.
	Br.	Ind.	Br.	Ind.					
17th Lancers			10		17		1		
6th Cavalry				2	4		1		
19th Lancers				2	4				
6th Dragoons	3		5		20		1		
2nd Lancers			10		5				
38th Horse				5	8				
1st K.D.G.			28		1		1		
29th Lancers				5					
36th Horse				6	2	2			
"Q" Bty, R.H.A.	1		2			4			
Divnl Ammn: Col.			11						
Total	4		66	20	61	6	4		

G.R. Maitland
Captain
D.A.A. & Q.M.G.

APPENDIX V

Weekly Wastage in Sickness. 22. 1. 16

Unit	Officers		Other Ranks		Remarks
	Br.	Ind.	Br.	Ind.	
17th Lancers			1		
6th Cavy				2	
6th Dragoons			2		
2nd Lancers				3	
38th Horse				4	
1st K.D.G.			2		
29th Lancers				1	
Field Sqdn:			2		
Divnl Supply Col.			4		
Total	—	—	11	10	

G.R. Maitland
Capt.
D.A.A. & Q.M.G.

APPENDIX VI

Deficiencies in Establishments of Fighting Units. 23.1.16

Unit	Officers Br.	Officers Ind.	Other Ranks Br.	Other Ranks Ind.	Horses Riding	Horses Draught	Mules Draught	Mules Ordnance	Remarks
17th Lancers			7		7	1			
6th Cavy		1		2					
19th Lancers				2	4				
6th Dragoons	4		7		13				
2nd Lancers				12					
38th Horse				9	4				
1st K.D.G.			33		4	1			
29th Lancers				8					
36th Horse				5					
"Q" Bty. R.H.A	1		4			9			
Divnl. Amm. Col.			1		1	7			
Total	5	1	52	38	33	16	2	.	

E.R. Maitland
Captain
D.A.A. & Q.M.G.

APPENDIX VII

Weekly Wastage in Sickness. 29.1.16.

Unit	Officers		Other Ranks		Remarks
	Br.	Ind.	Br.	Ind.	
17th Lancers			5		
6th Cavy				1	
6th Dragoons			3		
2nd Lancers				2	
1st K.D.G.			10		
29th Lancers				1	
Divnl Supply Col			6		
Auxy: H.T. Coy.			2		
Total	—	—	26	4	

G.R. Maitland
Capt.
D.A.A. & Q.M.G.

APPENDIX VIII

Deficiencies in Establishment of Fighting Units. 30.1.16.

Unit	Officers Br.	Officers Ind.	Other Ranks Br.	Other Ranks Ind.	Horses Riding	Horses Draught	Mules Draught	Mules Ordnance	Remarks
17th Lancers			10		2				
6th Cavy.				3	2			1	
19th Lancers								1	
6th Dragoons	1		4		8				
2nd Lancers				4	6				
38th Horse					5				
1st K.D.G.			6		6				
29th Lancers				6					
36th Horse				1				1	
"Q" Bty. R.H.A.	1		5						
Divnl. Ammn. Col.			1			1			
Total	2		26	14	29	1	1	2	

C.R. Maitland
Captain
D.A.A. & Q.M.G.

SERIAL NO. 2.

Confidential
War Diary
of

D.A.A. & Q.M.G., 1st Indian Cavalry Division.

FROM 1st February 1916 TO 29th February 1916

1ºA 2175

CONFIDENTIAL

WAR DIARY - ADMINISTRATIVE BRANCH - 1st INDIAN CAVALRY DIVISION

FEBRUARY 1st To 29th 1916

WAR DIARY or INTELLIGENCE SUMMARY

Army Form C. 2118.

Hour, Date, Place	Summary of Events and Information	Remarks and references to Appendices
DARGNIES 31.1.16	Departure of the dismounted Indian clipping party for 7th Corps, 3rd Army, for work connected with defences.	
	Composition.	
	1 B.O. 1 I.O. 5.1. O.R. from each of the 6 Indian Regts in the Bde.	
— " — 3.2.16	Formation of a Bde. Machine Gun Squadron in each Bde. each squadron consisting of 4 guns, 2 Indian sections of 2 guns each, and 4 Indian sections of 2 guns each. The personnel to form these squadrons being withdrawn from the Regiments in the Brigade, and replaced in Regts from the 100 dismounted reinforcements, with exception of the Reg.tl M.G. detachments (each 40 strong) which will not be replaced. The 100 D.M. to be brought up to strength by dismounts as reqd.	

(73989) W4141—463. 400,000. 9/14. H.&J.Ltd. Forms/C. 2118/10.

Army Form C. 2118.

WAR DIARY
OF
INTELLIGENCE SUMMARY.
(Erase heading not required.)

Hour, Date, Place	Summary of Events and Information	Remarks and references to Appendices
DARGNIES. 5.2.16	"U" Bty, R.H.A. reported been taken from 10th Corps. Casualties. Nil.	APP. I/II } B.
" 6.2.16	Weekly wastage in Liehman. Deficiencies in Establishment of Fighting Unit.	
" 11.2.16.	Orders issued for the formation of Ice M.G. Squadron in the Canadian Cavy. Bde. Consisting of 6 Sections of 2 Guns each.	
" 13.2.16.	Weekly wastage in Liehman. Deficiencies in Establishment of Fighting Unit.	APP III/IV } B.
" 14.2.16.	"A" Bty, R.H.A. reported been from 5th Divn. Casualties - 1 O.R. killed.	

WAR DIARY
INTELLIGENCE SUMMARY

Army Form C. 2118.

(3)

Hour, Date, Place	Summary of Events and Information	Remarks and references to Appendices
DARGNIES. 17.2.16.	British digging parties for defence work at 7th and 17th Corps left today, strength 50 B.O. Ranks from each British Regt. & Fd Troop 32 all Ranks.	
" — 20.2.16.	Weekly wastage in Vehicles experienced in Establishment of Fighting Units.	APP. I / VI
" — 22.2.16.	The Canadian (newly told now being organised as an "Independent Cavy Bde") allotted to a scheme, instructions been issued for the Brigade to be administered as a self contained formation and to carry out its own interior administration as such.	
" — 27.2.16.	Arrival of feed and become hunc with the Fort Garry Horse which unit joins the Bde	

Army Form C. 2118.

WAR DIARY
INTELLIGENCE SUMMARY.
(Erase heading not required.)

Hour, Date, Place	Summary of Events and Information	Remarks and references to Appendices
DARNIES 27.2.16	Weekly montage to Lichnes. Reference in Establishment of Fighting truck	APP. VII / VIII
" 28.2.16	"Thaw Scheme" put into operation. Under this scheme no motor vehicles are allowed to circulate (with certain exceptions) All lorries are down with the as of the horse transport of the 46th Div. Park, The Army H.T. Coy, 9 Regt Transport. Arrival of remainder of the Fort Garry Horse.	
" 29.2.16		
" 29.2.16	Canadian Cavy are almost complete in its organization with the exception of approximately 400 horses, and a few item of transport of Bde M.G. Squadron.	

E.P.Martin, t. Captain,
D.A.Q.M.G., 1st Ind Cavy Divn.

APPENDIX I

Weekly Wastage in Sickness. 6.2.16

Unit	Officers		Other Ranks		Remarks
	Nr.	Ind.	Nr.	Ind.	
17th Lancers	-	-	5	-	
6th Cavy.	-	-	-	3	
6th Dragoons	-	-	2	-	
2nd Lancers	.	.	.	1	
38th C.I. Horse	1	.	.	.	
36th Horse	-	-	-	1	
H.Q. R.H.A. Bde.	-	-	1	-	
Divnl. Ammn. Col.	-	-	3	-	
" Supply Col.	-	-	3	-	
Field Squadron	-	-	5	-	
Royal Can. Drag.	-	-	8	-	
Lord Strathcona's Horse	1	-	7	-	
R.C.H.A. Bde	-	-	11	-	
Can. Supply Col.	-	-	5	-	
Total	2	-	50	5	

G.R. Maitland
Captain,
D.A.A. & Q.M.G., 1st Ind. Cavy. Divn.

APPENDIX II

Deficiencies in Establishment of Fighting Units. 6.2.16

Unit	Officers		Other Ranks		Riding Horses	Draught Horses	Mules	Ord: Mules	Remarks
	Br.	Ind	Br.	Ind					
17th Lancers	–	–	21	–	3	–	–	–	
6th Cavy	–	–	7	4	4	–	–	–	
19th Lancers	–	–	–	–	1	–	–	–	
6th Drags.	–	–	6	–	11	–	–	–	
2nd Lancers	–	–	–	3	6	–	–	–	
38th C.I.H.	–	–	–	7	8	–	–	–	
1st K.D.G.	–	–	17	–	10	–	–	–	
29th Lancers	–	–	–	6	–	–	–	1	
36th Horse	–	–	–	2	2	–	–	–	
"Q" Bty, R.H.A.	–	–	4	–	–	5	–	–	
"U" – " –	–	–	–	–	–	6	–	–	
Divnl Ammn: Col.	–	–	1	–	2	5	–	–	
Royal Can: Drags	–	–	30	–	520	77	–	–	
Lord Strathcona's Horse	5	–	10	–	528	56	–	–	

W.Maitland
Captain,
D.A. & Q.M.G., 1st Indian Cav: Dn.

APPENDIX III

Weekly wastage in Sickness. 13. 2. 16

Unit	Officer		Other Ranks		Remarks
	Br.	Ind.	Br.	Ind.	
17th Lancers	-	-	7	-	
6th Cavy.	-	-	-	5	
19th Lancers	-	-	-	3	
6th Dragoons	-	-	1	-	
2nd Lancers	-	-	-	1	
38th C.I. Horse	-	-	-	1	
29th Lancers	-	-	-	2	
Lucknow Bde M.V.S.	-	-	1	-	
"U" Bty, R.H.A.	-	-	1	-	
Divl Amm: Col.	-	-	5	-	
Amm: Park	-	-	1	-	
Signal Sqdn.	-	-	1	-	
Royal Can: Drags.	-	-	7	-	
Lord Strathcona's Horse	-	-	6	-	
R.C.H.A. Bde	-	-	7	-	
Can: Supply Col.	-	-	5	-	
Total	-	-	42	12	

G R Waitham
Captain
D.A.A & Q.M.G., 1st Ind Cavy Dn

APPENDIX IV

Deficiencies in Establishment of Fighting Units. 13.2.16

Unit	Officers Br.	Officers Ind.	Other Ranks Br.	Other Ranks Ind.	Riding Horses	Draught Horses	Mules	Ord. Mules	Remarks
17th Lancers	–	–	60	–	52	–	–	–	
6th Cav.	1	1	–	52	41	–	–	1	
19th Lancers	2	–	–	35	18	–	–	–	
6th Drags.	1	–	56	–	57	2	–	–	
2nd Lancers	1	1	–	64	57	–	–	–	
38th C.I. Horse	1	–	–	41	31	–	–	–	
1st K.D.G.	–	–	65	–	48	–	–	–	
29th Lancers	1	–	–	41	31	–	–	–	
36th Horse	1	–	–	21	38	–	–	1	
Royal Can: Drags.	–	–	34	–	434	77	–	–	
L. Strathcona's Horse	5	–	–	–	530	57	–	–	
"B" Bty. R.C.H.A.	–	–	2	–	–	2	–	–	

G.R. Maitland
Captain
D.A.A. & Q.M.G. 1st Ind. Cav. Div.

APPENDIX V

Weekly wastage in Sickness. 20.2.16.

Unit	Officers		Other Ranks		Remarks
	Br.	Ind.	Br.	Ind.	
6th Cavy	-	-	-	2	
19th Lancers	-	-	-	1	
29th Lancers	-	-	-	4	
"A" Bty, R.H.A	-	-	2	-	
Mhow Bde M.G. Sqdn	-	-	1	-	
Lucknow Bde — " —	-	-	2	2	
Divnl Ammn: Col.	-	-	7	-	
Field Squadron	-	-	2	-	
Divnl Supply Col.	-	-	2	-	
Royal Can: Drags.	-	-	5	-	
L. Strathcona's Horse	-	-	5	-	
C.H.A. Bde	-	-	1	-	
Can: Supply Col.	-	-	2	-	
Total	-	-	29	9	

G.R. Maitland
Captain
D.A.A. & Q.M.G., 1st Ind Cavy Divn.

APPENDIX VI

Deficiencies in Establishment of Fighting Units 20.2.16

Unit	Officers Est.	Officers Ind.	O.R. Est.	O.R. Ind.	Riding Horses	Draught Horses	Mules	Bat Mules	Remarks
17th Lancers	–	–	23	–	–	–	–	–	
6th Cavy	–	–	–	2	–	–	–	–	
19th Lancers	–	–	–	2	–	–	–	–	
6th Drags	1	–	6	–	–	2	–	1	
2nd Lancers	–	–	–	5	–	–	–	–	
38th C.I. Horse	2	–	–	11	–	–	–	–	
1st K.D.G.	–	–	3	–	–	–	1	–	
29th Lancers	–	–	1	7	–	–	–	–	
Divnl Ammun: Col.	–	–	7	–	–	8	–	–	
Royal Can: Drags	–	–	–	–	49	23	–	6	
L. Strathcona Horse	4	–	12	–	260	24	–	–	
"A" Bty, R.C.H.A.	1	–	–	–	–	1	–	–	
"B" " "	–	–	–	–	1	3	–	–	
Cav: Bde. Ammun: Col.	–	–	–	–	–	10	–	–	

G.R. Maitland
Captain
D.A.A. & Q.M.G., 1st Ind Cavy Dn.

APPENDIX VII

Weekly wastage in Sickness. 27.2.16

Unit	Officers		Other Ranks		Remarks
	No.	Sick	No.	Sick	
6th Cavy	—	—	—	3	
19th Lancers	—	—	—	2	
6th Dragoons	—	—	1	—	
38th C.I. Horse	—	—	—	1	
29th Lancers	—	—	—	4	
Lucknow Bde M.G. Squadron	—	—	—	1	
36th Horse	—	—	—	2	
Signal Squadron	—	—	1	—	
Auxy: H.T. Coy, A.S.C	—	—	2	—	
Divnl Supply Col.	—	—	4	—	
R. Can: Dragoons	—	—	4	—	
L. Strathcona's Horse	—	—	2	—	
H.Q. R.C.H.A. Bde	—	—	2	—	
"B" Bty. R.C.H.A.	—	—	2	—	
Bde. Ammn: Column	—	—	1	—	
" Field Troop	—	—	1	—	
" Supply Column	2	—	—	—	
" Ammn: Park	—	—	1	—	
Total	2	—	21	13	

APPENDIX VIII

Deficiencies in Establishment of Fighting Units. 27.2.16

Unit	Officers		O.R.		Riding Horses	Draught Horses	Mules	Od. Mules	Remarks
	Br.	Ind	Br.	Ind					
17th Lancers	–	–	3	–	8	–	–	–	
6th Cavy.	2	2	–	26	10	–	–	–	
19th Lancers	2	1	–	22	7	–	–	–	
6th Drag.	1	–	30	–	10	–	–	–	
2nd Lancers	3	–	–	26	–	–	–	–	
38th C.I. Horse	2	–	–	44	–	–	–	–	
1st K.D.G.	–	–	24	–	–	–	–	–	
29th Lancers	2	1	–	25	10	–	–	–	
36th Horse	3	–	–	20	3	–	–	–	
"A" Bty. R.H.B.	–	–	2	–	–	–	–	–	
"Q" " "	–	–	4	–	–	–	–	–	
Divnl. Amm: Col.	–	–	6	–	–	–	–	–	

G.R. Whatham
Captain
D.A.A. & Q.M.G., 1st Ind. Cav. Bde.

(30)

CONFIDENTIAL.

WAR DIARY - ADMINISTRATIVE BRANCH - 1st INDIAN CAVALRY DIVISION.

MARCH 1st to 31st 1916.

Army Form C. 2118.

WAR DIARY
INTELLIGENCE SUMMARY.
(Erase heading not required.)

Instructions regarding War Diaries and Intelligence Summaries are contained in F. S. Regs., Part II. and the Staff Manual respectively. Title pages will be prepared in manuscript.

Hour, Date, Place	Summary of Events and Information	Remarks and references to Appendices
DARGNIES. 2.3.16	The Indian Cavalry Corps having been abolished the Division with the Indian Cavalry Corps Signal Squadron and Jodhpur Lancers composing it, is allotted to 3rd Army as Reserve and come under the orders of the Army direct.	
" — 5.3.16.	Weekly wastage in sickness. Deficiencies in Establishments.	
" — 9.3.16.	Return of Mitzed digging parties from 10th Corps.	Appx. I ⎱ H.Q. — II ⎰
" — 9.3.16.	Canadian Cavalry Regts. having been allotted to 4th Army the Bde is now attached to 2nd Ind. Cavy. Divn. for administration.	
" — 12.3.16.	Return of the Field Troop of the Field Sqdn. from 3rd Army School of Instruction.	

Army Form C. 2118.

WAR DIARY
INTELLIGENCE SUMMARY.
(Erase heading not required.)

Instructions regarding War Diaries and Intelligence Summaries are contained in F.S. Regs., Part II. and the Staff Manual respectively. Title pages will be prepared in manuscript.

Hour, Date, Place	Summary of Events and Information	Remarks and references to Appendices
DARGNIES. 12.3.16	Weekly wastage in dishes references	App. III/IV } HWS
" 19.3.16.	— ditto —	
" 20.3.16	Return of British Digging Party from 48th Div.	{ App. V/VI } HWS
WAIL. 26.3.16.	Division moved to new billeting area. Accommodation Instructions for the move. List of billets. Weekly wastage in dishes. Deficiencies in establishments of fighting units.	App. VII / VIII } HWS — " — IX/X } HWS
" 31.3.16.	As a large number of French horses suffering from mange had been in the new area no horses will be put under cover till it has been disinfected and passed by a Vety Officer.	

J.W. Fleming
Captain
D.A.A. & Q.M.G. 1st Indian Cav. Div.

(73989) W4141—463. 400,000. 9/14. H.&J.Ltd. Forms/C. 2118/10.

APPENDIX I

Weekly wastage in Sickness. 5. 3. 16

Unit	OFFICERS		OTHER RANKS		Remarks
	BRIT.	IND.	BRIT.	IND.	
6th Cavy	–	–	–	3	
19th Lancers	–	–	–	4	
2nd —	–	–	–	4	
38th C.I. Horse	–	–	–	4	
1st K.D.G.	–	–	8	–	
29th Lancers	1	–	–	1	
36th Jacobs Horse	–	–	–	7	
"U" Bty, R.H.A.	–	–	3	–	
Divnl: Ammn. Col.	–	–	6	–	
Lucknow Bde M.G. Sqdn.	–	–	–	1	
Signal Squadron	–	–	1	–	
Field Squadron	–	–	2	–	
Lucknow Bde Signal Troop	–	–	1	–	
Divnl: Supply Column	–	–	3	–	

H.W. Fleming
Captain,
D.A.A. & Q.M.G., 1st Indian Cav. Divn.

APPENDIX II

Deficiencies in Establishments of Fighting Units. 5.3.16.

Unit	Officers		Other Ranks		Riding Horses	Draught Horses	Mules	Ordnance Mules	Remarks
	BRIT.	IND.	BRIT.	IND.					
17th Lancers	-	-	32	-	36	-	-	-	
6th Cavalry	2	-	-	15	29	-	-	1	
19th Lancers	-	-	-	23	44	-	1	-	
6th Dragoons	1	-	41	-	17	-	-	-	
2nd Lancers	3	-	-	29	8	-	-	-	
38th C.I. Horse	3	-	-	20	16	-	-	-	
1st K.D.Gs	-	-	29	-	30	-	-	-	
29th Lancers	2	-	-	24	20	-	-	-	
36th Jacob's Horse	4	-	-	25	26	-	-	-	
"Q" Bty, R.H.A.	-	-	6	-	-	1	-	-	
"U" -"-	-	-	2	-	-	1	-	-	
Divnl. Ammn. Column	-	-	5	-	5	5	-	-	

A.W.Fleming
Captain,
D.A.A. & Q.M.G., 1st Indian Cav. Dn.

APPENDIX III

Weekly wastage in Sickness.   12.3.16

Unit	Officers BRIT	Officers IND	Other Ranks BRIT	Other Ranks IND	Remarks
17th Lancers	1	—	6	—	
6th Cavalry	—	—	—	3	
19th Lancers	—	—	—	1	
"A" Bty. R.H.A.	—	—	2	—	
6th Dragoons	—	—	1	—	
2nd Lancers	—	—	—	3	
38th C.I. Horse	—	—	—	5	
1st K.D.G.	—	—	2	—	
29th Lancers	—	—	2	—	
36th Jacob's Horse	—	—	—	4	
Divnl. Ammn. Col.	—	—	6	—	
Sialkot Kdl. M.T. Squadron	—	—	1	1	
Field Squadron	—	—	1	—	
Lucknow Kdl. Signal Troop	—	—	—	1	
Divnl. Supply Col.	1	—	3	—	
Auxy. H.T. Coy.	—	—	1	—	

H.W. Fleming
Captain.
DAA & QMG, 1st Ind Cavy Dn.

APPENDIX IV

Deficiencies in Establishment of Fighting Units.   12.3.16

Unit	Officers BRIT.	Officers IND.	Other Ranks BRIT.	Other Ranks IND.	Riding Horses	Draught Horses	Mules	Ordnance Mules	Remarks
17th Lancers	2	–	24	–	43	–	–	–	
6th Cavy.	1	–	–	1	45	–	–	–	
19th Lancers	–	–	–	2	23	–	–	–	
6th Dragoons	–	–	33	–	17	–	–	1	
2nd Lancers	2	–	–	13	27	–	–	–	
38th C.I. Horse	1	–	–	22	33	–	–	–	
1st K.D.G.	–	–	24	–	38	–	–	–	
29th Lancers	2	–	–	3	38	–	–	–	
36th Jacob's Horse	1	–	–	10	36	–	–	–	
"A" Bty, R.H.A.	–	–	2	–	–	–	–	–	
"Q" —"—	–	–	6	–	–	2	–	–	
"U" —"—	–	–	2	–	–	1	–	–	
Divnl Ammn. Column	–	–	–	–	6	10	–	–	

JW Fleming
Captain,
D.A.A. & Q.M.G., 1st Ind Cavy Divn.

APPENDIX V

Weekly wastage 1st Lucknow. 19. 3. 16.

Unit	OFFICERS		OTHER RANKS		Remarks
	Brit.	Ind.	Brit.	Ind.	
17th Lancers	—	—	4	—	
6th Cavy.	—	—	—	4	
19th Lancers	—	—	—	1	
Sialkot Bde M.G. Sqdn.	—	—	3	4	
"N" Bty, R.H.A.	—	—	1	—	
6th Dragoons	—	—	1	—	
2nd Lancers	—	—	—	2	
38th Horse	—	—	—	2	
29th Lancers	—	—	—	4	
36th J. Horse	—	—	—	8	
Lucknow Bde M.G. Sqdn.	—	—	—	2	
Divnl Ammn. Column	—	—	2	—	
Field Squadron	—	—	1	—	
Divnl Supply Column	—	—	2	—	
Auxy. H.T. Coy.	—	—	1	—	
Jodhpur Lancers	—	—	—	1	

H.W.Fleming
Captain,
DAA & QMG, 1st Lucknow Div.

APPENDIX VI

Deficiencies in Establishment of fighting units. 19.3.16

Unit	OFFICERS		O.R.		Riding Horses	Draught Horses	Mules	Ordnance Mules	Remarks
	Brit.	Ind.	Brit.	Ind.					
17th Lancers	–	–	41	–	42	–	1	–	
6th Cavy.	2	–	18	1	31	–	–	–	
19th Lancers	–	–	–	3	–	–	–	–	
6th Dragoons.	–	–	33	–	53	2	–	1	
2nd Lancers	2	–	–	9	21	–	–	–	
38th Horse	2	–	–	19	26	–	–	–	
1st K.D.G.	–	–	23	–	28	–	–	–	
29th Lancers	2	–	–	10	6	1	–	–	
36th Horse	1	–	–	19	2	–	–	1	
"Q" Bty. R.H.A.	–	–	5	–	–	–	–	–	
"U" —"—	–	–	2	1	–	–	–	–	
Divnl Ammn. Col.	–	–	1	–	6	5	–	–	

H.W.Fleming
Captain,
D.A.A & Q.M.G, 1st Indian Cavy Divn.

APPENDIX VII

No Q-1596.

Headquarters.
1st Indian Cavalry Division.
21st March 1916.

MEMORANDUM.

The new billeting area is allotted as below.

2. Horses will not be placed under cover.

3. The villages have been considerably damaged by the late occupants and units should be careful to get from the Maires a clear statement of damages already done, in order to avoid heavy claims soon after arrival.

4. Enquiries should be made regarding infection from mange and other infectious diseases.

5. The northern boundary of the area is the River CANCHE; between AUXI-LE-CHATEAU and FROHEN-LE-PETIT the boundary of the area is the River AUTHIE. These boundaries are to be strictly observed.

6. Halting places for MHOW Brigade on night 24th/25th and for Divisional Troops on night 25th/26th are NEUF MOULIN, ST RIQUIER and ONEUX; for SIALKOT Brigade on night 24th/25th are NEUILLY-LE-DIEN, MAISON-PONTHIEU, HIERMONT, BERNATRE.

7. Supply Railhead will open at AUXI-LE-CHATEAU on 26th.

8. AUXI-LE-CHATEAU is allotted to Third Army Infantry School, which is attached to this division for rations and administration from 26th instant.

9. Lists of billets to reach Divisional Headquarters on 26th.

10. One Ambulance will open at BACHIMONT.

11. O.C., A.S.C. will distribute the rug wagons of the A.H.T.Coy at once as follows :-

        Three G.S. wagons per regiment
        One   - do -   per battery
        Two   - do -   per M.G.Squadron.
        One   - do -   for Divisional Headquarters
        One   - do -   for Field Squadron.

12. These wagons will remain with units till after arrival in the new area.

13.

13. O.C., A.S.C. will detail one lorry for O.C. Signal Squadron on the day on which Divisional Report Centre moves.

14. The men left behind with surplus stores should remain dismounted: they will rejoin on the lorries which pick up the stores.

15. The D.M. will march with "B" echelon: O.C., A.S.C. will provide one lorry per Brigade for carriage of their kits.

                     sd/- W.K. Bourne, Lieut-Colonel,
         A.A. and Q.M.G. 1st Indian Cavalry Division.

To,

     Brigades and Divisional Units.

DIVISIONAL AREA.

DIVISIONAL TROOPS.

```
Divisional Headquarters   ....... WAIL
O.C. R.H.A. Brigade      )       (QUOEUX - MONTORGUEIL
Divnl Ammn Park          ) ......(SELLANDRE

Divnl Ammn Column         ............. VIEIL-HESDIN
Field Squadron            ................. AUXI-LE-CHATEAU.
Three Ambulances          )
Sanitary Section          ) ...... BACHIMONT - HAUTMAISNIL
Motor Ambulance Workshop  )
Aux H.T. Company          ................ WILLENCOURT
Supply Column             )       (
D.A.D.O.S.                )......(BUIRE-AU-BOIS
```

SIALKOT BRIGADE.

VACQUERIETTE - CHATEAU DU FORESTEL - GALAMETZ - FILLIEVRES - CONCHY-SUR-CANCHE - HARAVESNES - HAUTMAISNIL (exclusive) - ENQUIERES.

LUCKNOW BRIGADE.

FONTAINE-L'ETALON - SELLANDRE (exclusive) - VAUIX - WILLENCOURT (exclusive) - NEUILLY-LE-DIEN - GUESCHART - TOLLENT - CAUMONT.

MHOW BRIGADE.

MAISON-PONTHIEU - WILLENCOURT (exclusive) - AUXI-LE-CHATEAU (exclusive) - WAVANS - FROHEN-LE-PETIT - ST ACHEUL - HIERMONT.

APPENDIX VIII

No Q-1694.

Headquarters.
1st Indian Cavalry Division.
27th March 1916.

BILLETING AREA — 1ST INDIAN CAVALRY DIVISION.

UNIT	Where BILLETED.
Divisional Headquarters	WAIL.
Signal Squadron	WAIL.
C.O., A.S.C.	WAIL.
A.D.M.S.	St GEORGES.
A.D.V.S.	St GEORGES.
D.A.D.O.S.	WAIL.
SUPPLY COLUMN, WORKSHOPS & 1 ECHELON	WILLENCOURT.
SUPPLY COLUMN, 1 ECHELON	AUXI-LE-CHATEAU.
R.H.A. Bde Headquarters	QUOEUX.
DIVNL AMMN COL	St GEORGES.
DIVNL AMMN PARK	BUIRE-AU-BOIS.
FIELD SQUADRON	AUXI-LE-CHATEAU.
SIALKOT CAV FD AMBULANCE	HAUT-MAISNIL.
AMBALA " " "	QUOEUX.
LUCKNOW " " "	BACHIMONT.
MOTOR AMBULANCE WORKSHOP	BACHIMONT.
SANITARY SECTION	HAUT MAISNIL.
AUX H.T. Company	LANNOY.

SIALKOT BRIGADE.
- Headquarters .... Ch^{au} du FORESTEL.
- "Q" Battery R.H.A. .... Out of Division.
- 17th Lancers .... @FILLIEVRES : GALAMETZ.
- 6th Cavalry .... @VACQUERIETTE : ERQUIERES.
- 19th Lancers .... @AUBROMETZ : CONCHY-SUR-CANCHE.
- Machine Gun Squadron .... VIEIL HESDIN.
- Mobile Veterinary Section .... QUATREVAUX.

LUCKNOW BRIGADE.
- Headquarters .... VAULX.
- "U" Battery R.H.A. .... TOLLENT.
- 1st K.D. Guards .... GUESCHART.
- 29th Lancers .... @FONTAINE-L'ETALON : CHERIENNE.
- 36th Jacob's Horse .... @GENNE-IVERGNY : BOUFFLERS.
- Jodhpur Lancers .... @VITZ-VILLEROY : VILLEROY-SUR-AUTHIE LE PONCHEL.
- Machine Gun Squadron .... CAUMONT.
- Mobile Veterinary Section .... CUMONVILLE.

MHOW BRIGADE.
- Headquarters .... MAIZICOURT.
- "A" Battery R.H.A. .... BERNATRE.
- 6th Inn. Dragoons .... @WAVANS : BEAUVOIR-RIVIERE.
- 2nd Lancers .... @BEALCOURT : St ACHEUL : FROHEN-LE-PETIT.
- 38th Horse .... @MAISON-PONTHIEU : St LOT.
- Machine Gun Squadron .... HEIRMONT.
- Mobile Veterinary Section .... MAIZICOURT.

W H C Brown
Lieut-Colonel,
A.A. and Q.M.G. 1st Indian Cavalry Division.

@ Denotes Headquarters of Units.
To;
   Third Army "Q".
   Brigades and Divisional Units.

APPENDIX IX

Weekly wastage in Sickness. 26.3.16

Unit	OFFICERS		O.R.		Remarks
	Brit.	Ind.	Brit.	Ind.	
17th Lancers	–	–	1	–	
6th Cavy	–	–	1	3	
19th Lancers	–	–	–	2	
Sialkot Bde M.G. Sqdn.	–	–	1	3	
"A" Bty, R.H.A.	–	–	2	–	
6th Dragoons	–	–	1	–	
2nd Lancers	–	–	–	1	
38th Horse	–	–	–	7	
"U" Bty, R.H.A.	–	–	2	–	
1st K.D.G.	–	–	1	–	
29th Lancers	–	–	–	11	
36th Horse	–	–	–	5	
Lucknow Bde M.G. Sqdn.	–	–	2	3	
Divnl Ammn. Col.	–	–	5	–	
Field Squadron	–	–	6	–	
Army H.T. Coy.	–	–	1	–	
Divnl Supply Col.	–	–	4	–	
Jodhpur Lancers	–	1	–	8	
Divnl Ammn. Park	–	–	1	–	

H.W. Fleming
Captain
D.A.A.Q.M.G., 1st Ind Cavy Divn.

APPENDIX X

Deficiencies in Establishment of Fighting Units. 26.3.16

Unit	Officers Estb.	Officers Def.	O.R. Estb.	O.R. Def.	Remarks
17th Lancers	—	—	29	—	
6th Cavy.	1	—	—	1	
19th Lancers	—	—	—	2	
6th Drags.	—	—	11	—	
2nd Lancers	—	—	—	1	
38th Horse	—	—	—	13	
1st K.D.G.	—	—	16	—	
29th Lancers	2	—	—	24	
36th Horse	1	—	—	6	
"U" Bty., R.H.A.	—	—	3	1	
Divnl Ammn. Col.	—	—	1	—	

H.W. Fleming
Captain,
D.A.A. & Q.M.G., 1st Indian Cavy. Divn.

CONFIDENTIAL

WAR DIARY - ADMINISTRATIVE BRANCH - 1st INDIAN CAVALRY DIVISION

APRIL 1st to 30th 1916.

Army Form C. 2118.

WAR DIARY
INTELLIGENCE SUMMARY.
(Erase heading not required.)

Instructions regarding War Diaries and Intelligence Summaries are contained in F. S. Regs., Part II, and the Staff Manual respectively. Title pages will be prepared in manuscript.

Hour, Date, Place.	Summary of Events and Information.	Remarks and references to Appendices.
WAIL. 2.4.16.	Weekly wastage in Sickness.	APP. I } A.
" 9.4.16.	Deficiencies in Establishment of Fighting Unit.	" II }
" 16.4.16.	— ditto —	APP. III } A.
	— ditto —	" IV }
		APP. V } A.
		APP. VI }
YRENCH. 22.4.16.	Division moved here from divisional training area. In the ST RIQUIER training area. List of Billets.	APP. VII } A.
		APP. VIII } A.
" 23.4.16.	Weekly wastage in Sickness.	" IX }
" 30.4.16.	Deficiencies in Establishment of Fighting Unit. Division still carrying out divisional training.	
" 30.4.16.	Weekly wastage in Sickness. Deficiencies in Establishment of Fighting Unit.	APP. X } A.
		" XI }

G.P.Waitad
Captain
Head Quart. 1st Ind. Cav. Division.

APPENDIX I

Weekly wastage in Sickness. 2.4.16.

Unit	Officers Brit.	Officers Ind.	O.R. Brit.	O.R. Ind.	Remarks
Sialkot Bde. HQ.			1	-	
17th Lancers			6	-	
6th Cav.			-	4	
19th Lancers			-	2	
Sialkot Bde. M.G. Sqdn.			-	1	
" " Signal Troop			-	1	
6th Dragoons			4	4	
2nd Lancers			-	1	
38th Horse			1	5	
Mhow Bde. M.G. Sqdn.			1	-	
"U" Bty. R.H.A. Bde.			2	-	
1st. K.D.G.			4	-	
29th Lancers			-	4	
36th Horse			-	1	
Lucknow Bde. M.G.Sq			6	-	
Jodhpur Lancers (F.A)			1	-	
Divl Ammn. Col.			6	-	
Field Sqdn.			1	-	
Auxc. H.T. Co.			5	-	
Divl Supply Col.		1	3	-	

G.C. Maitland
D.A.A. & Q.M.G
Captain
1st Indian Cav. Divn

APPENDIX II

2.4.16

Deficiencies in Establishment of fighting units.

Unit	Officers		O.R.		Remarks
	Brit.	Ind.	Brit.	Ind.	
17th Lancers	2	.	27	.	
6th Cavy	3	.	.	5	
19th Lancers	.	1	.	4	
6th Dragoons	.	.	3	.	
2nd Lancers	.	.	.	1	
38th Horse	.	.	.	15	
1st K.D.G.	.	.	10	.	
29th Lancers	2	.	.	24	
36th Horse	1	.	.	8	
Jodhpur Lcrs	.	3	.	7	
"U" Bty, R.H.A.	.	.	4	1	

GR Maitland
Captain
D.A.A. & Q.M.G. 1st Ind. Cav. Divn.

APPENDIX III

Weekly Wastage Return 9-4-16

Unit	Cas. Brit	Cas. Ind	R Brit	R Ind	Remarks
6th Cav.	-	-	-	5	
19th Lancers	-	-	1	-	
Mhow Bde. H.Q.	-	-	2	-	
"A" Bty R.H.A.	-	-	2	-	
6th Dragoons	-	-	1	-	
2nd Lancers	-	-	-	2	
38th Horse	-	-	-	2	
Mhow Bde. M.G. Sqdn	-	-	1	-	
1st K.D.G.	-	-	1	-	
29th Lancers	-	-	-	1	
36th Horse	-	-	-	4	
Jodhpur Lancers	-	-	-	4	
Lucknow Bde M.G. Sqdn	-	-	-	2	
Divnl Ammn Col	-	-	2	-	
Field Sqdn.	-	-	3	-	
Divnl Supply Col.	-	-	3	-	

G.K. Mattam
Captain
D.A.A. & Q.M.G. 1st Indian Cavalry Divn.

APPENDIX IV

Deficiencies in Establishment of Fighting Units. 9/4/16

Unit	Officers		O.R.		Remarks
	Brit	Ind	Brit	Ind	
17th Lancers	2	.	10	.	
6th Cavy	.	.	.	7	
19th Lancers	.	1	.	5	
2nd Lancers	1	.	3ˣ	.	ˣBatmen
38th Horse	3	.	.	15	
1st K.D.G.	.	.	17	.	
29th Lancers	2	.	.	31	
36th Horse	1	.	.	10	
Jodhpur Lancers	.	3	.	.	
"U" Bty, R.H.A.	.	.	3	1	

G.E. Maitland
Captain
D.A.A. & Q.M.G., 1st Indian Cav. Division

APPENDIX V

Weekly wastage in sickness — 16-4-16.

UNIT.	Officers		O.R.		REMARKS.
	BRIT.	IND.	BRIT	INDIAN	
17th Lancers	-	-	1	-	
6th Cav.			-	1	
Sialkot Brig: M.G. Sqdn			-	1	
"A" Bty R.H.A.			1	-	
6th Dragoons			1	-	
2nd Lancers			-	3	
38th Horse			-	5	
Mhow Bde M.G. Sqd			-	1	
"U" Bty R.H.A.			2		
1st K.D.G.			4	-	
29th Lancers			-	3	
36th Horse			-	5	
Jodhpur Lancers			-	4	
Divl Ammn. Col.			2	-	
Divl A.S.C.			1		
Divl Supply Col.			2		

G R Maitland

Captain
D.A.A. & Q.M.G. 1st Indian Cavalry Division

APPENDIX VI

16.4.16

Deficiencies in Establishment of Fighting Units.

Unit	Officers		O.R.		Remarks
	Brit	Ind	Brit	Ind	
17th Lancers	2	.	12	.	
6th Cavy	1	.	.	.	
19th Lancers	.	1	.	.	
6th Drags	.	.	1	.	
1st K.D.G.	.	.	4	.	
29th Lancers	1	.	.	8	
36th Horse	1	.	.	8	
Jodhpur Lancers	.	2	.	.	
"U" Bty, R.H.A.	2	.	2	.	

G W C Maitland

Captain
D.A.A & Q.M.G., 1st Indian Cav. Division

APP. VII

No Q-2020.

Headquarters,
1st Indian Cavalry Division,
23rd April 1916.

BILLETING AREA - 1ST INDIAN CAVALRY DIVISION.

UNIT	WHERE BILLETED.
Divisional Headquarters	YVRENCH.
Signal Squadron	"
O.C., A.S.C.	"
A.D.M.S.	"
A.D.V.S.	"
D.A.D.O.S.	WAIL.
SUPPLY COLUMN, WORKSHOPS & 1 ECHELON	WILLENCOURT.
SUPPLY COLUMN, 1 ECHELON	AUXI-LE-CHATEAU.
R.H.A. BRIGADE HEADQUARTERS	MILLENCOURT.
DIVNL AMMN COLUMN	ST GEORGES : MILLENCOURT : ARGENVILLERS.
DIVNL AMMN PARK	BUIRE AU BOIS.
FIELD SQUADRON	AUXI-LE-CHATEAU.
SIALKOT CAV FD AMBULANCE	HAUT-MAISNIL.
AMBALA " " "	QUOEUX.
LUCKNOW " " "	BACHIMONT.
SANITARY SECTION	HAUT MAISNIL.
AUX H.T. COMPANY	LANNOY.
DIVNL TRAINING SCHOOL	VACQUERIETTE.

SIALKOT BRIGADE.

Headquarters	DRUCAT.
"Q" Battery R.H.A.	Out of division.
17th Lancers	@NEUF MOULIN : CACURS.
6th Cavalry	CANCHY.
19th Lancers	@MILLENCOURT : LEPLESSIEL : DRUCAT.
Machine Gun Squadron	CANCHY.
Mobile Veterinary Section	L'HEURE.

LUCKNOW BRIGADE.

Headquarters	VAULX.
"U" Battery R.H.A.	ARGENVILLERS.
1st K.D. Guards	GUESCHART.
29th Lancers	@FONTAINE-L'ETALON : CHERIENNE.
36th Horse	@GENNE-IVERGNY : BOUFFLERS.
Jodhpur Lancers	@VITZ-VILLEROY : VILLEROY-SUR-AUTHIE : LE PONCHEL.
Machine Gun Squadron	CAUMONT.
Mobile Veterinary Section	CUMONVILLE.

MHOW BRIGADE.

Headquarters	NOYELLES-EN-CHAUSSEE.
"A" Battery R.H.A.	ARGENVILLERS.
6th Inn. Dragoons	GAPENNES.
2nd Lancers	@YVRENCHEUX : GAPENNES.
38th Horse	@MAISON PONTHIEU : ST LOT.
Machine Gun Squadron	HEIRMONT.
Mobile Veterinary Section	MAIZICOURT.

Lieut-Colonel,
A.A. and Q.M.G. 1st Indian Cavalry Division.

@Denotes Headquarters of Units.

To,
Third Army "Q",
Brigades and Divisional Units.

Appendix VIII

Weekly wastage in Sickness. 23-4-16.

Unit	Officers		Other Ranks	
	Brit.	Ind.	Brit.	Ind.
17th Lancers	-	-	3	-
6th Cav.	-	-	-	2
19th Lancers				3
6th Dragoons			1	
2nd Lancers			-	2
38th Horse			-	4
Mhow Bde M.G. Sqdn			1	1
1st K.D.G's			5	-
29th Lancers				4
36th Horse				2
Jodhpur Lancers				1
Lucknow Bde M.G. Sqdn				2
H.Q. R.H.A Bde			1	
Ammn Colm			4	
"U" Baty R.H.A.			1	
Aux H.S. Coy			3	
Field Sqdn.			1	
Div'l Supply Col.			3	
a. Bty R.H.A			1	

G.R. Maitland

Captain
D.A.A & Q.M.G. 1st Indian Cavalry Divn.

APPENDIX IX

23.4.16

Deficiencies in Establishment of fighting Units

Unit	Officers		O.R.		Remarks
	Brit.	Ind.	Brit.	Ind.	
17th Lancers	2	.	17	.	
6th Cavy.	.	.	.	11	
19th Lancers	.	.	.	5	
6th Drag.	.	.	13	.	
2nd Lancers	.	.	.	10	
38th Horse	.	.	.	9	
1st K.D.G.	.	.	5	.	
29th Lancers	.	.	.	15	
36th Horse	.	.	.	11	
Jodhpur Lancers	.	3	.	.	

GEMaitland
Captain
D.A.A. & Q.M.G. 1st Indian Cav. Divn

APPENDIX:- X

Weekly wastage in Sickness 30.4.16

Unit	Officers		O.R.	
	Brit	Ind	Brit	Ind
17th Lancers	-	-	5	-
6th Cavalry	-	-	-	2
Sialkot M.G. Sqdn	-	-	1	-
6th Dragoons	-	-	9	-
2nd Lancers	-	-	1	4
38th Horse	-	-	-	5
Mhow Bde. M.G. Sqdn	-	-	-	1
29th Lancers	-	-	-	3
36th Horse				4
Jodhpur Lancers				8
Divnl. Ammn. Col			8	
Field Sqdn			3	

G R Maitland
Captain.
D.A.A. & Q.M.G. 1st Indian Cavalry Divn.

APPENDIX XI

30.4.16

Deficiencies in Establishment of fighting Units.

Unit	Officers		O.R.		Remarks
	Brit.	Ind.	Brit.	Ind.	
17th Lancers	.	.	13	.	
6th Cavy.	.	.	.	8	
6th Drag.	.	.	3	.	
2nd Lancers	.	.	1	15	
38th Horse	3	.	.	12	
29th Horse	2	.	.	12	
36th Horse	1	.	.	12	
Jodhpur Lancers	.	3	.	11	
Divnl. Ammn: Col.	.	.	4	.	

G.C. Maitland

Captain
D.A.A. & Q.M.G. 1st. Indian Cav. Divn

CONFIDENTIAL

WAR DIARY – ADMINISTRATIVE BRANCH – 1st INDIAN CAVALRY DIVISION

MAY 1st to 31st 1916.

Army Form C. 2118.

WAR DIARY
of
INTELLIGENCE SUMMARY.
(Erase heading not required.)

Instructions regarding War Diaries and Intelligence Summaries are contained in F.S. Regs., Part II. and the Staff Manual respectively. Title pages will be prepared in manuscript.

Hour, Date, Place		Summary of Events and Information	Remarks and references to Appendices
WAIL.	7. 5. 16.	Division returned from the St Riquier training area.	APPX: I & II.
		Weekly wastage & sickness. Deficiencies & establishment of fighting units.	
LE CAUROY.	10. 5. 16.	Division moved to new billeting area. List of billets.	APPX: III
— " —	14. 5. 16.	Weekly wastage & sickness. Deficiencies in Establishment of fighting units.	APPX: IV & V
— " —	18. 5. 16.	H.Q. 1st Ind. R.H.A. Bde with "A" & "U" Batteries and 3 Sections Divnl Ammn Column proceeded to join 31st Division for attachment.	
— " —	21. 5. 16.	Weekly wastage & sickness. Deficiencies in Establishment of fighting units.	APPX: VI & VII
— " —	22. 5. 16.	Cavalry Divisional Reserve Park joined the Division. This Park forms part of Third Army Troops but is to be administered by the formation controlling the area.	
— " —	28. 5. 16.	Weekly wastage & sickness. Deficiencies in Establishment of fighting units.	APPX: VIII & IX

W. M. [signature] Captain,
Gen & A.Q.M.G. 37th (new) Army Division

7.5.16.

Weekly Wastage in Sickness. APPX. I

Unit	OFFICERS		O.R.		Remarks
	Brit	Ind	Brit	Ind	
17th Lancers	.	.	5	.	
6th Cavy.	.	.	.	2	
19th Lancers	.	.	.	4	
Sialkot Bde M.G. Sqdn.	.	.	2	1	
6th Drag.	.	.	2	.	
2nd Lancers	.	.	.	1	
38th C.I.H	.	.	.	3	
Mhow Bde M.G. Sqdn.	1	.	1	.	
"U" Bty. R.H.A.	.	.	1	1	
29th Lancers	.	.	.	9	
Jodhpur Lancers	.	.	.	2*	*followers
Lucknow Bde M.G. Sqdn.	.	.	.	1	
Divnl Ammn: Col.	.	.	5	.	
Field Sqdn.	.	.	3	.	
H.Q. Divnl A.S.C.	.	.	1	.	
No. 577 Aux: M.T. Coy	.	.	1	.	
Divnl Supply Col.	.	.	3	.	

C R Maitland
Captain
D.A.A & Q.M.G, 1st Ind. Cavy. Dd.

APPX. II

Deficiencies in Establishment of Fighting Units. 7.5.16.

Unit	Officers Brit	Officers Ind	O.R. Brit	O.R. Ind	Remarks
17th Lancers	.	.	19	.	
6th Cavy	2	.	.	3	
19th Lancers	1	.	.	.	
6th Dragoons	.	.	11	.	
2nd Lancers	.	.	1	12	
38th C.I.H.	3	.	.	12	
1st K.D.G.	.	.	3	.	
29th Lancers	2	.	.	16	
36th Horse	1	.	.	.	
Jodhpur Lancers	.	2	.	11	

G R Maitland
Captain,
D.A. & 2 M.G., 1st Ind: Cav: Div:

APPX: III

No Q-2205.

Headquarters.
1st Indian Cavalry Division.
11th May 1916.

BILLETING AREA - 1ST INDIAN CAVALRY DIVISION.

UNIT	WHERE BILLETED.
Divisional Headquarters	LE CAUROY.
Signal Squadron	LE CAUROY.
O.C., A.S.C.	LE CAUROY.
A.D.M.S.	LIENCOURT.
A.D.V.S.	LIENCOURT.
D.A.D.O.S.	LE CAUROY.
Supply Column	GRAND BOURET.
R.H.A. Brigade Headquarters	LIENCOURT.
Divnl Ammunition Column	ETREE-WAMIN.
Divnl Ammunition Park	LIGNEREUIL.
Field Squadron	LIENCOURT.
Sialkot Cavalry Field Ambulance	HOUVIN HOUVIGNEUL.
Ambala Cavalry Field Ambulance	HOUVIN HOUVIGNEUL.
Lucknow Cavalry Field Ambulance	HOUVIN HOUVIGNEUL.
Sanitary Section	HOUVIN HOUVIGNEUL.
Aux. H.T. Company	Pit BOURET-SUR-CANCHE.

SIALKOT Brigade.

Headquarters	HOUVIN.
"Q" Battery R.H.A.	Out of division.
17th Lancers	@ BERLENCOURT : DENIER.
6th Cavalry	MAGNICOURT.
19th Lancers	AMBRINES.
Machine Gun Squadron	SARS LEZ BOIS.
Mobile Veterinary Section	DENIER.

LUCKNOW Brigade.

Headquarters	REBREUVE.
"U" Battery R.H.A.	REBREUVE.
1st K.D. Guards	@ SIBIVILLE : SERICOURT.
29th Lancers	CANETTEMONT.
36th Jacob's Horse	MONCHEAUX.
Jodhpur Lancers	REBREUVE.
Machine Gun Squadron	HONVAL.
Mobile Veterinary Section	HONVAL.

MHOW Brigade.

Headquarters	IVERGNY.
"A" Battery R.H.A.	BROUILLY.
6th (Inniskilling) Dragoons	REBREUVIETTE.
2nd Lancers	@ IVERGNY : BEAUDRICOURT : OPPY.
38th Horse	ROZIERE.
Machine Gun Squadron	WAMIN.
Mobile Veterinary Section	IVERGNY.

WKBourne
Lieut-Colonel,
A.A. and Q.M.G. 1st Indian Cavalry Division.

@ Denotes Headquarters of Units.

To,
   Third Army "Q".
   Brigades and Divisional Units.

14.5.16

Weekly wastage in Sickness APPX. IV

Unit	Officers		O.R.		Remarks
	Brit	Ind	Brit	Ind	
17th Lancers	1	.	3	.	
19th Lancers	.	.	.	2	
Sialkot Bde M.G. Sqdn.	.	.	2	.	
6th Drags.	.	.	5	.	
2nd Lancers	.	.	1	5	
38th C.I.H.	.	.	.	3	
Mhow Bde M.G. Sqdn.	1	.	.	.	
1st K.D.G.	.	.	6	.	
29th Lancers	.	.	.	2	
Lucknow Bde M.G. Sqdn.	.	.	6	1	
H.Q. R.H.A. Bde.	.	.	1	.	
"A" Bty. R.H.A.	.	.	1	.	
Divnl Ammn: Col.	.	.	2	.	
" Supply Col.	.	.	2	.	
No. 577 Aux: H.T. Coy	.	.	3	.	
Field Sqdn:	.	.	2	.	
Ambala C.F. Amb.	.	.	1	.	

G.R. Maitland
Captain

APPX. V

Deficiencies in Establishment of Fighting Units: 14.5.16

Unit	Officers Brit	Officers Ind	O.R. Brit	O.R. Ind	Remarks
17th Lancers	.	.	15	.	
6th Cavy.	3	.	.	9	
19th Lancers	2	.	.	4	
6th Dragoons	.	.	6	.	
2nd Lancers	.	.	.	13	
38th C.I. Horse	.	.	.	2	
1st K.D.G.	.	.	14	.	
29th Lancers	1	.	.	19	
36th Horse	1	.	.	4	
Jodhpur Lancers	.	2	.	5	

G.K. Maitland
Captain
D.A.A. & Q.M.G, 1st Ind: Cav: Dv:

APPX. VI

Weekly wastage in Sickness. 21.5.16.

Unit	Officers		O.R.		Remarks
	Brit	Ind	Brit	Ind	
17th Lancers	.	.	2	.	
6th Cavy.	.	.	.	2	
Sialkot Bde M.G. Sqdn.	.	.	2	1	
6th Drag.	.	.	3	.	
2nd Lancers	.	.	.	2	
38th C.I.H.	.	.	.	3	
Mhow Bde M.G. Sqdn.	.	.	.	3	
29th Lancers	.	.	.	5	
36th Horse	.	.	.	4	
Jodhpur Lancers	.	.	.	4	
Lucknow Bde M.G. Sqdn.	.	.	1	.	
Field Sqdn.	.	.	2	.	
Divnl Ammn. Col.	.	.	7	.	
" Supply Col.	.	.	2	.	
No. 577 Aux: H.T. Coy.	.	.	1	.	
Divnl Ammn. Park	.	.	1	.	
Sialkot C.F. Amb	.	.	2	1×	×Followers

G.R. Maitland
Captain,
DAA&QMG, 1st Ind. Cav: Dn:

APPX. VII.

Deficiencies in Establishment of Fighting Units. 21.5.16

Unit	OFFICERS		O.R		Remarks
	Brit.	Ind.	Brit	Ind	
17th Lancers	.	.	18	.	
6th Cavy	.	.	.	9	
19th Lancers	2	.	.	3	
6th Dragoons	.	.	17	.	
2nd Lancers	.	.	.	11	
38th C.I. Horse	.	.	.	12	
1st K.D.G.	.	.	18	.	
29th Lancers	.	.	.	17	
36th Horse	1	.	.	14	
Jodhpur Lancers	.	1	.	4	

W. M. Martin
Captain.
D.a.a&2.M.G., 1st Ind. Cav. Du.

APPX. VIII

Weekly wastage in Sickness. 28.5.16.

Unit	Officers Brit	Officers Ind	O.R. Brit	O.R. Ind	Remarks
17th Lancers	.	.	2	.	
6th Cavy.	.	1	.	1	
19th Lancers	.	.	.	2	
Sialkot Bde M.G. Sqdn:	.	.	1	1	
6th Dragoons	.	.	6	.	
2nd Lancers	.	.	.	5	
38th C.I.H	.	.	.	3	
29th Lancers	.	.	.	3	
36th Horse	.	.	.	3	
Lucknow Bde M.G. Sqdn:	.	.	3	.	
Field Squadron	.	.	5	.	
No. 577 Aux: H.T. Coy	.	.	1	.	

G.R. Maitland
Captain
D.A.A. & Q.M.G. 1st Ind. Cav. Dv:

APPX. IX

Deficiencies in Establishment of fighting units. 28.5.16.

Unit	OFFICERS		O.R.		Remarks
	Brit	Ind	Brit	Ind	
17th Lancers	1	.	15	.	
6th Cavy.	.	.	.	8	
6th Dragoons	.	.	8	.	
2nd Lancers	.	.	.	15	
38th C.I. Horse	1	.	.	13	
29th Lancers	.	.	.	17	
36th Horse	.	.	.	18	
Jodhpur Lancers	.	.	.	12	

G.E. Maitland
Captain,
S.C. and 2 i/c, 1st Ind. Cav. Bde.

SERIAL NO. 2

Confidential
War Diary
of

D.A.A. & Q.M.G. Hq. 1st Indian Cavalry Division

FROM 1st June 1916 TO 30th June 1916

Army Form C. 2118.

WAR DIARY

INTELLIGENCE SUMMARY.

(Erase heading not required.)

Instructions regarding War Diaries and Intelligence Summaries are contained in F. S. Regs., Part II, and the Staff Manual respectively. Title pages will be prepared in manuscript.

Hour, Date, Place.	Summary of Events and Information.	Remarks and references to Appendices.
LE CAUROY. 1st to 27th June, 1916.	A Divl. Salvage Squadron was formed to deal with the collection and custody of surplus stores in the event of an advance. The Squadron consists of 3 troops:- 1 R.O. - C.O. 1 Sergt. in Bearer for Cavy. Regt. 1 man per Squadron. " M.G. Squadron. * Total Salvage Sqdn:- 1 R.O., 10 N.C.O., 43 men. Under this scheme stores collected are arranged in a central position near a railway, to dispose as circumstances of the moment admit. The object of the scheme is to avoid preventable waste of Government stores which have accumulated owing to the nature of the present warfare and to ensure that all army equipment etc. abandoned by casualties or cavalry left behind by troops pursuing attack, are safeguarded. The Auxiliary M.T. lorry allotted to the Division for the carriage of horselings has now been made available for the carriage of rations during the summer months.	B.

Continued. 2.

Army Form C. 2118.

WAR DIARY
INTELLIGENCE SUMMARY.
(Erase heading not required.)

Instructions regarding War Diaries and Intelligence Summaries are contained in F. S. Regs., Part II, and the Staff Manual respectively. Title pages will be prepared in manuscript.

Hour, Date, Place.	Summary of Events and Information.	Remarks and references to Appendices.
	Wagons are fitted with 33 Neelaugulan 200 gallon tanks.	
	Following circulars were drawn up and issued to all concerned in the Divisions:—	
	(1). Notes on the rear of the battlefield — Appx: I	
	(2). Summer Marching Dress. — II	
	(3). Selections regarding supplies in the event of a forward move — III	
	A certain number of men in the Divn. were medically classified during the month, but majority were subsequently withdrawn being required to make up deficiencies in certain Infantry Battns.	
	Begging parties as follows from the Divn. were sent up during the month to work in the 7th & 17th Corps areas:—	
	23 B.O.R. and 730 I.O.R.	

Even

Continued 3.

Army Form C. 2118.

WAR DIARY

INTELLIGENCE SUMMARY.

(Erase heading not required.)

Instructions regarding War Diaries and Intelligence Summaries are contained in F. S. Regs., Part II, and the Staff Manual respectively. Title pages will be prepared in manuscript.

Hour, Date, Place.	Summary of Events and Information.	Remarks and references to Appendices.
	1800 S.O.R. with proportion of Officers. The total number of casualties among these ranks were:—	A
	Brit. O.R. Ind. O.R. K. W. K. W. 1 3 17 (5 pm)	
LE CAUROY. 28.6.16.	Brere having received orders to move to another area certain detailed instructions were issued to all concerned in the Bde.	Appx. IV B
" 29.6.16.	Hqrs 1st Ind. R.H.A. Bde with "A" & "U" Batteries and 3 Sections Brere Signal Annex Col. reported him from 51st Infantry Bde. today; Also "Q" Bty, from 5-17 Bde. The Bde has been re-armed with 18-pounder guns, wagons and limbers.	A
DOULLENS. 30.6.16.	Bde moved to new area today. Billeting List. Minialtard aft: Brare 2nd Bde, 1st Ind. Cav. Divn.	Appx. V B

No A-4657. Headquarters.
1st Indian Cavalry Division.
10th June 1916.

To,
Brigades and Divisional Units.

The following notes on the rear of the battlefield are forwarded for information and guidance. The methods of evacuation of sick are now clearly laid down and have not been touched on in these notes.

1. The normal methods of evacuation have been modified in trench fighting, and Stragglers' Posts and prisoners' Collecting Posts have been established in certain places in advance. When the Cavalry get on the move we return to the normal plan; and the three main links in working the services of collection and evacuation will be as follows :-
(a) Stragglers' Patrols will follow the fighting troops;
(b) in rear of them will be one main A.P.M's Collecting Post;
(c) "B" echelon.
    If a Brigade is detached, portions of these three links go with it, and the system is worked on a smaller scale.
A. STRAGGLERS' PATROLS.
2. If the division is acting as such, not in the trenches, three patrols will be detailed to follow the fighting troops. Each patrol will be under a Provost Serjeant, and will consist of three British Provosts, two Indian Provosts and 10 Jodhpur Lancers. They will keep touch with the Brigade in front of them. They will search woods, valleys, villages, etc, for stragglers. They will not take over escorted prisoners, but will direct the escort to the A.P.M. They will take over any casual enemy not under escort, as far as circumstances permit. The care of wounded is not one of their duties; but prompt attention may save lives, and a few extra field dressings should be carried. They should also satisfy themselves that there are no skrimshankers among the apparently wounded; and they may obtain from the wounded arms and ammunition for the re-arming of stragglers. In such a case they should leave a receipt with the wounded man to justify his reaching the dressing station unarmed. The M.Os have instructions to take the names of any men who arrive unarmed or unequipped without sufficient justification.
3. The patrols will catch loose horses, if this can be done without delay; and will send them to the A.P.M. with parties of stragglers. F.S. Regulations lays down "Stray horses and mules if identified, are to be returned at once to their unit: if not identified they must be sent to the nearest mounted unit." But it is not intended during a Cavalry advance that Stragglers Patrols should spend their time in hunting for units; and unless a unit is close by and asking for horses, they will normally take everything back to the A.P.M.
    The mounted parties of the M.V.S. will be working up in rear of these Stragglers' Patrols.
4. Stragglers will be collected in batches and sent direct to the A.P.M. It is not proposed normally to send them straight to their Brigades from the Stragglers' Patrols, but they must be sent back to the A.P.M. under escort. If possible they should be sent to him with escorts who are on their way back with prisoners. If this is not possible the Patrol Leader must detail an escort.
B. A.P.M'S COLLECTING POST.
5. The A.P.M. will here take over all that comes. The men at his disposal are one British Provost Serjeant, and about 20 British Provosts, 12 Indian Provosts, 2½ to 3 troops Jodhpur Lancers, and part of the Salvage Squadron.
6. His normal position will be about 2 miles in rear of the fighting troops. He will usually select a village, or at any rate a place with water, on the main line of evacuation, and he will inform Divisional Headquarters of his position and any alteration in it. The "Q" Staff will keep him informed generally of the plans and progress of events, will inform Brigades of his position, and will tell him the position of Divisional and Brigade Headquarters, Dressing Stations and "B" echelon.
    The Divisional Troops V.O. will make his Headquarters here.

7. The Squadron or party which captures prisoners will disarm them, and send them to Regimental Headquarters. Regiments will send them direct to the A.P.M. not to Brigade Headquarters and will send, by their escort any papers they may have had time to take from them. A rapid examination of a preliminary nature is all that can be expected before prisoners reach the A.P.M. but officers, N.C.Os and men should be separated at as early a stage as is convenient. The Intelligence officer will thus know where to find prisoners for examination.

8. Should the A.P.M's post require to move forward the prisoners will be left in a church or other suitable enclosure under a small guard. If the Infantry are following up the Cavalry this may be a more economical method than sending them back. They can be handed over to the Infantry escorts as these arrive, and the guard will rejoin the A.P.M. at once.

9. Stragglers, loose horses, arms, equipment, when picked up will all be sent back to the A.P.M's post, and he will to some extent sort them there. He will divide stragglers into two groups -

(a) those who have horses or who have been remounted and are fit to rejoin;
(b) those who for any reason are unfit to rejoin at once.

(a) will consist of those who have lost their horses or who have become detached, and failed to find their unit. They will now when re-equipped or remounted be sent to their units in batches with returning prisoner escorts or under proper command.
(b) will be sent back to "B" echelon.

10. The D.A.D.O.S. will place one or more Armourers at the A.P.M's post and with the assistance of these, arms and equipment will be sorted; any that are needed to re-arm (a) will be taken; the remainder will be carried by (b) or sent strapped on to horses etc to "B" echelon.

11. A.P.M. will send periodically to the Dressing Station to collect the arms brought there by wounded men; and O.C. Dressing Station will take every opportunity of sending these across. The A.P.M's post, Dressing Station and M.V.S. will often only be a short distance apart.

C. <u>"B" ECHELON (OR PART OF "A" ECHELON IF "B" ECHELON HAS BEEN LEFT BEHIND.)</u>

12. The senior B.T.O. will be in command and will establish himself in a village or other suitable portion on the main line of evacuation. Here will be sent in all that comes back from the Front; except prisoners.

13. O.C. Salvage Squadron will be under the orders of the O.C. "B" echelon for looking after stragglers. The D.A.D.O.S. will make this his Headquarters; and the Armourers will be here.

14. Arms will be oiled, cleaned, repaired; equipment will be sorted out. Stragglers not fit to rejoin immediately will be brought here, rested, fed, and re-equipped. Loose horses, slightly wounded horses, etc, will be collected, fed and watered, and taken over by the M.V.S.

15. For clearing the battlefield one or more units will be placed at the disposal of the D.A.A. and Q.M.G. who will co-ordinate the work of the troops given him, the Stragglers' Patrols, A.P.M's Collecting Post and Salvage Squadron.

sd/- W.K.Bourne, Lieut-Colonel,
A.A. and Q.M.G. 1st Indian Cavalry Division.

NO. Q.2463

HEADQUARTERS,
1st Indian Cavalry Division.
15th June 1916.

To,
    Brigades and
    O.C.,A.S.C.
    Field Squadron.

1. The Summer Marching Order laid down in this Office Q.2116. dated 21st of the 5th, is cancelled, and the following substituted.

ON THE MAN

    Haversack containing two Gas Helmets, 1 pair of goggles.
    Haversack, cotaining Map, Notebook, and unexpended portion of the day's ration.
    Waterbottle, Bandolier, Bayonet, Field Glasses, Field Dressing and Wirecutters for those who carry them.

ON THE HORSE.

(a). In the Wallets.
    Mug, Handkerchief, pair of socks, towel, housewife, holdall containing: soap, toothbrush, comb, shaving brush, razor, laces, knife, fork and spoon.
    One Iron ration, or two if ordered.

(b) On the saddle:
    Coat warm, British.
    Waterproof sheet.
    Hay net.
    Body brush.
    Canvas bucket.
    Corn sack.
    Nose bags, 2.

Note-1. The picketing peg, heel rope and shackle will be carried on "B" Echelon.
2. The mans blanket will be carried on "B" Echelon, unless orders are given to carry it under the saddle.
3. If saddles are without numnah panels, two blankets will be carried under the saddle during Active Operations.
4. The normal amount of Oats to be carried will be the unexpended portion of the day's rations. If special orders are given, 16 lbs, will be carried in the corn sack and two nose bags.

DISTRIBUTION OF PACK MULES

2. The distribution of pack mules in a Cavalry Regiment will be :-

LOAD	PER SQDN.	PER REG'T.
(a) S.A.A.	1.	4.
(b) Grenades, entrenching tools, sand bags, camp kettles.	3.	12.
(c) Explosives		2
TOTAL		18

DISTRIBUTION OF S.A.A.

3. The distribution of S.A.A. will be :-
   (a). On the man and horse, 180 rds.per rifle
       (50 only for shoeing smiths and Signallers.

   (b). In regtl reserve. 50 rds per rifle for 480 rifles = 24,000.

   (a)
   1. 2,000 in leather carriers on 1 mule per sqdn = 8,000
   2. 4,000 in L.G.S.W. of each squadron.   =16,000
                                            Total   24,000

Note (a). In cases where the leather carrier will not hold the full 2,000, the balance will not be carried.

DISTRIBUTION OF TOOLS ETC.

4. The distribution of tools etc.will be:-

ARTICLE	ON PACK MULE	In.L.G.S.W.	Total per sqdn	Total per Regt.
Shovels	30	10	40	160.
Picks	8	8	16	64.
" helves	-	4	4	16.
Hand axes	4	12	16	64.
Felling axes	1	2	3	12.
Bill hooks	4	12	16	64.
Hand saws	2	6	8	32.
Hedging gloves	4	4	8	32.
Sand bags	25	25	200	900.
Grenades	72	-	72	288.
Camp kettles	3	6	9	36.

EXPLOSIVES

5. The load for two mules, carrying explosives, will include:-

Guncotton,wet, Charges 1503		96.
" ,dry primers.		240.
Detonators.		144.
Fuse, instantaneous.	yds	300.
" , safety	fathoms.	72.
Matches.		468.
Bar boring,or crowbar.		1.
Hammers, about 7 lbs.		1.
Pliers.		2.
Twine.	lbs	2.
Wire.	"	6.

L.G.S.W.

6. The load of the squadron L.G.S.W. will include :-
   The tools given in para.4, col. 3.
   The remainder of the Pioneer Equipment.

Horse shoes	boxes	4.
Very pistols.		1.
" " ammn. box.		1.
Veterinary chest, 25 lbs.		1.
Lanterns, tent folding		4.
Rifle oil.	gallom	1.
Flannelette.	yds	66.
pull through strings		50.

(continued on No3)

Continued :-
Trench stretchers
Butchers' implements.
Saddlers' repairing material.
Horse gear and Drivers kit
Ration packs.

If Troops are likely to be away from their base for more than 48 hours the available space will be filled up with oats pup to the maximum weight of 1 ton per L.G.S.W.

ENTRENCHING TOOLBAGS.

7. One pair of entrenching toolbags per squadron can be indented for on the authority of G.H.Q. O/B 1682, dated 2-6-16.
    If the tools are carried on two mules per squadron this will suffice. If toolbags for 3 mules per squadron are needed, the pioneer panniers should be converted locally.

Provision of tools
8. Brigades will submit to Divnl Headquarters by the 17th inst., a statement showing by units the tools required to fill up to the scale given in paras. 4. 5.

(Sd) W.K.BOURNE, Lieut-Col
A.A .&%.Q.M.G. 1st Indian Cavalry Division.

No Q-2589.

Appx: III

Headquarters.
1st Indian Cavalry Division.
26th June 1916.

To,
Brigades and Divisional Units.

The present situation regarding supplies in the event of a forward move is as follows :-

1. **Available resources at noon each day at present.**

Ordinary issue	(1)	Unexpended portion of current day's rations for men and horses.
	(2)	One day's iron ration (emergency) on the man.
Iron rations within the Division	(3)	One day's iron ration for men <u>at present</u> in Bde S.O. charge.
	(4)	Another day's iron ration for men <u>at present</u> in Bde S.O. charge.
	(5)	One day's ration (ordinary) for men and horses for next day's use.
Ordinary issue	(6)	One day's ration (ordinary) for men and horses just drawn on H.T. for distribution next day and consumption on the day after next and in units charge.
Park Reserve near the Division	(7)(8)	2 days' iron rations and grain for animals carried on the Supply Reserve Park (H.T.) of 1st Indian Cavalry Division.

Note A. The present system of drawing rations in the morning at Railhead on units' Transport is the cause of (5) and (6) being in units' charge so early. Before the Division moves as a mounted force, a return to the <u>normal system</u> will be made, when the position will be modified as regards (5) and (6) thus -

Ordinary issue
(5) One day's ration on lorries for delivery in the afternoon for next day's use.
(6) One day's ration just drawn at Railhead on lorries for consumption on the following day to (5).

2. Once the Division returns to the normal system and is on the move or liable to move at any hour the following day's ration (No 5) will not be distributed till the evening meal time as a rule. Lorries will deliver daily to units transport or at regimental Headquarters when possible, and once the delivery is made it becomes the "unexpended portion" - (namely (1) above) and must be carried by the man or horse. The fodder alone presents difficulty and this must be consumed as far as possible during the night as no carrying power exists for this.

(Ordinary daily issues Nos 1, 2 and 6 above.)

3. The carrying power and method of distribution when on the move will be as follows :-
(1) The "unexpended portion" (as explained above) on the man or horse.
(2) One iron ration for the man - in the wallets. Those without wallets carry this ration in the haversack as heretofore.
(3) One iron ration now in charge of B.S.O. will also be carried in the wallets. For those without wallets this ration will be carried on pack.

Note B. As regards (2) and (3) for <u>Indians</u>, the gur is carried in the gur tin provided for the purpose in the case of (2) and in tins now being collected in the case of (3). These 2 tins will be carried in the wallets or in the haversack. The biscuits of (2) will be in the wallets or on the man as heretofore: the biscuits

of (3) in the wallets or on pack as heretofore.
(4) One iron ration for the man (now in B.S.O's charge) will be carried on the cook's wagon.
(5) One day's ordinary ration will be carried on M.T. lorries until the evening it is issued to units and becomes (1).
(6) One day's ordinary ration will be similarly carried until during the next evening it is issued to units from lorries.
(7)
& 2 days' rations and corn will be carried on the H.T. Park.
(8)

4. In order that units may be able to carry 16 lbs of oats including the unexpended portion of the day's ration in the 2 nose bags and the cornsacks, an issue of 5 lbs per horse will be made as soon as possible. This must be turned over daily, but the amount must be kept as a reserve in case of emergency.

W K Bourne

Lieut-Colonel,
A.A. and Q.M.G. 1st Indian Cavalry Division.

Appx: IV

SECRET.   No Q-2615.

Headquarters.
1st Indian Cavalry Division.
28th June 1916.

Reference G-899.
The new billeting area is as follows :-

Sialkot Brigade .... LUCHEUX.
Lucknow Brigade .... GROUCHES, LA FOLIE Fm, BOUT DES
                                PRES, MILLY.
Mhow Brigade .... AUTHIEULE.
Divnl Headquarters)
Signal Squadron   )
O.C.,A.S.C.   )
A.D.M.S.   ) .... DOULLENS.
A.D.V.S.   )
D.A.D.O.S.   )
R.H.A.Brigade (complete) .... DOULLENS.
Cavalry Field Ambulances .... "
Sanitary Section .... "
Divnl Ammunition Park .... "
Field Squadron .... LE MARAISSEC.
Jodhpur Lancers .... BREVILLERS.
Aux H.T.Company .... OCCOCHES.

2.   Details of the accommodation available in these areas are given in Appendix "A".

3.   The permanent detachments stationed in LUCHEUX and AUTHIEULE are not to be disturbed. These are :-

   At LUCHEUX   (37th Divnl School.
                    (Casualty Clearing Station.
                    (Detachment Labour Battalion.

   At AUTHIEULE   Detachment Labour Battalion.

4.   The billeting in Doullens is arranged by the Town Major who has handed over a certain number of billets for this Division. Details of these billets and a plan of DOULLENS will issue later.

5.   By arrangement with VII Corps, the Jodhpur Lancers may make use of billets in LE JOUICH, which are unoccupied at present.

6.   One copy of report on water supply in area - REMAISNIL: BEAUMETZ : BASSEUX : MEZEROLLES is forwarded to each Brigade herewith.

7.   There are water troughs and lift and force pumps in several of the villages. More may be needed at LUCHEUX. The Field Sqdn will assist if called upon.

8.   Staff Captain Sialkot Brigade will obtain much detailed information if he calls on the 37th Division Staff Officer in charge of the School.

9.   A sketch of MILLY and BOUT DES PRES, and details of accommodation are forwarded to Lucknow Brigade herewith. These are to be left, when done with, with the Maire.

10. Staff Captain Mhow Brigade will obtain detailed information regarding AUTHIEULE from O.C. 3rd Labour Battalion, who is stationed there.

11.

11. There are four lift and force pumps working from the river, and one from a well in AUTHIEULE; O.C. Field Squadron will place a Sapper in charge.

12. The horses of Divisional Headquarters, the Ambulances and some of the R.H.A. will be picketed in the Boulevards of DOULLENS. Strict orders are to be issued by each O.C. concerned that no horses are to be tied to trees, and that the trees are to be preserved from all damage.

13. All surplus stores, beyond those authorised for units in the field, will be dumped in the present billeting area, and will be collected by the Salvage Squadron into the Divisional Dump at LE CAUROY as soon as the troops have left. No extra transport will be provided. The surplus stores of the R.H.A. will be deposited at LE CAUROY, en route.

14. In DOULLENS the men will be billeted in the town, and stable guards will be left with the horses. Tents for these stable guards at the rate of three tents per Battery, three per Divnl Ammunition Column, one per Field Ambulance, one for Divnl Hqrs, will be picked up by D.A.D.O.S. from the tents in charge at present of the 17th Lancers, and will be issued at DOULLENS on the afternoon of the 30th.

15. D.A.D.O.S. will also pick up tents from the following units
    6th Cavalry - 14
    19th Lancers - 16
    Skot M.G.Sqdn - 8
    R.T.O. FREVENT - 10
and distribute in the new area at the rate of
    3 per regiment
    1 per Bde Hqrs
    3 per M.G.Sqdn
    1 per M.V.S.
    3 per Aux H.T.Coy.
These will be available for stable guards.

16. The dismounted men will be in REBREUVE while Railhead remains at FREVENT.

W.K.Browne

Lieut-Colonel,
A.A. and Q.M.G. 1st Indian Cavalry Division.

APPENDIX "A".
BILLETING ACCOMMODATION.

	Billets		Huts
	Officers	Other ranks	
LUCHEUX	160	3000	600 400 (Forest)
LA FOLIE FME	8	500	
AUTHIEULE	20	1220	2200
MILLY	17	400	
GROUCHES) BOUT DES PRES)	45	1000	
BREVILLERS	10	900	

No.Q-2642.

Headquarters,
1st Indian Cavalry Division.
30th June 1916.

BILLETING AREA - 1ST INDIAN CAVALRY DIVISION.

UNIT.	WHERE BILLETED.
Divisional Headquarters	DOULLENS.
Signal Squadron	do.
O.C.,A.S.C.	do.
A.D.M.S.	do.
A.D.V.S.	do.
D.A.D.O.S.	do.
R.H.A.Bde.Hdqrs. & 3 Batteries	do.
Divisional Ammunition Column	do.
Divisional Ammunition Park	do.
Jodhpur Lancers	BREVILLERS.
Field Squadron	LE MARAIS SEC.
Sialkot Cavalry Field Ambulance	DOULLENS.
Ambala Cavalry Field Ambulance	do.
Lucknow Cavalry Field Ambulance	do.
Sanitary Section	do.
Supply Column	GRAND BOURET.
Aux. H.T.Company	OCCOCHES.
No.1 Indian Cavalry Reserve Park	BOUBERS SUR CANCHE.

SIALKOT BRIGADE:-
Headquarters	LUCHEUX.
17th Lancers	do.
6th Cavalry	do.
19th Lancers	do.
Machine Gun Squadron	do.
Mobile Veterinary Section	do.

LUCKNOW BRIGADE:-
Headquarters	GROUCHES.
1st K.D.Guards	do.
29th Lancers	MILLY.
36th Jacob's Horse	BOUT DES PRES.
Machine Gun Squadron	LA FOLIE FERME.
Mobile Veterinary Section	GROUCHES.

MHOW BRIGADE:-
Headquarters	DOULLENS.
6th (Inniskilling) Dragoons	AUTHIEULE.
2nd Lancers	do.
38th C.I.Horse	do.
Machine Gun Squadron	do.
Mobile Veterinary Section	DOULLENS.

Dismounted men	REBREUVE.

W K Brown
Lt.Colonel,
A.A.& Q.M.G.,1st Indian Cavalry Division.

To,
Third Army "Q"
Brigades and Divisional Units.

SECRET

WAR DIARY — ADMINISTRATIVE BRANCH — 1st INDIAN CAVALRY DIVISION.

JULY 1st to 31st 1916.

Army Form C. 2118.

WAR DIARY
INTELLIGENCE SUMMARY.
(Erase heading not required.)

Instructions regarding War Diaries and Intelligence Summaries are contained in F.S. Regs., Part II. and the Staff Manual respectively. Title pages will be prepared in manuscript.

Hour, Date, Place	Summary of Events and Information	Remarks and references to Appendices
DOULLENS. 2.7.16.	3.30 p.m. Orders received from Third Army for Bion to move at once to new area. Bion was clear of the area within two hours from receipt of the order. List of billets.	APPX: I A.
AUXI-LE-CHATEAU. 12.7.16.	Approval having been given for representatives of the British Army to take part in the Review at PARIS on the 14th inst., a party was sent from the Brigade consisting of :- 2 B. Os. 2 I. Os. 21 Indian N.C.Os. 7 O. Rs.	A.
" 17.7.16.	"U" Bty. R.H.A. placed at disposal of 5th Division.	A.
" 18.7.16.	Orders received for Bion to move to new area. Administrative instructions issued.	APPX: II A.
VILLERS CHATEL. 19.7.16.	Division arrives in new area today. List of billets.	III A.
" 19.7.16.	R.H.A. Bde (less "U" Bty), and Field Squadron placed at disposal of XIII Corps.	A.

Army Form C. 2118.

WAR DIARY
INTELLIGENCE SUMMARY.
(Erase heading not required.)

Instructions regarding War Diaries and Intelligence Summaries are contained in F.S. Regs., Part II. and the Staff Manual respectively. Title pages will be prepared in manuscript.

Hour, Date, Place	Summary of Events and Information	Remarks and references to Appendices
VILLERS CHATEL. 20.7.16.	Party of 900 dismounted men relieving equal proportion of officers from Lucheux Rd. (K.O.), 29th Lancers & 36th Horse, and 100 from Joothieur Lancers proceeded to 60th Siege Trenches for mining fatigue.	P.
" — 26.7.16	Strength table places at disposal of VI Corps. working parties as under to take into work in 14th Divn at midnight 28/29th:- 17th Lancers R.O. 3. N.C.O. 9. O.R. 135 (three shifts) 6th Carry " 3. " 3. 103 N.C.O. 12 " 120 " " 19th Lancers " 3. " " 12 " 180 " " Rations for 29th to be taken in Limbers and issued-generally sent up daily by units.	R.
" — 30/31.7.16.	Julius Isle relieves the Lucheux Rd. working parties in 60th Siege trenches. Joothieur Lancers also relieves them.	R.

P.T.O.

Army Form C. 2118.

WAR DIARY
INTELLIGENCE SUMMARY.
(Erase heading not required.)

Hour, Date, Place	Summary of Events and Information	Remarks and references to Appendices
VILLERS CHATEL. 31.7.16.	Total casualties in working parties - Killed - I.O.R. 3. Wounded - B.OS. 2. B.O.R. 5. I.O.R. 9. Total Casualties in "U" Bty, R.H.A. - Killed. B.OS. 2 Wounded. " 3. B.O.R. 3 C.R. MacHardy Captain, D.A. and Q.M.G. 1st Ind. Cav. Div.	

No. Q-2665

APPX: I.

Headquarters,
1st Indian Cavalry Division.
3rd July 1916.

BILLETING AREA — 1ST INDIAN CAVALRY DIVISION.

UNIT	WHERE BILLETED
Divisional Headquarters	AUXI - LE - CHATEAU.
Signal Squadron	do.
O.C., A.S.C.	do.
A.D.M.S.	do.
A.D.V.S.	do.
D.A.D.O.S.	do.
R.H.A. Bde. H.Qrs.	Chateau DRUCAS.
"A", "Q" & "U" Batteries R.H.A.	WAVANS & BEAUVOIR RIVIERE.
Divisional Ammunition Column	
Divisional Ammunition Park	NOYEUX.
Jodhpur Lancers	LANNOY.
Field Squadron	AUXI - LE - CHATEAU.
Sialkot Cavalry Field Ambulance	NOYEUX.
Ambala Cavalry Field Ambulance	do.
Lucknow Cavalry Field Ambulance	do.
Sanitary Section	do.
Supply Column	GRAND BOURET.
Aux. H.T. Company	OCCOCHES.
No. 1 Indian Cavalry Reserve Park	BOUBERS SUR CANCHE.

SIALKOT Brigade:-
Headquarters	REMAISNIL.
17th Lancers	MEZEROLLES.
6th Cavalry	OUTRE BOIS.
19th Lancers	do.
Machine Gun Squadron	REMAISNIL.
Mobile Veterinary Section	do.

LUCKNOW Brigade:-
Headquarters	FROHEN-LE-GRAND.
1st K.D. Guards	do & FROHEN-LE-PETIT.
29th Lancers	VILLERS L'HOPITAL.
36th Jacob's Horse	do.
Machine Gun Squadron	FROHEN-LE-PETIT.
Mobile Veterinary Section	do.

MHOW Brigade:-
Headquarters	MAIZICOURT.
6th (Inniskilling) Dragoons	MAIZICOURT.
2nd Lancers	MAIZICOURT.
38th C.I. Horse	ST. ACHEUL.
Machine Gun Squadron	MONTLOUIS FERME.
Mobile Veterinary Section	MAIZICOURT.

Dismounted Men	REBREUVE.

G.R. Maitland
Capt for Lt. Colonel,
A.A. & Q.M.G., 1st Indian Cavalry Division.

To
Third Army "Q"
Brigades and Divisional units.

Q.-2816.

APPX: II

Headquarters,
1st Indian Cavalry Division
18th July 1916.

ADMINISTRATIVE INSTRUCTIONS
Issued in accordance with "G" 64

1.- The billeting areas will be as follows:-

Divisional Headquarters	(VILLERS CHATEL.
	(MINGOVAL.
Jodhpur Lancers	BETHONSART & GUESTREVILLE.
R.H.A. Brigade	(ACQ & ECOIVRES.
less S.A.A.Secn of D.A.C.	(Same billets as before
S.A.A.Secn D.A.C.	SAVY.
Divnl Ammn Park	SAVY.
Field Squadron	AGNIERES, just North of AUBIGNY.
Cav Fd Ambulances	One at ECOIVRES; remainder in TINCQUES.
Sanitary Section	TINCQUES
Divnl Supply Column	TINCQUES
A.H.T.Company	GAUCHIN VERLOINGT, west of ST POL.
Reserve Park	Remain at BOUBERS.
Mhow Brigade.	ST MICHEL - SUR - TERNOISE: GRAND CAMP : RO COURT ST LAURENT : ROELLECOURT.
Sialkot Brigade.	In the valley of R.GY.Area will be given later.
Lucknow Brigade	
Brigade Headquarters, advanced	ECOIVRES.
Brigade Area	VILLERS CAMBLIGNEUL and VILLERS BRULIN and BERLETTE.

Troops already in these billets are not to be moved. Details are sent herewith to those concerned.

2. Divisional Headquarters will water at VILLERS CAMBLIGNEUL. Jodhpur Lancers will water at troughs South of main road between TINCQUES and BERLES.
3. O.C.Field Squadron will obtain some extra water troughs from CE XVII Corps.
4. Staff Captain of Lucknow Brigade and Billeting officers of Field Squadron, D.A.P. and D.A.C. will meet a Divnl Staff Officer at SAVY Railway Station at 10 a.m. 19th.   10 a.m.
5. There are 127 tents pitched on rising ground at ST MICHEL on South side of ST POL - ARRAS main road. These are available for the Mhow Brigade; and will be taken over there from D.D.O.S. XVII Corps.
6. Railhead opens at TINCQUES on 19th. 20
7. All units will send back two men to-day on the empty Supply lorries to accompany the Supply Column to-morrow and take charge of dumped rations at new billets.
8. Orders for the move of the D.M. will follow. They will rejoin their units in the new billets.
9. Ordnance and postal lorries will move with the Supply Column Hqrs.

W K Bourne
Lieut-Colonel,
A.A. and Q.M.G. 1st Indian Cavalry Division.

No. Q.-2831

Headquarters,
1st Indian Cavalry Division.
19th July 1916.

BILLETING AREA- 1ST INDIAN CAVALRY DIVISION.

UNIT	WHERE BILLETED.
Divisional Headquarters	VILLERS CHATEL.
Signal Squadron	do.
O.C.,A.S.C.	MINGOVAL.
A.D.M.S.	SAVY.
A.D.V.S.	SAVY.
D.A.D.O.S.	VILLERS CHATEL.
R.H.A.Bde. H.Qrs	ECOIVRES.
"A", "Q" Batteries R.H.A.	ACQ & FREVENT CAPELLE.
Divisional Ammunition Column	ACQ.
Divisional Ammunition Park	SAVY.
Jodhpur Lancers	BETHONSART GUESTREVILLE.
Field Squadron	AGNIERES.
Sialkot Cavalry Field Ambulance	TINQUES.
Ambala Cavalry Field Ambulance	TINQUES.
Lucknow Cavalry Field Ambulance	MARCEUIL.
Jodhpur Cavalry Field Ambulance	TINQUES.
Sanitary Section	do.
Supply Column	do.
Aux H.T.Company	GAUCHIN VERLOINGT.
No.1.Indian Cavalry Reserve Park	BOUBERS SUR CANCHE.
Field Cashier	TINQUES.

SIALKOT Brigade:-

Headquarters	AGNEZ-LES-DUISANS.
17th Lancers	GOUVES.
6th Cavalry	AGNEZ-LES-DUISANS.
19th Lancers	do.
Machine Gun Squadron	GOUVES.
Mobile Veterinary Section	AGNEZ-LES-DUISANS.

LUCKNOW Brigade:-

Headquarters	VILLERS-BRULIN.
1st K.D.Guards	CAMBLIGNEUL.
29th Lancers	do.
36th Jacob's Horse	VILLERS-BRULIN.
Machine Gun Squadron	BETHENCOURT.
Mobile Veterinary Section	VILLERS-BRULIN.

MHOW Brigade:-

Headquarters	ROELLECOURT.
6th (INNISKILLING) Dragoons	ST MICHEL.
2nd Lancers	Grand Camp-Rocourt-Boirin.
38th C.I.Horse	ROELLECOURT.
Machine Gun Squadron	do.
Mobile Veterinary Section	do.

CKBourne
Lieut-Colonel,
A.A.&.Q.M.G. 1st Indian Cavalry Division.

To,
Third Army "Q"
Brigades and Divisional Units.

SECRET

WAR DIARY - ADMINISTRATIVE BRANCH - 1st INDIAN CAVALRY DIVISION.

AUGUST 1st to 31st 1916.

Army Form C. 2118.

WAR DIARY
or
INTELLIGENCE SUMMARY
(Erase heading not required.)

Instructions regarding War Diaries and Intelligence Summaries are contained in F. S. Regs., Part II. and the Staff Manual respectively. Title Pages will be prepared in manuscript.

Place	Date	Hour	Summary of Events and Information	Remarks and references to Appendices
VILLERS CHATEL.	1.8.16	—	Departure of the Exchange Party — 50 all ranks from each Indian Cavalry Regiment proceeding Jodhpur Lancers — for MARSEILLES BASE.	A.
— " —	7.8.16	—	Further allotment of 500 Steel helmets for the Division.	A.
— " —	8.8.16	—	Additional allotment of 1000 Steel helmets for the Division.	A.
— " —	9.8.16	—	Move of Lucknow Bde into VIIth Corps area. Railhead for all rations except Indian rations, at LARBRET-SAVLTY for loading and for distribution on 9th, and for concentration on 10th. Indian rations to continue to be sent from the Division direct by lorry. Billets:— Bde Hdqrs. .... PAS. M.V.S. ..... — " — 1st H.Bg .... — " — M.G. Sqn.(less 1 section each with 29th Lancers and 36th Horse) ... HUMBERCOURT. 29th Lancers and 1 Section M.G. Sqdn .... WARLINCOURT.	A.

P.T.O.

Continued - 2.

Army Form C. 2118.

WAR DIARY
INTELLIGENCE SUMMARY
(Erase heading not required.)

Place	Date	Hour	Summary of Events and Information	Remarks and references to Appendices
VILLERS CHATEL.	9.8.16		36th Horse and 1 Section M.G. Sqdn - GUADIEMPRE. Lucknow Cav: Fd: Ambulance - ST AMAND.	
— " —	10.8.16		Issue of Instructions regarding changes to take place in billeting area. Issued revised billeting list of the Divn.	APPX: I II
— " —	29.8.16		Further S.S.O. Steel helmets allotted to the Divn.	III.
— " —	— " —		Divn. completed with additional 80 Hotchkiss guns, each British and Indian Cavalry Regiment in the Divn. including Jodhpur Lancers is now equipped with 16 of these guns.	III.
— " —	— " —		Third Army intimated that in consequence of Rations of Corn having fallen so low arrangements have been made for increased amounts to be sent to Railhead. This Division to receive 80 tons per week.	IV.
			Total casualties among working parties in The	

Continued – 3.

Army Form C. 2118.

WAR DIARY
INTELLIGENCE SUMMARY
(Erase heading not required.)

Place	Date	Hour	Summary of Events and Information	Remarks and references to Appendices

The line during the month –

        B.O. Io. B.OR. I.OR.

Killed – 2. – 7. 4.
Wounded – 1. 2. 21. 21.

Names of Officers killed –
Captain E.B. EGERTON, 17th Lancers.
2nd Lieut. B.A. CARVER, 6th Dragoons.

E R Whitam
Major.
B.M. & ? ? , 1st Indian Cavalry Division.

APPX: I

SECRET. No. Q-3019 Headquarters,
1st Indian Cavalry Division.
9th August 1916.

ADMINISTRATIVE INSTRUCTIONS.

The following changes will take place in billeting areas on the morning of the 10th instant.

Mhow Brigade)	CAMBLIGNEUL, PENIN,
Sialkot Cav.F.Amb.)	DOFFINE Farm, and
Sanitary Section)	part of TINQUES.
Jodhpur Lancers	SAVY.
Jodhpur Cav.F.Amb.	AGNIERES.

2. If Mhow Brigade wish to place their Brigade Hd.Qrs. in TINQUES, they will allot billets in PENIN for the Sialkot Cav.F.Amb. If Brigade Hd.Qrs. goes to PENIN, the Sialkot Cav.F.Amb. will be billeted in TINQUES.
   Mhow Brigade will inform Divl.Hd.Qrs. of dispositions by 2.00 p.m., 9th instant.

3. One Squadron Hampshire Carabineers are moving out of SAVY to make room for the Jodhpur Lancers.

4. Billets are allotted in TINQUES and SAVY by the Town Majors of those places. The Town Major of SAVY has his office in AUBIGNY.

5. O.C., A.S.C. will detail 6 lorries to be at CAMBLIGNEUL at 6.00 p.m. on 9th to move men back, who are required to assist in moving the horses of Mhow Brigade.

6. XVIIth Corps have arranged to place 15 C.S.L. tents at the disposal of the Town Major TINQUES, in order to free billets there for the Division

WK Browne
Lt.Colonel,
A.A.& Q.M.G., 1st Ind.Cav.Division.

To
Three Brigades	A.D.M.S.	D.A.D.O.S.
R.H.A. Bde.	A.D.V.S.	A.P.M.
Jodhpur Lancers	O.C., A.S.C.	O.C., Salvage Sqdn.
Field Squadron	Signal Squadron	Postal Inspector.
	General Staff.	Field Cashier.

Copy to XVII Corps. Q
Town major SAVY.
" " TINQUES.

SECRET.   No. Q 3031   Headquarters,
                      1st Indian Cavalry Division.
                      10th. August. 1916.

APPX: II

BILLETING AREA - 1ST INDIAN CAVALRY DIVISION.

UNIT.	WHERE BILLETED
Divisional Headquarters	VILLERS CHATEL.
Signal Squadron	Do.
O.C., A.S.C.	MINGOVAL.
A.D.M.S.	SAVY
A.D.V.S.	SAVY
D.A.D.O.S.	VILLERS CHATEL.
R.H.A. Bde. H.Qrs.	Maroeuil.
"A"."Q", Batteries R.H.A.	ACQ & FREVIN CAPELLE.
Divisional Ammunition Column	FREVIN CAPELLE.
Divisional Ammunition Park	SAVY.
Field Squadron	AGNIERES.
Jodphur Lancers	SAVY.
Sialkot Cavalry Field Ambulance	TINCQUETTES.
Ambala Cavalry Field Ambulance	ACQ.
Lucknow Cavalry Field Ambulance	St AMAND.
Jodphur Cavalry Field Ambulance	AGNIERES.
Sanitary Section	TINCQUETTES.
Supply Column	TINQUES.
Aux H.T. Company	Fm duBOIS de la TELUSE.
No 1, Indian Cavalry Reserve Park	HERNICOURT.
Field Cashier	TINQUES.

SIALKOT Brigade, attached VI Corps :-

Headquarters	AGNEZ-LEZ-DUISANS.
17th Lancers	GOUVES.
6th Cavalry	AGNEZ-LEZ-DUISANS.
19th Lancers	Do.
Machine Gun Squadron	GOUVES.
Mobile Veterinary Section	AGNEZ-LEZ-DUISANS.

LUCKNOW Brigade attached VII Corps.

Headquarters	PAS.
1st, K. D. Guards	HUMBERCOURT. BERLES-AU-BOIS. LA CAUCHIE.
29th Lancers.&.1.sec.M.G.Sqdn.	WARLINCOURT. SOUASTRE.
36th Jacobs' Horse. & 1 sec M.G.Sqdn.	GAUDIEMPRE. SOUASTRE.
Machine G. Sqdn.(less 1 sec with each 29th L, and 36th J.H.)	HUMBERCOURT.
Mobile Veterinary Section	PAS

MHOW Brigade :-

Headquarters	CAMBLIGNEUL.
6th (INNISKILLING) Dragoons	PENIN.
2nd Lancers	MAGNICOURT-SUR-CANCHE.
38th, C.I. Horse	CAMBLIGNEUL.
Machine Gun Squadron	Do.
Mobile Veterinary Section	Do.

W K Browne
Lieut-Colonel.
A.A. & Q.M.G. 1st Indian Cavalry Division

To,
    Third Army "Q"
        Three Brigades.   A.D.M.S.   D.A.D.O.S.
        R.H.A. Bde.   A.D.V.S.   A.P.M.
        Jodphur Lancers.   O.C.,A.S.C.   O.C. Salvage Sqdn.
        Field Squadron.   SIGNAL SQDN.   Postal Inspector.
            GENERAL STAFF.   Field Cashier.

SECRET

WAR DIARY — ADMINISTRATIVE BRANCH — 1st INDIAN CAVALRY DIVISION.

SEPTEMBER 1st — 30th. 1916.

Army Form C. 2118.

WAR DIARY
INTELLIGENCE SUMMARY
(Erase heading not required.)

Instructions regarding War Diaries and Intelligence Summaries are contained in F.S. Regs., Part II. and the Staff Manual respectively. Title Pages will be prepared in manuscript.

Place	Date	Hour	Summary of Events and Information	Remarks and references to Appendices
VILLERS CHATEL.	1.9.16.	—	Administrative instructions issued to all concerned regarding move of Divn to new area.	APPX: I.
FROHEN LE GRAND.	3.9.16.	—	Division arrived today and billeted for the night en route to ST RIQUIER Training area.	
ST RIQUIER	4.9.16.	—	Division arrived today. To carry out Training. Billeting list.	APPX: II.
— do —	9.9.16.	—	Divisional (?) Train moved by Rail to ALBERT for work under Corps. To be [struck through] supplied by 2nd Ammunition Store.	
DOULLENS.	11.9.16.	—	Division arrived today. R.H.A. Bde less "R" Bty rejoined Divn from duty with XVII Corps.	
ALLONVILLE	13.9.16.	—	Division arrived today. Railhead to be FRECHENCOURT.	
— " —	13.9.16.	—	Conversion of the Auxiliary H.T. Coy into a Horse Reserve Park consisting of 40 Bn wagons for carriage of ammunition and approximately the same amount as to carriage by a Coly. Ammn. Park Coy to be loaded under Divisional arrangements and to be attached to, and remain with, the heavy section of the Divnl Ammn. Column, being moved up as opportunity offers under orders from Corps Hdqrs. Formation of two Ammunition dumps, one at LA BOISSELLE and one at BRIQUETERIE each containing 200 rounds per gun for 18 pr. and 13 pr., and	

Army Form C. 2118.

WAR DIARY
INTELLIGENCE SUMMARY

(Erase heading not required.)

Instructions regarding War Diaries and Intelligence Summaries are contained in F.S. Regs., Part II and the Staff Manual respectively. Title Pages will be prepared in manuscript.

Place	Date	Hour	Summary of Events and Information	Remarks and references to Appendices
Continued.			100 rounds per 3-pr Hotchkiss, and 500,000 rounds of S.A.A. to be drawn from the dumps at any time when impossible to draw from Railhead in the normal manner. Orders issued for S.A.A. & Bela and such to continue to demand as normally from the Divnl Ammn. Column, which in turn draws from The Park.	
ALLONVILLE	13.9.16		Formation of a Limbered Wagon Train of 58 lorries to carry a further 2 days supplies per man at a somewhat reduced ration, and 4 lbs of oats per horse.	
MORLANCOURT	15.9.16		Division moved to a position of readiness SOUTH of DERNANCOURT and went into bivouac, opening Divnl Report Centre at MORLANCOURT, and leaving "B" Echelon, Divnl Ammn. Park, M. Vet. of Divnl Ammn. Column behind in bivouac NORTH of QUERRIEU.	
"	15.9.16		Divisions Reserves dumped at Dernancourt also.	
"	17.9.16		Railhead now at ALBERT.	
"	18.9.16		Steel Helmets complete to 1 per man all authorised.	
"	18.9.16		Divnl Ammn. Park moved up to CACHILLOT FARM - EAST of MEAULTE.	

WAR DIARY or INTELLIGENCE SUMMARY

Army Form C. 2118.

Place	Date	Hour	Summary of Events and Information	Remarks and references to Appendices
(continued) MORLANCOURT	18.9.16	-	Field Squadron to various order of Cavalry Corps for work, and went to R from R.E.S.E of FRICOURT. To continue to be supplied by Divn.	
"	25.9.16	-	Divn. moved up to FRICOURT leaving "B" Echelon detail at GUERRIEU. Cavalry Advanced Report Centre at MONTAUBAN with Rear Report Centre at FRICOURT. Returned to bivouac in the evening.	
BUSSY LES DAOURS	27.9.16	-	Divn. returned back to BUSSY area, and "B" Echelon rejoined. Railhead CORBIE.	
PICQUIGNY	28.9.16	-	Divn. arrived today. Limbers Ammn. Pars after returning loads to CORBIE Bugs and E.S.C. Dump returned to No.10 Reserve Park.	
AILLY LE HAUT CLOCHER	29.9.16	-	Divn. arrived in this area today. Railhead changed to ST RIQUIER.	
"	29.9.16	-	Completing M.T. Coy handed over all ammunition in charge to O.L. CONTAY, and returned all spare parts etc to R.H.H. Base, and toy remaining ments Coy to Div.	
LIGESCOURT	30.9.16	-	Division arrived in CRECY area today. Railhead changed to BEAURAINVILLE. List of billets.	APPX III
"	30.9.16	-	Dismounted Men rejoined the Divn.	

Army Form C. 2118.

WAR DIARY
or
INTELLIGENCE SUMMARY

(Erase heading not required.)

Place	Date	Hour	Summary of Events and Information	Remarks and references to Appendices
LIGNESCOURT.	30.9.16.		Total number of casualties in Division during the month:-	
			KILLED.	
			3 - B.O.R.	
			5 O.R.	
			WOUNDED	
			1 B.O. (Capt. E.W. SPURRIN, 329th Lancers).	
			7 B.OR.	
			28 O.R.	
			A.E.Whittorne	
			Major	
			Brd Bde., 1st Mounted Div.	

SECRET.   O. 3142.   Headquarters.
                              1st Indian Cavalry Division.
                              1st September, 1916.

ADMINISTRATIVE INSTRUCTIONS.
Reference O.O.22.

1. **MOVEMENTS OF DISMOUNTED MEN.**

    (1). One lorry per regiment will report at Brigade Headquarters and Jodphur Lancers Headquarters at 7 a.m., on 3rd inst, to carry kits only of dismounted men, to the FROHEN-LE-GRAND billeting area. They should leave units, loaded with the kits and units representatives, by 7-30 a.m., and be released after dumping kits in the new billet, by 10-30 a.m.

    (2). These lorries will then proceed to MANIN Church at 2 p.m., The dismounted men of the Sialkot Brigade will be at MANIN at that hour and go on the lorries to VILLERS L'HOPITAL whence the dismounted men will march to their billets.
    The lorries when released will proceed back to the units whose kits they lifted in the morning.

    (3). The D.M., of Lucknow and Mhow Brigades will march to their billeting area.

    (4). In addition 5 lorries will be at Jodphur Lancers H.Q., at Savy at 2 p.m., on the 3rd and will carry their D.M., to billets at BARLEY.

2. On 4th inst, these lorries (one per regiment) will lift the D.M. kits to BUIRE-AU-BOIS, and dump them in charge of the regimental representatives by 8 a.m. when the lorries will be released.
    Dismounted parties will march to BUIRE-AU-BOIS.

3. The dismounted men will remain in BUIRE-AU-BOIS from the 4th inst, during the stay of the Division in the training area.
    Capt H. Clarke, 6th Dragoons will command the D.M., as long as they remain together.

4. POSTAL. Mails will be delivered in new billets each day.

5. There will be no delivery of Ordnance Stores till the 4th inst in the ST RICQUIER area (except for R.H.A Brigade.).

6. Tents that cannot be lifted will be left with Maires and lifted later under Divisional arrangements.
    A report on number of tents left and where left will be furnished to Divisional Headquarters by 4th inst.

7. Notes on FROHEN-LE-GRAND Billeting area are attached.

                                        G R Maitland
                                        ─────────────
                                        Major.
                    D.A.A.& Q.M.G. 1st Indian Cavalry Division.

To, No 1. Sialkot Bde.   6. Signal Sqdn.   13. Camp Commdt.
    2. Mhow Bde.   7. R.H.A. Bde.   14. "G"
    3. Lucknow Bde.   8. O.C., A.S.C.   15. Third Army.
    4. Jodphur Lrs.   9. A.D.M.S.
    5. Field Sqdn.   10. A.D.V.S
                          11. Liaison Offr.

APPX.II

No. Q. 3156.   Headquarters,
                                          1st Indian Cavalry Division.
S E C R E T   4th September, 1916.

BILLETING AREA - 1ST INDIAN CAVALRY DIVISION.

UNIT.	WHERE BILLETED.
Divisional Headquarters	ST RICQUIER.
Signal Squadron	-do-
O.C., A.S.C.	-do-
A.D.M.S.	-do-
A.D.V.S.	-do-
D.A.D.O.S.	-do-
R.H.A. Bde. Hd Qrs	MARIEUIL.
"A", "Q", Batteries R.H.A.	ACQ & FREVIN CAPPELLE.
Divisional Ammunition Column S.A.A	CONTEVILLE.
Divisional Ammunition Park "A" Sect.	-do-
Field Squadron	ST RICQUIER.
Jodhpur Lancers	NEUF MOULIN.
Sialkot Cavalry Field Ambulance	MILLENCOURT
Ambala Cavalry Field Ambulance	ARGEN VILLERS.
Lucknow Cavalry Field Ambulance	-do-
Jodhpur Cavalry Field Ambulance	MILLENCOURT.
Sanitary Section	-do-
Supply Column	ST RICQUIER.
Aux H.T. Company	Fm du BOIS de la TELUSE.
No 1 Indian Cavalry Reserve Park	HERNICOURT.
Field Cashier	ST RICQUIER.

SIALKOT Brigade:-
Headquarters	DRUCAT.
17th Lancers	DRUCAT. CAOURS. L'HEURE.
6th Cavalry	NEUILLY. L'HOPITAL.
19th Lancers	LE PLESSIEL.
Machine Gun Squadron	NEUILLY L'HOPITAL.
Mobile Veterinary Section	MILL L'HEURE.

LUCKNOW BRIGADE :-
Headquarters	BRAILLY.
1st K.D. Guards	CANCHY.
29th Lancers	DOMVAST.
36th Jacob's Horse	GAPENNES.
Machine Gun Squadron	BRAILLY.
Mobile Veterinary Section	BRAILLY.

MHOW BRIGADE.
Headquarters	NOYELLE-EN-CHAUSSEE.
6th (Inniskilling) Dragoons	GUESCHART.
2nd Lancers	GUESCHART & CUMONVILLE.
38th C.I. Horse	MAISON-PONTHIEU.
Machine Gun Squadron	NEUILLY LE DIEN.
Mobile Veterinary Section	NOYELLE-EN-CHAUSSEE.

G R Maitland
                                                    Major.
                    D.A.A. & Q.M.G., 1st Indian Cavalry Division.

To,
Third Army "Q"	A.D.M.S.	A.P.M.
Three Brigades.	A.D.V.S.	O.C. Salvage Sqdn.
R.H.A. Bde.	O.C., A.S.C.	Postal Inspt.
Jodhpur Lrs.	Signal Sqdn.	Field Cashier.
Field Squadron	D.A.D.O.S.	R.T.O. Railhead.
		General Staff.

To be substituted for list issued with No. Q-3973
dated 30th September, 1916.

APPx: III

Headquarters,
1st Indian Cavalry Division.
3rd October, 1916.

No. Q-4008.

BILLETING AREA - 1ST INDIAN CAVALRY DIVISION.

UNIT	WHERE BILLETED.
Divisional Headquarters	LIGESCOURT.
Signal Squadron	,,
O.C., A.S.C.	,,
A.D.M.S.)	WADICOURT.
A.D.V.S.)	
D.A.D.O.S.	LIGESCOURT.
O.C., R.H.A.	Ch. South of last E of BOIS de St. SAULVE.
Divisional Ammn Column	ESTREE-LES-CRECY.
Divisional Ammn Park	LABROYE - LE BOISLE.
Field Squadron	Fm. ½ m. North of CRECY on LIGESCOURT Road.
Jodhpur Lancers	FONTAINE-SUR-MAYE.
Jodhpur Lancers Escort	ROSSIGNOL.
Sialkot Cav Field Ambulance	ESTREE-LES-CRECY.
Ambala --do--	WADICOURT.
Jodhpur --do--	ESTREE-LES-CRECY.
Lucknow --do--	CRECY.
Sanitary Section	ESTREE-LES-CRECY.
Divisional Supply Column	LABROYE - LE BOISLE
Aux. H.T.Coy	Out of Division.
No. 1. Indian Cav. Reserve Park	--do--
Field Cashier	LABROYE.

SIALKOT Brigade.
Headquarters	Pt. PREAUX.
17th Lancers	VIRONCHEAUX.
"Q" Battery. R.H.A	ARGOULES.
6th Cavalry	DOMINOIS.
19th Lancers	LE PETIT CHEMIN.
Machine Gun Squadron	ARGOULES.
Mobile Veterinary Section	Fm. ½ m. West of A of ARGOULES

LUCKNOW Brigade.
Headquarters	CRECY.
1st K.D.Guards	MACHY.
"U" Battery. R.H.A	CRECY.
29th Lancers	† CAUMARTIN - MACHIEL.
36th Jacob's Horse	CRECY.
Machine Gun Squadron	CRECY.
Mobile Veterinary Section	SAW MILL.

MHOW Brigade.
Headquarters	DOURIEZ.
6th (Inniskilling) Dragoons	† DOMPIERRE - VOISIN.
"A" Battery. R.H.A	† LE BOISLE - VERGEOLLAY.
2nd Lancers	RAYE-SUR-AUTHIE.
38th C.I.Horse	DOURIEZ.
Machine Gun Squadron	LABROYE.
Mobile Veterinary Section	DOURIEZ.

† Denotes H.Q.

G.R.Maitland Major
for Lieut-Colonel.
A.A. & Q.M.G. 1st Indian Cavalry Division.

To,
G.H.Q.Troops.	A.D.M.S.	O.C. Salvage Squadron.
Cavalry Corps Q.	A.D.V.S.	A.D.P.S.
Three Brigades.	O.C., A.S.C.	Postal Inspector.
O.C., R.H.A.	Signal Squadron.	Field Cashier.
Jodhpur Lancers.	D.A.D.O.S.	R.T.O.Railhead.
Field Squadron.	A.P.M.	General Staff.
		Camp Commdt.

Original

Secret

WAR DIARY.

ADMINISTRATIVE BRANCH – 1ST INDIAN CAVALRY DIVISION.

1st October to 31st October, 1916.

Army Form C. 2118.

WAR DIARY
or
INTELLIGENCE SUMMARY
(Erase heading not required.)

Instructions regarding War Diaries and Intelligence Summaries are contained in F. S. Regs., Part II. and the Staff Manual respectively. Title Pages will be prepared in manuscript.

Place	Date	Hour	Summary of Events and Information	Remarks and references to Appendices
LIGESCOURT	19th/18th October		Division remains in temporary billets.	
"	19th Oct.		HdQrs R.H.A. Bde, 3 Batteries, and four Sections of Divl Ammn. Park proceeded to HAVERNAS for attachment to 1st British Cavalry Division.	
"	-"-		The Three B.de Machine Gun Squadrons detailed for attachment to Reserve Army proceed to work in the Trenches. The number of the three Squadrons to move on 21st inst. to the area OUTREBOIS—OCCOCHES West of DOULLENS and march to SAILLY—AU—BOIS on 22nd at which place they will report to Town Major for instructions and billets. The personnel of the three Squadrons to be moved by Motor Lorries on 22nd inst. The British personnel to be entrained by XIII Corps, and the Indian personnel being rationed by the Bde from our Railhead. Lorry to run out on alternate days carrying two days rations commencing with issues on 23rd to accommodate 24th and 25th Inst. to report XIII Corps Troops Supply Column.	
"	22nd Oct.		R.H.A. Bde rejoined the Division today.	
"	28th Oct.		A working party of 100 dismounted men will form proportion of	

2449 Wt. W14957/M90 750,000 1/16 J.B.C. & A. Forms/C.2118/12.

Army Form C. 2118.

WAR DIARY
INTELLIGENCE SUMMARY
(Erase heading not required.)

Place	Date	Hour	Summary of Events and Information	Remarks and references to Appendices

continued			Officers for work in XIII Corps area moved out to-day. Party to continue to be fed from this Bric, a Lorry being sent daily to XIII Corps Troops Supply Column, and being sent on from there. Mails for this party to be sorted by unit- and sent back to Supply Column & returning lorries and to go up with rations on following day.
			
			Casualties during M.C. Sgdn. and Dismounted party during month:—
			
			    KILLED. Nil.
			    WOUNDED. 6. B.O.R.	

E.M. Waterman Major,
O.H.Q. H.Q., 1st Ind. Cav. Div.

WAR DIARY

ADMINISTRATIVE BRANCH, 4th CAVALRY DIVISION.

NOVEMBER 1st to 30th, 1916.

Army Form C. 2118.

WAR DIARY
INTELLIGENCE SUMMARY

(Erase heading not required.)

Instructions regarding War Diaries and Intelligence Summaries are contained in F. S. Regs., Part II. and the Staff Manual respectively. Title Pages will be prepared in manuscript.

Place	Date	Hour	Summary of Events and Information	Remarks and references to Appendices
ST VALERY.	2.11.16.		Division moved into Winter billets today. Billeting list —	APPX. I.
-"-	6.11.16.		The Auxiliary M.T. Coy, A.S.C., reporied Division, and billeted temporarily at FRESSENNEVILLE.	
-"-	11.11.16.		Dismounted men reported the Division from XIII Corps today.	
-"-	17.11.16.		G.O.C. Division presented ribbons of medals recently awarded to officers and other ranks of the Division today in the Square at ESCARBOTIN.	
-"-	19.11.16.		"A" and "H" Batteries, R.H.A. less Indian personnel proceeded to join Fourth Army. "N" Bty. Horse Artillery Section of Ammn. Column or Park to be attached to Fourth Army Artillery School at VAUX-EN-AMIENOIS; "A" Bty. with Section of Ammn. Column and Park to be attached to 3w Corps for duty in the line on 3w Corps front. Mules for these two batteries to be diverted at BOULOGNE. Rations for them being drawn at the	A.R.

2449 Wt. W14957/M90 750,000 1/16 J.B.C. & A. Forms/C.2118/12.

Continued—page 2.

Army Form C. 2118.

WAR DIARY
or
INTELLIGENCE SUMMARY

(Erase heading not required.)

Place	Date	Hour	Summary of Events and Information	Remarks and references to Appendices
ST VALERY.	20.11.16.	—	Reinforcements for the last time today, rationing them up to and for 21st inst.	
— " —	20.11.16.	—	Party of one Indian officer per Indian cavalry Regiment from the Division with 3 Indian Orderlies proceed to England as representatives of the Indian Army for a flag and Shield given to India by the League of Empire, which H.M. Queen Alexandra has graciously consented to present on 23rd inst.	
— " —	20.11.16.	—	Indian Brigade M.G. Squadron rejoins Division from the Trenches today.	
— " —	21.11.16.	—	The C. in C. having sanctioned a proposal made by G.O.C. Cavy Corps, that each Cavy Rgt. should form a dismounted Pioneer Battn. from about the end of November until the end of Jany. to work in whatever part of the line they are most required, the Pioneer Battns. from each of the Lucknow & Mhow Bdes. proceeded today to join 3rd Corps and 1st Anzac Corps.	

(contd - page - 3)

WAR DIARY
INTELLIGENCE SUMMARY
(Erase heading not required.)

Army Form C. 2118.

Instructions regarding War Diaries and Intelligence Summaries are contained in F.S. Regs., Part II. and the Staff Manual respectively. Title Pages will be prepared in manuscript.

Place	Date	Hour	Summary of Events and Information	Remarks and references to Appendices
			respectively. Indian ratios for these two Battns to be drawn from ALBERT. British rations and animals from respective Corps Echelons.	
ST VALERY	21.11.16.		Lucknow Cav. Field Ambulance proceeded to join Fourth Army for attachment to 14th Corps, arrangements regarding rations to be the same as for the Pioneer Battns.	
- " -	22.11.16.		Exchange Party of Indians consisting of 1 I.O. and 131 I.O.R. arrived from Base, ROUEN, today.	
- " -	25.11.16.		Similar exchange party left for Base, MARSEILLES, today.	
- " -	26.11.16.		Lucknow Field Ambulance M.G. Section left for the M.G. Squadrons reported to be from Trenches.	
- " -	28.11.16.		In consequence of decisions from G.H.Q. to practically replace the Indian Sections of the M.G. Squadrons by Irregular Cavalry	R.

Army Form C. 2118.

WAR DIARY
INTELLIGENCE SUMMARY

(Erase heading not required.)

contd- page 6t

Instructions regarding War Diaries and Intelligence Summaries are contained in F. S. Regs., Part II. and the Staff Manual respectively. Title Pages will be prepared in manuscript.

Place	Date	Hour	Summary of Events and Information	Remarks and references to Appendices
ITYALERY	28.11.16.	—	Divisions by British sections thus bringing these sections in to an all British basis. The below Brigade M.G. personnel and transports completed to the new establishment, i.e. to that laid down in War Establishment, Part VII, dated 18.9.16. the Indian personnel involved implied rejoining their respective units.	
—	30.11.16.	—	Detachment of the Divnl Reserve Park - strength 3 officers, 141 O.R., and 173 horses - rejoined Divn.	
—	30.11.16.	—	"Q" Bty, R.H.A. was re-armed today with 13 pr. guns, number of ammunition wagons. the 18 pr. equipment being loaded the same Frame day and returned to Base. Casualties amongst the various units detached from the Divn during the month. B.O. B.O. I.O. B.O.R. I.O.R. killed - — 1 1 8 wounded - 4 — 10 24. missing - — — — 1.	Major D.A.Q.M.G. 15th Cav Divn

CONFIDENTIAL.   No. Q-4742.

Appx: I

Headquarters,
1st Indian Cavalry Division.
24th November. 1916.

BILLETING AREA - 1ST INDIAN CAVALRY DIVISION.

UNIT.	WHERE BILLETED.
Divisional Headquarters	ST VALERY.
Jodhpur Durbar	SAUCOURT.
Field Cashier	FRESSENNEVILLE.
Signal Squadron	ST VALERY.
Field Squadron. R.E.	BOISMONT.
C.R.H.A.	ST VALERY.
1st Ind. R.H.A. Bde. Ammunition Col.	FRESSENNEVILLE.
Ammunition Park	PINCHEFALISE.
Divisional Supply Column	FRESSENNEVILLE.
Sanitary Section	- do -
Auxiliary Horse Transport Co.	FRIVILLE.
No.1. Indian Cav. Res. Park	FRIVILLE.
Lucknow Casualty Clearing Station	FRESSENNEVILLE.
Divisional School	CAYEUX.
Divisional Gas School	CAYEUX.
Divisional Rest Camp	FRESSENNEVILLE.
Horse Dip	FRIVILLE.
Railhead	WOINCOURT.

SIALKOT BRIGADE :-

Brigade Headquarters	PENDE.
17th Lancers	ST BLIMONT. VAUDRICOURT. TILLOY.
6th Cavalry	ARREST. ESTREBOEUF. RIBEAUVILLE.
19th Lancers	CAYEUX. WATHIEHURT.
"Q" Battery. R.H.A.	SALLENELLE.
Machine Gun Squadron	MONS. BOUBERT.
Sialkot Cavalry Field Ambulance	Out of Division.
Mobile Veterinary Section	PENDE.

LUCKNOW BRIGADE :-

Brigade Headquarters	MOYENNEVILLE.
1st (King's) Dragoon Guards	MIANNAY. BOUILLANCOURT. LAMBERCOURT
29th Lancers	CHEPY. ACHEUX.
36th Jacob's Horse	CAHON. LE MONTANT. QUESNOY.
"U" Battery. R.H.A.	Out of Division.
Machine Gun Squadron	HYMMEVILLE. CAMPAGNE. QUESNOY.
Lucknow Cavalry Field Ambulance	ACHEUX.
Mobile Veterinary Section	HYMMEVILLE.

MHOW BRIGADE :-

Brigade Headquarters	ESCARBOTIN. BELLOY.
6th (Inniskilling) Dragoons	ESCARBOTIN.
2nd Lancers	BRUTELLES. LALEU. LANCHERES.
38th C.I.Horse	NIBAS. OCHANCOURT. LE BOCQUET.
"A" Battery. R.H.A.	Out of Division.
Machine Gun Squadron	OFFEUX.
Ambala Cavalry Field Ambulance	BOUBERT.
Mobile Veterinary Section	BELLOY.

Jodhpur Lancers	VALINES, ST MARC, SAUCOURT. FRIREULLES.
Jodhpur Cavalry Field Ambulance	MONCHEAUX.

W.K.Bourne
Lieut-Colonel.
A.A. & Q.M.G. 1st Indian Cavalry Division.

To, Cavalry Corps "Q" & "G"
 Three Brigades.
 O.C., R.H.A. Bde.
 Jodhpur Lrs.
 D.A.D.O.S.
 A.D.M.S.
 A.D.V.S.
 O.C., A.S.C.
 Signal Sqdn.
 Camp Commandant.
 Salvage Sqdn.
 A.B.P.S.
 Postal Inspector.
 Field Cashier.
 A.P.M.

SECRET.

WAR DIARY

ADMINISTRATIVE BRANCH — ~~HEAVY~~ 1 DIV DIVISION

1st to 31st December, 1916.

Army Form C. 2118.

WAR DIARY
INTELLIGENCE SUMMARY
(Erase heading not required.)

Place	Date	Hour	Summary of Events and Information	Remarks and references to Appendices
ST VALERY	1st Dec. 1916.	—	Routine.	
"	2nd	—	Partial use of Horse Transport instead of mechanical transport for supply of units within reach of Railhead.	
"	3rd & 9th	—	Routine	
"	10th	—	Advanced Parks, Sialkot Pioneer Battn. Officers 5, O.R. 20 proceeded to III rd Corps.	
"	11th & 12th	—	Routine.	
"	13th	—	Sialkot Pioneer Battn. strength as under, relieved when P.B. (incl. Corps). Officers 22, O.R. 794, Horses 72, Vehicles 2-wheeled 25, 4-" 4	
"	14th	—	Lucknow P.B. carries out its own disp. Transport not changed. (1 Anzac Corps).	GP.

Army Form C. 2118.

WAR DIARY
INTELLIGENCE SUMMARY

Part 2.

Instructions regarding War Diaries and Intelligence Summaries are contained in F. S. Regs., Part II. and the Staff Manual respectively. Title Pages will be prepared in manuscript.

(Erase heading not required.)

Place	Date	Hour	Summary of Events and Information	Remarks and references to Appendices
ST VALERY	13th Dec. 30th			
"	31st Dec. 1916.		Telegrams received from Chief General Staff, India, conveying sanction of Government of India to:—	
			(1) Free rations to all combatant Indian ranks of Indian Army except when on leave or furlough.	
			(2) Increase of pay to Indian ranks. The grant of special field allowances not to have the effect by these increases of affecting retiring and special pensions.	
			(3) Increase of rates of family allotment for combatant ranks of the Indian Army with effect from 4th August 1914.	
			(4) Issue of meritorious service medals without annuity to Indian troops under rank of commissioned officer as a reward for meritorious service or devotion to duty in The Field. No limit to number decorations. Authority to award delegated to D.A.G. Indian Section, Base.	
"			A list of Honours & Rewards awarded to officers and men	J.

WAR DIARY
INTELLIGENCE SUMMARY

Page 3.

Army Form C. 2118.

Place	Date	Hour	Summary of Events and Information	Remarks and references to Appendices
Continued.			during the month were published in Divere Orders and attached as an Appendix.	APPX. I
			Casualties among Pioneer Natives during the month -	
			killed. 6. B.O.R.	
			wounded. 10. B.O.R.	
			3. I.O.R.	

E.P.Mathew
Major,
D.A.A. & Q.M.G.
4th Cav. Div.

APPX: I

No. 326.

DIVISIONAL ORDERS
BY
MAJOR-GENERAL A.A.KENNEDY. C.M.G.
COMMANDING 4TH CAVALRY DIVISION.

PART II.　　　　　5th January, 1917.

1.— HONOURS & REWARDS.

The Divisional Commander has much pleasure in notifying that the following decorations have been awarded :-

INDIAN ORDER OF MERIT, 2nd Class.

No. 3094. A/Lce Dafadar DHURAM SINGH.
　　　　　14th Jat Lancers, I.A. attached
　　　　　Lucknow M.G.Squadron.

No. 2786. Dafadar HAJEE AHMED.
　　　　　36th Jacob's Horse. I.A. attached
　　　　　Lucknow M.G.Squadron.

INDIAN DISTINGUISHED SERVICE MEDAL.

No. 2334. Dafadar DARAYO SINGH.
　　　　　29th Lancers. I.A. attached
　　　　　Lucknow M.G.Squadron.

No. 2673. Lance Dafadar MAHOMED HAFIZ.
　　　　　29th Lancers. I.A. attached
　　　　　Lucknow M.G.Squadron.

MILITARY CROSS.

No. 50864. Sqdn Sergt-Maj G.W.WEBB
　　　　　Machine Gun Corps. attached
　　　　　Lucknow M.G.Squadron.

DISTINGUISHED CONDUCT MEDAL.

No. 50867. Sergt J.W.STRATFORD.
　　　　　Machine Gun Corps. attached
　　　　　Lucknow M.G.Squadron.

The Fifth Army Commander's congratulations should be conveyed to the recipients.

(Authority A.M.S.Fifth Army No.H.R/538 (1) d/- 30-12-16)

2.— HONOURS & REWARDS.

The Divisional Commander has much pleasure in notifying the following Honours and Rewards, which have been awarded in the New Years Gazette for services rendered in connection with Military operations in the Field and for distinguished service in the Field :-
(Authority Supplement to the London Gazette dated Jan: 1st 1917).

COMPANION OF ST MICHAEL & ST GEORGE. (C.M.G).

Colonel (Temp. Brig-Gen) Neil Wolseley HAIG.
　　Commanding Mhow Cavalry Brigade.

Lieut-Col. (Temp. Brig-Gen) Laurence Lockhart MAXWELL, I.A.
　　Commanding Sialkot Cavalry Brigade.

P.T.O.

TO BE MAJOR-GENERAL.

Colonel (Temp Maj-Gen) H.P.LEADER. C.B.
    late Commanding 4th Cavalry Division.

TO BE BREVET LIEUT-COLONELS.

Major (Temp Brig-Gen) M.F.GAGE. D.S.O.
    Commanding Lucknow Cavalry Brigade.

Major (Temp Lieut-Col) H.F.WICKHAM.
    Commanding 1st (King's) Dragoon Guards.

DISTINGUISHED SERVICE ORDER.

Lieut-Col Claude Edward Charles Graham CHARLTON. R.A.
    late Commanding 1st Indian R.H.A.Brigade.

Major Ronald Hastings LASCELLES.
    late Commanding "U" Battery. R.H.A.

Major William Pattinson PAYNTER.
    Commanding "Q" Battery R.H.A.

Lieut-Col John Arthur SHAW. C.,A.S.C.
    Commanding 4th Cavalry Division A.S.C.

MILITARY CROSS. (M.C).

Lieut (Temp Capt) Rowan Scrope RAIT-KERR.
    Commanding 4th Field Squadron.

MERITORIOUS SERVICE MEDAL. (M.S.M).

9714. Sergt W.HOLDEN. 13th Hussars, Divnl H.Q. (already presented)
6559. Sqdn-Sergt-Maj F.WHITE. 7th Hussars. 4th Signal Sqdn.

FOR GALLANTRY AND DEVOTION TO DUTY WHILE SERVING IN FRANCE AND FLANDERS.

INDIAN ORDER OF MERIT, 2nd Class.

Jemadar ABDUL RAHIM KHAN.   29th Lancers.

2581. Sowar INDAR SINGH.   -do-
3636. Dafadar HARDITT SINGH.   36th Jacob's Horse.
2266. L/Dafadar UDEY SINGH.   2nd Lancers.
1392. Sowar JULAB SINGH.   Jodhpur I.S.Lancers.

INDIAN DISTINGUISHED SERVICE MEDAL.

6th Cavalry.

Jemadar AMIR SINGH.
"   BACHITTAR SINGH.

1436. Dafadar (Hon Jem) ARJAN SINGH.
1919. Dafadar MAZAR ALI SHAH.
 829. Q.M.Dafadar ODEY CHAND.
2671. Ward Orderly. ABDUL WAHAB KHAN, Att'd Sialkot C.F.A.

19th Lancers.

Ressaidar GHULAM HUSAIN.

2780. Dafadar MAHAN SINGH.
2949.   "   GULBAR KHAN.

P.T.O.

29th Lancers.

Risaldar CHANDA SINGH.
Jemadar MAHAN SINGH. Attached M.G.Squadron.

O.T. 1405. Kot Dafadar LALL SINGH.
2193. Kot Dafadar IMDAD ALI. Attached A.V.C.

36th Jacob's Horse.

615. Kot Dafadar SAHEB SINGH.
2896. Sowar HAZRAT SHAH.
2143. Kot Dafadar ABDUL KHALIK. Attached M.G.Sqdn.

35th Horse.

3562. Dafadar DALIP SINGH. Attached 36th J.Horse.

2nd Lancers.

Ressaidar ABDUL LATIF KHAN.
Jemadar DHARA SINGH. Attached M.G.Squadron.

1329. Kot Dafadar RAM PERSHAD.
1396. Dafadar JIWAN SINGH.

22nd Cavalry.

Risaldar AZAM ALI. Attached 2nd Lancers.

38th Central India Horse.

Jemadar RAM SINGH.

2143. Kot Dafadar GHILZAI KHAN.
2613. Dafadar LAL KHAN.
O.T. 2749. Lce Dafadar MEHR SINGH.
2421. Dafadar SHERJAN KHAN.

Jodhpur I.S.Lancers.

1121. Dafadar BHUR SINGH.
1263. Dafadar RUP SINGH.
1485. Lce Dafadar ZALIM SINGH.

Alwar I.S. Lancers.

777. Jemadar KEHAR SINGH. Attached Jodhpur I.S.Lancers.

23rd Cavalry.

964. Dafadar SHER SINGH. Attached Ambala C.F.A.

3.-- PROMOTIONS.

19th Lancers.

To be Risaldar :-
Ressaidar ASMAT ULLAH KHAN, dated 11th December 1916, vice Risaldar KHUSHAL KHAN, transferred to Permanent Base.

To be Ressaidar :-
Jemadar KHWAJA MUHAMAD, dated 11th December 1916, vice Ressaidar ASMAT ULLAH KHAN, promoted.

To be Jemadars.
O.T. No. 2417. Kot Dafadar SHAM SINGH, dated 11th October 1916, vice Jemadar KAPUR KHAN, proceeded to India.

To be Jemadars.

No. 2939, Kot Dafadar HASHAM KHAN, dated 11th December 1916, vice Jemadar KHWAJA MUHAMAD, promoted.

No. 3247, Kot Dafadar ABDUL JABAR, dated 11th December 1916, vice Jemadar BISHEN SINGH, transferred to permanent Base.

No. 2961. Kot Dafadar INSAF ALI, dated 11th December 1916, vice Jemadar JUMA KHAN, transferred to Permanent Base.

4.-- BICYCLES - CARE OF.

It is quite clear from the state in which bicycles are received in the Armourer's Shop that reasonable care is not exercised in looking after them. In nearly every case the bearings are found to be worn out through neglect to lubricate them, and frequently the whole frame and wheels are badly rusted through not having been cleaned for prolonged periods.

In future O.C's units, will see that all bicycles are inspected at least once a week, to see that they are properly cleaned and oiled, and that fittings and accessories are complete.

When bicycles require repairs that cannot be carried out regimentally, they will be sent to the Armourer's Shop in the Ordnance lorry, Clearly labelled to show what Unit they come from. Indents to replace these bicycles will not be submitted until intimation is received from the D.A.D.O.S. that the bicycles are past repair.

Any damage that is found on inspection in the Armourer's Shop to have been caused by negligence, will be charged against the Unit concerned.

It is thought that most units have men who can do the simple repairs and adjustments to bicycles, but any who wish to have a man trained in this work should apply to the D.A.D.O.S. who will arrange for a short course of instruction in the Armourer's Shop.

5.-- PAY & ALLOWANCES.- INDIAN ARMY.

With the approval of Secretary of State, Government of India have sanctioned with effect from 1st January 1917 (1) grant of free rations to all combatant Indian ranks of Indian Army except when on leave or furlough; (2) Increases of pay to Indian ranks as follows :-

Subadar-Major and Risaldar-Major............ Rs 30.
Subadar, Risaldar & Ressaidar............... Rs 20.
Jemadar..................................... Rs 10.
Havildar and Dafadar........................ Rs 2.
Naick and Lance Dafadar..................... Rs 1.

The existing special field allowances will not be affected by these increases of pay.

(Auth: Chief of General Staff, India No.101226 dated 29th December.1916).

6.-- PROMOTIONS.

36th Jacob's horse, attached Lucknow M.G.Squadron.

To be Jemadar :-

No. 2786. Dafadar HAJEE AHMED, I.O.M. vice Jemadar GHULAM KHWAJA killed in action, dated 6th November.1916.

7.-- D.R.L.S.

Divisional Order No. 310, para 8 is cancelled.

Attention is drawn to G.R.O. 1136.

8.-- APPOINTMENTS.
19th Lancers.
Capt T.S.PATERSON having joined the regiment from India to be officiating Squadron Commander, vice Capt V.J.A.CONNEL, 13th Lancers dated 3-12-16.

C R Maitland
Major

Lieut-Colonel,
A.A. & Q.M.G. 4th Cavalry Division.

DIVINE SERVICES.

CHURCH OF ENGLAND   -   Sunday January 7th, 1917.

HYMMEVILLE...Parade Service, followed by Holy Communion.. 9-30 a.m.
MIANNAY........ do   do   do..... do   ..11-15 a.m.

ROMAN CATHOLIC.

ST BLIMONT....   Holy Mass .... 9-00 a.m.

-:-

LOST.

From NOYELLES Station between the 20th and 27th December last:-

A case of saddlery, 3'0" x 2'6" marked in stencil
Lt.J.H.CARPENTER. I.A.R.
    Attached 6th Cavalry.
        1st Indian Cavalry Division.

Kindly send any information to owner.

No. 323.

DIVISIONAL ORDERS
BY
BRIGADIER-GENERAL N.W.HAIG.
COMMANDING 4TH CAVALRY DIVISION.

PART 11.   27th December. 1916.
-:-

1.-- HONOURS & REWARDS.

   The Divisional Commander has much pleasure
in notifying that the undermentioned have been
awarded the Military Medal:-

No. 50868 Sergeant Arthur James CORLEY.
          Machine Gun Corps (attached
          Lucknow Machine Gun Squadron).

No. 51392 Private John Alexander McINTOSH.
          Machine Gun Corps. (attached
          Lucknow Machine Gun Squadron).

(Auth: XIII Corps A-5209 dated 23-12-16).

No. 50894 Private Andrew GIBB.
          Machine Gun Corps. (attached
          Lucknow Machine Gun Squadron).

(Auth: XIII Corps A-5209 dated 24-12-16).

2.-- COURTS MARTIAL.

   In future, all Proceedings of Courts Martial
held under the Indian Army Act, will be sent
to Divisional Headquarters.

                                Lieut-Colonel,
                A.A. & Q.M.G. 4th Cavalry Division.

         D I V I N E   S E R V I C E S

   CHURCH OF ENGLAND   - SUNDAY, December 31st.

CAYEUX, (Lecture Room),...Holy Communion..... 8-30 a.m.
CAYEUX.   Do   ....Parade Service..... 10-30 a.m.

SALLENELLE,(School House) Evening Service.... 5-30 p.m.

No. 317.

DIVISIONAL ORDERS
BY
MAJOR-GENERAL A.A.KENNEDY. C.M.G.
COMMANDING 4TH CAVALRY DIVISION.

PART II.   8th December. 1916.

1.-- HONOURS AND REWARDS.

The Divisional Commander has much pleasure in publishing the following notification :-

Under authority of H.M. the King, the General Officer Commanding in Chief has awarded decorations to the undermentioned :-

Fifth Army Commander and XIII Corps Commander's congratulations are to be conveyed to the recipients.

(Auth: 31st Division No. C/206/A dated 5-12-16).

MILITARY CROSS.

Lieut U.F.FALCONER.   29th Lancers. I.A.
                       Attached Lucknow M.G.Squadron.

2. EXTRACT FROM 93RD INFANTRY BRIGADE ROUTINE.

756. - The Corps Commander has been pleased to award the Military Medal to the undermentioned for gallantry in the Field.

No. 47105 Private J.VANCE.
Lucknow M.G.Squadron.

(Sd) W.K.BOURNE.
Lieut-Colonel.
A.A. & Q.M.G. 4th Cavalry Division.

x   x   x   x   x   x